Wong Kar-wai: Interviews

Conversations with Filmmakers Series
Gerald Peary, General Editor

Wong Kar-wai
INTERVIEWS

Edited by Silver Wai-ming Lee and Micky Lee

University Press of Mississippi / Jackson

www.upress.state.ms.us

The University Press of Mississippi is a member of the Association of
American University Presses.

First printing 2017

∞

Library of Congress Cataloging-in-Publication Data

Names: Wong, Kar-wai, 1958–author. | Lee, Silver Wai-ming editor. | Lee, Micky editor.
Title: Wong Kar-Wai : interviews / edited by Silver Wai-ming Lee and Micky Lee.
Description: Jackson : University Press of Mississippi, 2017. | Series: Conversations with
filmmakers series | Includes bibliographical references, filmography and index. |
Identifiers: LCCN 2017010478 (print) | LCCN 2017027866 (ebook) | ISBN 9781496812858
(epub single) | ISBN 9781496812865 (epub institutional) | ISBN 9781496812872 (pdf
single) | ISBN 9781496812889 (pdf institutional) | ISBN 9781496812841 (cloth : alk. paper)
Subjects: LCSH: Wong, Kar-wai, 1958-—Interviews. | Motion picture producers and
directors—China—Hong Kong—Interviews.
Classification: LCC PN1998.3.W65 (ebook) | LCC PN1998.3.W65 A5 2017 (print) | DDC
791.4302/33092—dc23
LC record available at https://lccn.loc.gov/2017010478

British Library Cataloging-in-Publication Data available

Contents

Introduction   vii

Filmography   xx

Chronology   xxiii

Wong Kar-wai on *As Tears Go By*   3
　　Lok Ching / 1988

Wong Kar-wai Takes Charge   8
　　Cheuk Chi / 1988

The Days of Being Wild: Eight-day Location Shooting in the Philippines   11
　　Angel / 1989

All about *Days of Being Wild*: A Dialogue with Wong Kar-wai   16
　　Jimmy Ngai / 1990

The This and That of Wong Kar-wai   21
　　Yeung Wai-lan and Lau Chi-kwan / 1994

Working like a Jam Session   36
　　Michel Ciment / 1994

The Northern Beggar and Southern Emperor in a Pleasant Forest:
Dialogue with Wong Kar-wai   47
　　Lin Yao-teh / 1994

A Coin of Wong Kar-wai   56
　　Gary / 1995

The Film Supermarket of Wong Kar-wai   61
　　Gary Mak / 1995

Open Communication: Wong Kar-wai   70
　　Yik Ming / 1997

Each Film Has Its Own Ounce of Luck   76
  Michel Ciment and Hubert Niogret / 1997

Interview with Wong Kar-wai: *In the Mood for Love*   85
  Michel Ciment and Hubert Niogret / 2000

Muse of Music: Interview with Wong Kar-wai   94
  Tony Lan Tsu-wei / 2000

2046   100
  Mark Salisbury / 2004

All Memories Are Traces of Tears:
Wong Kar-wai on Literature and Aesthetics (Parts 1 & 2)   104
  Tony Lan Tsu-wei / 2004

Because of Norah Jones: *My Blueberry Nights*:
Exclusive Interview with Wong Kar-wai   115
  Hong Kong Film / 2007

The American Way   129
  Tony Rayns / 2008

Exclusive Interview: Wong Kar-wai (*Ashes of Time Redux*)   134
  Damon Houx / 2008

The Grandmaster or the Grand Barber? Multiple Choice Questions
for Wong Kar-wai   141
  Li Hongyu / 2013

The Grandmaster, Director Wong Kar Wai   151
  David Poland / 2013

Interview: Wong Kar-wai   162
  Jake Mulligan / 2013

Wong Kar-wai: *The Grandmaster* Should Have Been a Trilogy   166
  An Ying / 2015

Additional Resources   172

Index   000

Introduction

This volume collects twenty-two interviews of Wong Kar-wai conducted over nearly three decades. The contents and the order in which the interviews appear reflect a divide between what Wong's films mean to Hong Kong and international critics. The first four interviews are on Wong's first two films: *As Tears Go By* and *Days of Being Wild*.[1] The fourth film *Chungking Express* that made Wong's name known to an international audience is mentioned in the fifth interview. The last four interviews are all on *The Grandmaster*—the two American critics see it as a kung fu film while the Chinese critics see it as a period film about the Republic of China.

The first interview in this volume "Wong Kar-wai on *As Tears Go By*" was published in 1988 in the now defunct Hong Kong magazine *City Entertainment* (in Chinese *Film Biweekly*). In the interview, Wong talks about his first directed feature film, *As Tears Go By*, which not only received praises among Hong Kong critics, but also performed fairly well in the domestic box office. But it was Wong's second film, *Days of Being Wild*, that made him—for better or for worse—a household name in Hong Kong. The critics were pleased that Hong Kong cinema had a director who went against the commercial tide, but the mainstream press was keen on reporting on the lengthy production time and the extraordinary budget in gossip sections. More than two decades after the release of *Days of Being Wild*, Wong's films have been exhibited in the most prestigious film festivals and have received international accolades. However, Hong Kong mainstream media still complain about Wong's films being incomprehensible and taking too much time and money to make. For example, the critics still have not concluded whether Wong's latest film *The Grandmaster* is a frivolous "showing off" or a rich cinematic text.

Similarly, Wong's films receive polarized feedback from the audience. On one hand, Wong has a lot of devoted and enthusiastic fans who collect film memorabilia, discuss his films online, quote from his films, and create fan arts. On the other hand, Wong's films are rarely blockbusters, his latest *The Grandmaster* being an exception. Hong Kong locals use "Wong Kar-wai" in daily life as a derogatory term when describing something abstract and artistic.

Unlike the local audience who had already formed an opinion of Wong quite early on in his career, most of the international audience first learned of Wong

Kar-wai's work through his fourth feature film *Chungking Express*. International film festivals such as Cannes, Berlin, and Toronto offer critics and fans outside Asia a first glimpse at Wong's latest work. Film festivals generate buzz that excites Wong's fans around the world. They also prove his films are greatly admired among critics and judges. For example, Wong received the prestigious Best Director Award for *Happy Together* at Cannes, making him the first Chinese director to earn this award. In addition, Wong's films are frequent subjects of scholarly debate not only in the Chinese language, but also in English, French, Italian, German, and so on.

The text provided by critics on Wong Kar-wai is as rich as Wong's films. The collected interviews not only provide scholars, critics, and fans with materials for further criticism and interpretation, but they are texts themselves that reveal what Wong thinks and what critics think of Wong and his films. Framing the interviews as both resources and discourses about Wong, this introduction aims to do three things: first, situate Wong Kar-wai in the two new waves of Hong Kong cinema; second, summarize Wong's explanations of the development process of various films; and third, summarize how Wong sees his artistic influence and regular collaborators.

Over the span of more than two decades, Wong maintains a consistent auteur persona in the interviews. He is able to explain the creation process of every film and suggest how he worked with the cinematographers, art directors, editors, and actors. Unlike most Hong Kong directors who made films scripted by others and produced by major studios in the 1980s, his work is said to have a signature style reflected from story-telling, aesthetics, and acting. Wong's vision and artistic control of his films stems from his emerging from the Second Wave of new Hong Kong cinema.

When Hong Kong New Wave emerged in the late 1970s and early 1980s, it was more an accidental outcome than an intended movement. These directors include Ann Hui, Tsui Hark, Patrick Tam, Allen Fong Yuk-ping, Alex Cheung Kwok-ming, and Yim Ho. They neither made any joint declaration nor regularly cooperated with each other. Nonetheless, their background is very similar: most of them returned to Hong Kong after studying films in the UK and the US. Before making films, some of these directors worked for public television channel Radio Television Hong Kong; others worked for commercial television station TVB.

New Wave directors produced genre films with experimental elements. They produced refreshing and exciting TV dramas and genre films because they were aware that television shows and films could be art, political statements, as well as mass entertainment. These directors renewed and transformed conventional genres by introducing new techniques they learned from the West. For example, Tsui Hark introduced elements of Hollywood sci-fi and horror to the *wuxia* genre. New Wave directors believed filmmaking is not only about storytelling, but film scoring and art direction are also key components. They explored lesser-known social issues and the Hong Kong identity. With on-location shooting, the cityscape has become an important part of New Wave films. For example, Ann Hui's *The Secret* (1979) shows Chinese-styled apartment buildings in an old district Sai Wan.

At the same time, New Wave directors were aware that the Hong Kong film industry privileges commercial production, and they would be hard-pressed to change the status quo. Rather than challenge the market and the studio system, they sought a new space for their work to survive. Cheuk Pak-tong, a New Wave scholar, calls these directors "reformists not revolutionists."[2] Meanwhile, the emergence of independent film production companies encouraged more young people to enter the industry, but those newcomers did not want to serve the big studios. They also wanted to become auteurs by creating signature works.

The Second Wave emerged in the mid-1980s. Directors such as Stanley Kwan, Clara Law, Mabel Cheung, and Wong Kar-wai are seen as the successors of the first New Wave because some came from a television background and some had worked as screenwriters or assistants for New Wave directors. The Second Wave is even more experimental in storytelling, film aesthetics, and techniques. As a result, some of the Hong Kong audience feel the Second Wave is strictly art house cinema. Interestingly, whenever Wong Kar-wai is asked about being an art house director, he denies being one and says his films are actually very commercial.

Wong never calls himself a Second Wave director or an art house director in the interviews, but it is hard not to connect the dots between Wong Kar-wai and the two new waves. First, Wong began his production training at local television station TVB after dropping out of college as a graphic design student, and he was a scriptwriter who wrote a wide range of film genres from comedy to drama to gangster movies. Second, he collaborated with many New Wave filmmakers as a scriptwriter and an editor. For example, he wrote the script for *Final Victory* for Patrick Tam, who in turn would later edit Wong's film *Days of Being Wild*. Third, Wong worked with actresses who starred in New Wave films, most notably Maggie Cheung and Brigitte Lin, who have appeared in *Song of the Exile* (Ann Hui, 1990), *Farewell China* (Clara Law 1990), *Love Massacre* (Patrick Tam 1981), and *Zu: Warriors from the Magic Mountain* (Tsui Hark 1983). Fourth, Wong worked with art directors and producers who first made their mark in New Wave. Wong's art director, William Chang, was the art director for *Love Massacre*, *Nomad* (Patrick Tam 1982) and *Homecoming* (Yim Ho 1984). Jeff Lau, Wong's good friend and Jet Tone Films partner, produced *The Imp* (Dennis Yu 1981) and *Nomad*. Fifth, Tony

Rayns, a British critic who specializes in East Asian cinema and introduced many New Wave films to the West, is a fan of Wong and provides many English subtitles for his films. Lastly, Wong believes he makes genre films. He compares *In the Mood for Love* to a Hitchcock suspense and labels *The Grandmaster* an epic.

In many ways, Wong Kar-wai has moved beyond the Second Wave—he continues to make films, while maintaining his style and vision. Unlike Patrick Tam, who has retired from the film industry, Wong continues to focus on making films; and unlike Tsui Hark, who has become a major film producer and a mainstream director, Wong produces few films and is not considered to be part of the mainstream. However, he is also more business savvy than he appears to be. In the interviews, he emphasizes the importance of selling distribution rights abroad, and he understands how to set up his own company and acquire funding from international investors, as well as keep production costs within budget, despite what most people believe.

Seventeen of the twenty-two interviews collected here were originally published in Chinese or French. In addition, the earliest interviews mostly come from the Hong Kong publication, *City Entertainment*, and are not available online. These particular interviews provide resources to readers who have no access to Hong Kong archives. Since *Chungking Express* was the film that introduced Wong to the world beyond Hong Kong and Asia, the editors looked for interviews in Hong Kong publications that focus on Wong's first three films: *As Tears Go By, Days of Being Wild*, and *Ashes of Time*. From *Chungking Express* onwards, the editors looked for interviews appearing in publications for film scholars and serious fans in the UK, the US, and France.

Wong Kar-wai speaks Cantonese, Mandarin Chinese, and English. It can be assumed that he used Cantonese for interviews appeared in Hong Kong publications, Mandarin Chinese for Taiwanese and mainland Chinese publications, and English for the rest. (For the interviews appeared in French, the interview was conducted in English and translated). Wong moved to Hong Kong from Shanghai when he was five and he did not speak Cantonese, but his Cantonese became fluent soon. It is unknown if he grew up speaking Mandarin Chinese because it was not the dominant language among Shanghainese until the communist party took over China. But he is fluent with his Mandarin Chinese during interviews. His English is also fluent but he is not as expressive with it as he is with Cantonese. He is able to express himself well in English but does not use idioms, slangs, or colloquial expressions. In each of the interviews, Wong is quite open to sharing his thoughts. He is more inclined to share personal anecdotes and his view of history with the Greater Chinese media. Local media, however, is keen on detailing what it views as Wong's excessive overspending, lengthy filmmaking process, harsh demands on actors, and shooting without a script. In truth, these excesses are common in Hong Kong, US, and European independent filmmakings. For example, during the heyday of Hong Kong films from the 1960s to the 1980s, most scripts were written quickly and the directors did not adhere to the scripts; however, directors usually made films much faster than Wong, often in a matter of a month if not a week. Wong's involvement in every step of the film development process is not unheard of in US and European independent filmmaking, but it is not a common practice in Hong Kong.

"Does Wong Kar-wai have a script or not?" is a common question from critics and fans. On the making of *Chungking Express*, Wong tells Michel Ciment in his 1995 interview the film was made during a two-month sabbatical while he was waiting for some postproduction equipment to arrive for *Ashes of Time*: "Since I had nothing to do, I followed my instincts and decided to direct *Chungking Express*." Wong further states, "When I started to film, I hadn't yet written [the screenplay] completely." Interestingly, the improvisational style is what caught the attention of fans who like its energy and Faye Wong's authentic performance. As for *Happy Together*, Wong tells Ciment and Niogret in 1997 that he only had a two-page synopsis before arriving in Argentina. He wrote the script on set just before filming started. He added it was a lot of fun to let Tony Leung Chiu-wai and Leslie Cheung improvise during the sex scenes because the improvisation highlighted the different personalities of the two actors. While Leslie Chueng wanted to test boundaries, Tony Leung was very concerned about gay sex.

Unfortunately, the "no-script" method did not work for the English-speaking film, *My Blueberry Nights*. In his interview with *Hong Kong Film* in 2007, Wong revealed novelist Lawrence Block was asked to co-write a screenplay before filming. Although there was a complete script before shooting, Wong reserved the right to change it. During shooting, he told the actors they were allowed to make changes, and he sought feedback from local crew members. In 2008, Wong told Tony Rayns he encouraged this "trying out approach" because "we've seen so many films about Chinese people made by foreigners which look very weird to us, and I didn't want to repeat that mistake!"

Wong insists his films are driven by characters, not plot. However, the characters in Wong's films are often a reflection of the actors themselves. Faye Wong is said to be as elusive in real life as her character in *Chungking Express*, Tony Leung Chiu-wai is as pensive as Lai Yiu-fai in *Happy Together*, and Norah Jones is as straightforward as the character in *My Blueberry Nights*. Wong spends a lot of time communicating with the actors about the characters. In his interviews with Angel in1990 and Ciment in 1995, Wong explained the earliest stage of shooting takes a long time because he does not give the actors a screenplay to rehearse. Instead he prefers to communicate with them and let them know the mentalities of the characters. For example, Zhang Ziyi was not familiar with how dancehall girls were portrayed in old Hong Kong movies, so Wong spent quite a bit of time talking with Zhang and asked her to rehearse in the dresses that women wore in that era. During the process of experimenting, shooting, and re-shooting, Wong looks for a common rhythm between the actors, and once that is established shooting becomes much smoother. In explaining why he does not want the actors to rehearse, he said, "it is not like I need to find a model to wear a piece of already-made clothing; that is not true [for me]. Usually I see a person; then I think of what clothing this person should wear" (*Hong Kong Film* 2007, 23). Wong's relationship with actors brings out their best performances, as evidenced by the numerous acting nominations and awards given by the Hong Kong Film Awards and the Hong Kong Film Critics Society that respectively represent the industry and the critics. The long list of winners can be found in the filmography in this volume.

Film auteurs usually produce, direct, and write their own films, and Wong Kar-wai is no exception. *My Blueberry Nights* and *The Grandmaster* notwithstanding, Wong is the sole-credited screenwriter for his films. In 1990, Jimmy Ngai asked why Wong does not collaborate with a scriptwriter, to which he replied, "No scriptwriter would like to be stuck with a director for such a long time. They have to make a living!"

In addition to the lengthy processes of preproduction and production, Wong Kar-wai also spends a long time on postproduction, especially in editing. In their 1994 interview Yeung and Lau wondered why Wong spends so much time in editing. Wong explained the process is so time-consuming because he films a lot of footage that could be used in the final cut. The uncut time is much longer than the screening time. However, Wong does not get tied up by the footage. If he deemed some scenes redundant or unsuitable for the final cut, Wong does not hesitate to exclude them from the final cut.

Sometimes the editing process takes so long due to his "rough script" approach where the story is constructed during the cutting process. For *Ashes of Time*, he told Yeung and Lau he stitched the many fragmented scenes into a coherent story. The same happened with *Happy Together*. He tried different cuts with different scenes and sequences; cutting was "more of a process of elimination than of addition" (Ciment and Niogret 1997, 11). As a result, all footage of the character played by Hong Kong singer Shirley Kwan was cut. (The scenes with Kwan's character were included in *Buenos Aires Zero Degree: The Making of "Happy Together."*) For *In the Mood for Love*, Wong told Ciment and Niogret in their interview in 2000 he had more than two hours of materials for the final cut, but he edited it scene by scene to figure out the story structure. "Going to Cannes" has become a synonym for deadline. But the feedback that Wong receives from Cannes prompts him to edit more. The existence of different film cuts excites fans; they want to see all other versions not played in their region. Die-hard fans usually acquire DVDs of different regions for comparison. In this way, Wong follows the long-standing practice of the Hong Kong film industry by releasing different cuts. Traditionally, the first cut is played at a midnight premiere. The feedback gathered from the audience prompts another round of editing, and then the film is further edited to meet overseas regulations and to respond to different market tastes.

Wong explains in several interviews why some films deserve so many cuts. For his first feature, *As Tears Go By*, Wong admitted to Lok Ching in 1998 that the ending of the Hong Kong cut in which Andy Lau is killed is "weak but acceptable." The Taiwanese cut has an alternative ending in which Andy Lau becomes mentally impaired. The Hong Kong audience compared its ending to the alternative ending and debated which one was better. The midnight premiere of *Chungking Express* was fifteen minutes longer with more scenes of Brigitte Lin than the final cut. According to Yeung and Lau (1994), Wong was responsible for editing the story of Brigitte Lin while William Chang was responsible for editing the story of Faye Wong. Neither of them had any idea how long the other's cut was until the very last minute. In the case of *Ashes of Time Redux*, Wong included scenes that did not appear in the original version because, during the re-making process, he found out the film is longer in Chinatown copies. More action scenes were included by overseas distributors to appeal to overseas Chinese (Houx 2008). The original film reels and the various Chinatown tapes provided much material for Wong to restore the film negative and to redo film scoring and coloring. He believes the re-edited film presents a clearer story structure.

Wong prefers to see some of his films as a collection of stories. *Days of Being Wild* was conceptualized as two films with multiple stories; however, its poor box office showing made investors withdraw funding so the already-planned sequel was never made. Wong envisioned a three-to-four-hour version of *Days of Being Wild* on VHS. Similarly, *Chungking Express* was conceptualized as a film with three stories, and one of them was later included in *Fallen Angels*.

The Grandmaster is rumored to have a six-hour ultimate version, but Wong denies this version exists. Nonetheless, there are four versions in the market: the 3D version, which is the longest; the Greater Chinese cut; the European cut; and, finally, the US cut, which is less than two hours long. These different lengths not only reflect the expectations of different markets, but they also reflect how the story of Ip Man appeals to different audiences. For example, the US version explicates the history of the Republic of China and highlights Ip Man's relationship with Bruce Lee while the Greater Chinese version downplays both. In the interviews with Poland (2013) and Mulligan (2013), Wong said he wanted to tell the story in different ways, although he thinks it is the same film regardless of length and has no preference of the three versions.

Two years after the domestic version release, Wong presented a 3D version of *The Grandmaster*, which focused more on the character Ip Man than the time period (An Ying 2015). Unlike most film directors, Wong supervised the entire production of the 3D version, thus reinforcing the talk about his ongoing editing. And in response to fans' requests, Wong included two deleted segments deemed unsuitable for the 3D version at the end of yet another version of the film. In explanation, Wong said, "the unknown is very attractive for the audience, and I would like to share the footage with them" (An Ying 2015).

Some critics claim the deleted scenes are mentioned in interviews as a marketing strategy. Once the fans know about deleted scenes, alternative endings, and different versions, they want to see them and, therefore, buy a copy of each version. However, some deleted scenes from Wong's films can be found online or are included as bonuses in DVDs. For example, the Criterion collection of *In the Mood for Love* contains a few deleted scenes in which Tony Leung and Maggie Cheung meet again in Cambodia.

Unlike most Hong Kong directors, Wong Kar-wai is not afraid of drawing from great film directors and literature. While some fans say his films are too literary, he says it only *appears* to be so (Yeung and Lau 1994).

To what extent should Wong's films be interpreted based on his life experience and arts that have inspired him? The "1960s Trilogy" (*Days of Being Wild*, *In the Mood for Love*, and *2046*) seems to reflect Wong's impression of Hong Kong when he first moved from Shanghai with his mother. In a number of interviews, Wong talks about his impressions of the city when he and his mother adopted Hong Kong as their new home. He was aware of his status as an outsider because he did not speak Cantonese.

After so many years in Hong Kong, Wong feels Shanghainese are losing their identity. Nowadays, there is no longer a distinction between Shanghainese and Cantonese; there are only Hong Kong people. *In the Mood for Love* is an attempt for him to show "how the Shanghainese communities [were] really like" (Ciment and Niogret 2000, 80) because even the contemporary Shanghainese do not know much about the history of their community, customs, and rituals. Wong strives to retain some of that history in his films. The English subtitles for *In the Mood for Love* have omitted subtle details of the Shanghainese way of life in 1960s Hong Kong. Because the film was first conceptualized as one about food, Wong paid a great deal of attention to what Maggie Cheung and her landlady's family eat throughout the film. The mention of a particular kind of vegetable in a Shanghai-nese household hints at the time of the year.

In addition to preserving his memory of the Shanghainese way of life, Wong also wants to preserve buildings and traditions that will soon disappear or have already disappeared. Wong uses film negative to catalog old buildings in Wan Chai—a district that has undergone tremendous change due to redevelopment (Gary Mak 1995). For example, the inn in 2046 was a prison that has been torn down since the release of the film. Wong believes future audiences will see these newly demolished buildings still standing in his films, and they will contemplate how Hong Kong looked in past years.

The Grandmaster also attempts to preserve something that will soon disap-pear—in this case, different schools of martial arts. The film was originally titled *The Grandmasters*, and Wong did not only want to show Ip Man and one school of martial arts. He wanted to show several schools of martial arts through the story of Ip and his colleagues. He regrets the cultural traditions associated with martial arts are dying because the Chinese government only sees martial arts as a sport where coaches train students, not as a school where the master represents the father figure to his apprentices. He hopes the film will renew public interest in learning martial arts, not as a sport, but as a traditional art (Li Hongyu 2013).

Much of the audience's fascination with Wong Kar-wai springs from his reticent answers to questions about his artistic point of view. In interviews, Wong is very good at explaining how his films are made, but he provides little information on how he views his body of work. As previously mentioned, whenever interviewers suggest Wong's films are art, he rebukes them and replies his films are actually very commercial. Wong's ambiguity towards his body of work is further illustrated when Gary Mak asks Wong in a 1995 interview if he prefers surface acting or dramatic acting. Wong answers both are fine as long as it is good; however, "most times good acting cannot be described." When asked if he prefers a specific kind of film genre, he says again anything goes as long as it is good.

While Wong hesitates to list film directors who have influenced him, he does not shy away from sharing his opinions of directors whose films he likes. In his early years in Hong Kong, Wong and his mother went to the theater daily. They would watch a few films a day, whether they were imports from Hollywood, Eu-rope, or Japan. During college and through his collaborator Patrick Tam, Wong started watching films by great masters such as Yasujirō Ozu, Akira Kurosawa, Bernardo Bertolucci, Michelangelo Antonioni, Éric Rohmer, and Robert Bresson. He mentions to Yeung and Lau in 1994 that Bresson taught him to not spend un-necessary effort to make films. Wong imitates Bresson's close-up frames to shoot in small, enclosed space in *In the Mood for Love*. Also in that interview, Wong comments on a number of other directors: Krzysztof Kieślowski, Martin Scorsese, Leos Carax, Gus Van Sant, Andrei Tarkovsky, Hou Hsiao-hsien, Zhang Yimou, and Zhang Yuan. He highly praises Tarkovsky's *Nostalgia* and Hou's *City of Sadness*, which he regards as the best film of all time. In another interview about his contribution of *The Hand* to the omnibus *Eros*, Wong points out that Antonioni's *The Eclipse* taught him film protagonists do not have to be the characters, they could also be the space.[3]

Cultural critics and fans admire Wong's films because they appreciate the literary quality of the dialogues, internal monologues, and narratives. Unsurprisingly, Wong is an avid reader and his love of literature is expressed in his films and interviews. Modern Chinese literature inspires Wong to make films. *Ashes of Time* focuses on the early life of the two protagonists, Eastern Heretic and Western Venom, characters introduced in Louis Cha's *The Legend of Eagle-shooting Heroes*. *In the Mood for Love* and *2046* were inspired by *Intersection* and *The Alcoholic*, written by Liu Yichang, a Hong Kong writer who was born and raised in Shanghai. *In the Mood for Love* and *2046* led Hong Kong scholars to revisit Liu's works (Tony Lan 2004). *The Hand* in *Eros* was adapted from Shi Zhecun's *The Taxi Dancer in the Dusk*.

Of course, Wong's repertoire of literary knowledge goes beyond modern Chinese literature. In a 1994 interview with Lin, Wong discusses books he read while growing up. Because his father believed one has to read all the classics during childhood, Wong began reading classical Chinese literature quite early on. To maintain a connection to his siblings who were stranded in mainland China during the Cultural Revolution, Wong wrote to them about world literature, such as Honoré de Balzac's *La Comédie Humaine* as well as the works of John Steinbeck and Ernest Hemingway. Later, Wong's reading list expanded to include Japanese writers such as Yasunari Kawabata, Kobo Abe, Osamu Dazai, and Riichi Yokomitsu; modern Chinese writers such as Lu Xun, Zhou Zuoren, Lu She, and Mu Shiying; and Latin American writers such as Gabriel García Márquez, whose *Chronicle of a Death Foretold* taught Wong about the possibility of nonlinear storytelling. Argentinian writer Manuel Puig's *Kiss of the Spider Woman* and *Heartbreak Tango* are also some of Wong's favorites.

Wong Kar-wai pays a lot of attention to the music and sound of his films. Some Hong Kong New Wave directors insisted on using scored music in their work, but Wong uses both original film scores and ready-made music. He sees himself as a DJ for his films and sometimes incorporates his favorite music into his films. For example, Wong uses "Take My Breath Away" in the climactic scene in *As Tears Go By* where Maggie Cheung and Andy Lau kiss in a telephone booth. That song was selected because they needed a song, and Wong liked that one. Wong had not thought of a song for this scene. The use of Latin music in *In the Mood for Love* and *2046*, reflects the music that he grew up listening to. His father was a manager of a night club and Filipino bands played a lot of cover version of Latin music. Although those films have ready-made music in them, Wong does not shy away from using original scores; however, choosing original scores can be uncertain. Wong believes that directors generally have a difficult time talking to musicians because they use different languages. His collaboration with Frankie Chan in *Ashes of Time* succeeded because he is both a musician and a director.

In addition to picking music, Wong Kar-wai has a few people he works with regularly—most notably art director and editor William Chang and cinematographer Christopher Doyle. The trio's frequent collaboration invites questions: To what extent is the director the only decisive author? Is Wong's authorship always a co-authorship? Wong often talks about Chang and Doyle in the interviews and acknowledges their imperative roles in his films. In an interview with Ciment in 1995, Wong describes himself as a team leader who has jam sessions with Chang and Doyle. Because of their early and constant collaborations, Chang and Doyle understand Wong's expectations and share his artistic visions.

William Chang has worked with Wong since the filming of *As Tears Go By*. Better known as Wong's art director, he is also the film editor (sometimes uncredited). Wong says of Chang, "He would not hesitate to cut a frame if it seems necessary to him, even if the décor had taken a lot of effort and time" (Ciment and Niogret 1997, 14). *Hong Kong Film* (2007) asked Wong whether a film's aesthetic is Wong's or Chang's vision. Wong replied that he and Chang have very similar ideas and they often know what each other is thinking without telling the other his thoughts.

Another long-time collaborator, Christopher Doyle, has been Wong's cinematographer since *Days of Being Wild*. Wong seldom gives instructions to Doyle about lighting, color, or framing as he already knows what Wong wants. "I don't even have to look at the video screen because, in following his movement, I know what his take will be like" (Michel and Niogret 1997, 10).

In the two earliest interviews on *As Tears Go By*, Wong Kar-wai reveals his thoughts on filming process, such as the need for research and working with the same people regularly. At the beginning of his directing career, Wong told an interviewer, "I don't believe in research because it is impossible to know someone's story by just chatting [to them] for one day or so," and he hoped he could "stay relaxed like Juzo Itami when making films" (Lok Ching 1988, 24, 25). Wong seemed to be very self-reliant—he scouted locations and did postproduction. At the end of his interview in 1988, Cheuk commented on that self-reliance, "Perhaps one day he would be the only person in the crew; this must give him an overwhelming satisfaction. And hopefully when he is a producer, he would suppress all his romantic thoughts and become sensibly realistic" (17). As Wong's filmmaking career continued, he learned that research and collaboration are important. He did extensive research for *The Grandmaster* before starting to film. And beyond his work with Chang and Doyle, Wong has expanded his group of collaborators in the last few years even though he prefers to work with the same few people (Cheuk Chi 1988).

The editors would like to remark on a number of translation choices in this concluding section. First, some of Wong's answers are further explained in endnotes in recognition of the audience outside the Greater China region. The endnotes elaborate on Wong's answers on a number of issues, such as what he intended to do in a film, the work from which he adapted, historical events in Hong Kong and China, as well as relationship between the characters.

Second, it has to be noted that Hong Kong Chinese speak Cantonese, a Chinese dialect that is very fluid. Most Hong Kong Chinese are bilingual, so they regularly use English words or phrases in daily conversation. However, these words are not used in the same ways as native English speakers. Some of the interviews from Hong Kong publications translated those English words to Chinese, but others kept them. In cases where English words and phrases appeared in an interview originally conducted in Cantonese, the editors kept and italicized those words. The English words might show how a local Hong Kong Chinese talks. The editors noted instances where the words are not used as a native speaker would. Concepts that are difficult to translate in English are presented in Mandarin *pinyin* in the body text and the meanings are stated in the endnotes.

Third, names are presented in the following way: For Chinese and Korean names, the last name precedes the given name. For Hong Kong Chinese who have an English name, the English name precedes the last name. Sometimes, the English name and the last name precede the given name. For example, Maggie Cheung is well-known, so her Chinese first name is not used. However, Wong has worked with two famous actors both called Tony Leung, so we spell out their full names the first time they appear in an interview. For actors and crew members who are less well-known, their names will be presented in the order of English name (if any), last name, and first name (such as Barry Wong Ping-yiu). For mainland Chinese actors and crew members, their first names are not hyphenated. For Japanese and non-Asian names, the first name precedes the last name.

ACKNOWLEDGMENTS

Silver Wai-ming Lee would like to thank all the publishers and authors who generously gave permission for reprinting and translating the interviews. He would also like to thank the following friends for their help: Lu Fang-long for contacting the publishers in Taiwan and Maurice Leung and Roy Chan for translating and proofreading some of the articles.

Micky Lee would like to thank the following people at Suffolk University for their help: Marjorie Salvodon at the Department of Modern Languages and Cultural Studies for her skillful translation from French to English; Michael DiLoreto, Josephine Ames, Andrew Hudson, Jessica Bartel, and Emily Thistle for their clerical support; Suffolk alumnus Jake Mulligan for his sharing of the full-length *Grandmaster* interview (abbreviated version originally appeared in *Slant*).

Needless to say, the editors are responsible for all errors.

NOTES

1. *As Tears Go By, Days of Being Wild*, and *Ashes of Time* were screened at the non-competition programs at Cannes, Berlin, and Venice Film Festival respectively. But it was *Chungking Express*, the relatively approachable film, that first won the critics' hearts and reached a wider audience in the West.

2. See Pak-tong Cheuk, *Hong Kong New Wave Cinema (1978–2000)*. Bristol: Intellect, 2008, pp. 15–16.

3. The conversation between Wong Kar-wai and Kevin Tsai (a renowned Taiwanese TV host whose family originated from Shanghai) is not included in this volume; however, it is included in the bonus tracks of the Taiwanese version of *Eros* DVD. Wong told Tsai when Antonioni invited him to make the omnibus film *Eros*, he thought of the short story, *The Taxi Dancer in the Dusk*, by neo-sensualist writer Shi Zhecun. In the story, Shi used conversations to show the circumstances of the taxi dancer. Wong mentioned in the interview that the film was about eavesdropping rather than peeping. He further said when he was young he would visit his classmate's neighbor whose sister was a nightclub dancer. Wong could hear sounds from her room but rarely saw her in person because she woke up very late. This "heard but not seen" fueled Wong's imagination. Another inspiration for the film is Gong Li's hand which is said to be very soft and sensuous, so Wong decided to make a film about her hand.

Chronology

1958   Born on July 17 in Shanghai. His father is a hotel manager and his mother is a housewife. He is the youngest of three children.

1963   Moves with his mother to Hong Kong and lives in the Tsim Sha Tsui district. His father and siblings are unable to join them due to onset of the Cultural Revolution.

1980   Attends Hong Kong Polytechnic (now Hong Kong Polytechnic University), majoring in graphic design.

1982   Quits college and enrolls in a director training program offered by Television Broadcasts Limited. Continues to work there as a scriptwriter after graduation. Produces first television drama 執到寶 (*Don't Look Now*) and is assistant director for 輪流轉 (*Five Easy Pieces*). Writes first screenplay 彩雲曲 (*Once upon a Rainbow*).

1985   Writes 吉人天相 (*Chase a Fortune*), a comedy. Meets Alan Tang Kwongwing, a former actor who became a film producer, at Wing Scope.

1986   Writes the screenplay for *The Final Victory*.

1988   Directs *As Tears Go By*, which receives positive reviews and good box office sales.

1989   At the 8th Hong Kong Film Awards, *As Tears Go By* wins Best Supporting Actor (Jacky Cheung) and Best Art Direction (William Chang) *As Tears Go By* screens at Cannes Film Festival at the International Critics' Week.

1990   *Days of Being Wild* released but is received poorly among audiences and is pulled from theaters.

1991   *Days of Being Wild* received five awards at the 10th Hong Kong Film Awards: Best Picture, Best Director, Best Actor (Leslie Cheung), Best Art Direction, and Best Cinematography. The film re-released in theaters but still receives poor reception among audiences.

1992   Founds Jet Tone Films with Jeff Lau.

1994   *Chungking Express* released. *Ashes of Time* released two months later. *Chungking Express* was made during the lengthy production of *Ashes of Time*.

1995   *Fallen Angels* released in Hong Kong. *Chungking Express* wins four awards at the 14th Hong Kong Film Awards: Best Picture, Best Director, Best

Actor (Tony Leung), and Best Editing. *Ashes of Time* wins another three: Best Art Direction, Best Cinematography, and Best Costume and Make-up Design. The two films compete with each other in seven categories, including Best Picture, Best Director, Best Screenplay, and Best Art Direction. At the Hong Kong Film Critics Society Awards, *Ashes of Time* wins Best Film, Best Director, Best Screenplay, and Best Actor (Leslie Cheung).

1996   *Fallen Angels* wins three awards at the 15th Hong Kong Film Awards: Best Supporting Actress (Karen Mok), Best Cinematography, and Best Original Score. *Chungking Express* was the first Wong's film screened in the US. It is released in DVD by Rolling Thunders, a distribution company launched by Quentin Tarantino. Wong made his first commercial, which is for the brand of Takeo Kikuchi.

1997   *Happy Together* released. Wong wins Best Director at the Cannes Film Festival; this is the first major international award won by Wong and the first Cannes award won by a director from the Greater China Region. *Happy Together* is nominated for the Palm d'Or. Tony Leung Chiu-wai wins Best Actor at the 16th Hong Kong Film Awards.

1998   *Fallen Angels* screens in the US. Wong mentions *In the Mood for Love* is in preproduction

2000   *In the Mood for Love* released. It premieres in May at the Cannes Film Festival, where Tony Leung Chiu-wai wins the Best Actor award. It wins the Best Technical Grand Prize and is nominated for the Palm d'Or. *In the Mood for Love* premieres at the Hong Kong Cultural Centre.

2001   *In the Mood for Love* screens in the US. The film wins five awards at the Hong Kong Film Awards, including Best Actor (Tony Leung Chiu-wai), Best Actress (Maggie Cheung), Best Art Direction, Best Costume and Make-up Design, and Best Film Editing. It also wins six "best foreign film" awards, including New York Film Critics Circle Awards and British Independent Film Awards. Wong directs a short promotion film for BMW. Wong is awarded the Bronze Bauhinia Star by the Hong Kong SAR Government for his contribution to society.

2004   *2046* released. It premieres at the Cannes Film Festival and is nominated for a Palme d'Or.

2005   *2046* screens in the US. It wins six awards at the Hong Kong Film Awards, including Best Actor (Tony Leung Chiu-wai), Best Actress (Zhang Ziyi), Best Cinematography, Best Art Direction, Best Costume and Make-up Design, and Best Original Film Score. *Eros* premieres in September at the Venice Film Festival.

2006   Wong chairs the jury at the Cannes Film Festival and receives the Ordre National de la Légion d'Honneur.

2007   *My Blueberry Nights*, Wong's first feature film in English, opens at Cannes. *The Hand* released in the omnibus *Eros*. Wong receives an Honorable Doctorate Degree in Social Sciences from the Open University of Hong Kong.

2008   *My Blueberry Night* opens in the US. *Ashes of Time Redux*, a remaster of the original, released with redubbed dialogue; however, Leslie Cheung's voice is retained due to the actor's suicide in 2003.

2013   *The Grandmaster* released. It is the opening film for the Berlin Film Festival. Wong receives the Ordre des Arts et des Lettres from the French government for his contribution to film.

2014   Wong receives a lifetime achievement award at the 45th International Film Festival of India. *The Grandmaster* wins twelve awards at the 33rd Hong Kong Film Awards, including Best Film, Best Director, Best Screenplay, Best Actress (Zhang Ziyi), Best Supporting Actor (Max Zhang), Best Cinematography, Best Film Editing, Best Costume and Make-up Design, Best Action Choreography, Best Original Film Score, and Best Sound Design. *The Grandmaster* receives two nominations at the Academy Awards: Best Cinematography and Best Costume Design. Wong chairs the Grand Jury at the Berlin Film Festival.

2015   The 3D version of *The Grandmaster* released in mainland China and Taiwan.

2016   To celebrate the twenty-fifth anniversary of Jet Tone, the 40th Hong Kong International Film Festival screens Wong's films produced by Jet Tone, including the 3D version of *The Grandmaster* and the sixty-minute version of *The Hand*.

Filmography

The Chinese title is followed by the Mandarin *pinyin* and the literal translation of the Chinese title (if applicable). All last names are capitalized.

AS DIRECTOR

Feature Films

AS TEARS GO BY (1988)
旺角卡門 / WANG JIAO KA MEN (MONG KOK CARMEN)
Hong Kong
Production company: In-Gear
Director: **WONG Kar-wai**
Screenplay: **WONG Kar-wai**
Producer: Alan TANG Kwong-wing
Director of photography: Andrew LAU Wai-keung
Editor: Peter CHIANG
Art director: William CHANG Suk-ping
Music: Danny CHUNG Deng-yat
Cast: Andy LAU, Jacky CHEUNG, Maggie CHEUNG, Alex MAN
Hong Kong Film Awards: Best Supporting Actor (Jacky CHEUNG) and Best Art Direction; nominated for Best Film, Best Director, Best Actor (Andy LAU), Best Actress (Maggie CHEUNG), Best Supporting Actor (Alex MAN), Best Film Editing, Best Cinematography, and Best Film Score
Golden Horse Awards (Taiwan): Nominated for Best Director, and Best Art Direction
Color, 102 minutes

DAYS OF BEING WILD (1990)
阿飛正傳 / A FEI ZHENG ZHUAN (THE STORY OF AH-FEI)
Hong Kong
Production company: In-Gear
Director: **WONG Kar-wai**

Screenplay: **WONG Kar-wai**
Producer: Alan TANG Kwong-wing
Director of photography: Christopher DOYLE
Editors: Patrick TAM Ka-ming, KAI Kit-wai
Art director: William CHANG Suk-ping
Music: Terry CHAN Ming-tao
Sound recordist: Steve CHAN Wai-hung
Cast: Leslie CHEUNG, Andy LAU, Maggie CHEUNG, Carina LAU, Jacky CHEUNG, Rebecca PAN
Hong Kong Film Awards: Best Film, Best Director, Best Actor (Leslie CHEUNG), Best Cinematography, and Best Art Direction; nominated for Best Screenplay, Best Actress (Carina LAU), and Best Film Editing
Golden Horse Awards (Taiwan): Best Director, Best Supporting Actress (Rebecca PAN), Best Film Editing, Best Art Direction, Best Makeup and Costume Design, and Best Sound Recording; nominated for Best Feature Film, Best Leading Actor (Leslie CHEUNG), and Best Leading Actress (Carina LAU)
Color, 90 minutes

CHUNGKING EXPRESS (1994)
重慶森林 / CHONG QING SEN LIN (CHUNGKING JUNGLE)
Hong Kong
Production company: Jet Tone
Director: **WONG Kar-wai**
Screenplay: **WONG Kar-wai**
Producer: Jeff LAU Chun-wai
Directors of photography: Christopher DOYLE, Andrew LAU Wai-keung
Editors: William CHANG Suk-ping, KAI Kit-wai, KONG Chi-leung
Art director: William CHANG Suk-ping
Music: Frankie CHAN, Roel A.GARCIA
Cast: Brigitte LIN, Tony LEUNG Chiu-wai, Faye WONG, Takeshi KANESHIRO, Valerie CHOW
Hong Kong Film Awards: Best Film, Best Director, Best Actor (Tony LEUNG), and Best Film Editing; nominated for Best Screenplay, Best Actress (Faye WONG), Best Supporting Actress (Valerie CHOW), Best Cinematography, Best Art Direction, and Best Original Film Score
Hong Kong Film Critics Society Awards: Film of Merit
Golden Horse Awards (Taiwan): Best Leading Actor (Tony LEUNG Chiu-wai); nominated for Best Feature Film, Best Director, Best Leading Actress (Faye WONG), Best Cinematography, Best Film Editing, Best Art Direction, and Best Original Film Score
Color, 98 minutes

ASHES OF TIME (1994)
東邪西毒 / DONG XIE XI DU (EASTERN HERETIC, WESTERN VENOM)
Hong Kong
Production companies: Scholar, Jet Tone
Director: **WONG Kar-wai**
Screenplay: **WONG Kar-wai**, based on the novel *The Legend of the Condor Heroes*
(*The Legend of Eagle-shooting Heroes* 射鵰英雄傳) by Jin Yong (Louis CHA, 金庸)
Producer: CHAN Pui-wah
Director of photography: Christopher DOYLE
Editors: Patrick TAM Ka-ming, William CHANG Suk-ping, KAI Kit-wai, KONG
Chi-leung
Art director: William CHANG Suk-ping
Music: Frankie CHAN, Roel A.GARCIA
Martial arts director: Sammo HUNG Kam-po
Casts: Leslie CHEUNG, Tony LEUNG Kar-fai, Brigitte LIN, Tony LEUNG Chiu-wai,
Carina LAU, Charlie YOUNG, Jacky CHEUNG, Maggie CHEUNG
Hong Kong Film Awards: Best Cinematography, Best Art Direction, and Best Costume and Makeup Design; nominated for Best Film, Best Director, Best Screenplay, Best Film Editing, Best Action Choreography, and Best Original Film Score
Hong Kong Film Critics Society Awards: Best Film, Best Director, Best Screenplay, and Best Actor (Leslie CHEUNG)
Golden Horse Awards (Taiwan): Best Cinematography and Best Film Editing; nominated for Best Adapted Screenplay, Best Art Direction, and Best Makeup and Costume Design
Venice Film Festival: Golden Osella Award for Best Cinematography
Color, 98 minutes

FALLEN ANGELS (1995)
墮落天使 / DUO LUO TIAN SHI (FALLEN ANGELS)
Hong Kong
Production company: Jet Tone
Director: **WONG Kar-wai**
Screenplay: **WONG Kar-wai**
Producers: **WONG Kar-wai**, Jeff LAU Chun-wai
Director of photography: Christopher DOYLE
Editors: William CHANG Suk-ping, WONG Ming-lam
Art director: William CHANG Suk-ping
Music: Frankie CHAN, Roel A.GARCIA
Cast: Leon LAI, Michele REIS, Takehi KANESHIRO, Charlie YOUNG, Karen MOK,
CHAN Fai-hung, CHAN Man-lui

Hong Kong Film Awards: Best Supporting Actress (Karen MOK), Best Cinematography, and Best Original Film Score; nominated for Best Film, Best Director, Best New Performer (CHAN Man-lui), Best Art Direction, Best Costume and Makeup Design, and Best Film Editing
Hong Kong Film Critics Society Awards: Film of Merit
Golden Horse Awards (Taiwan): Best Film Editing and Best Art Direction; nominated for Best Cinematography and Best Original Film Score
Color, 96 minutes

HAPPY TOGETHER (1997)
春光乍洩 / CHUN GUANG ZHA XIE (FIRST GLEAM OF THE SPRING LIGHT)
Hong Kong
Production companies: Block 2 Pictures, Jet Tone
Director: **WONG Kar-wai**
Screenplay: **WONG Kar-wai**
Producer: **WONG Kar-wai**
Director of photography: Christopher DOYLE
Editors: William CHANG Suk-ping, WONG Ming-lam
Art director: William CHANG Suk-ping
Music: Danny CHUNG Deng-yat
Sound editor: TU Duu-chih
Sound recordist: LEUNG Chi-tat
Cast: Leslie CHEUNG, Tony LEUNG Chiu-wai, CHANG Chen
Hong Kong Film Awards: Best Actor (Tony LEUNG Chiu-wai); nominated for Best Film, Best Director, Best Actor (Leslie CHEUNG), Best Supporting Actor (CHANG Chen), Best Cinematography, Best Film Editing, Best Art Direction, and Best Costume and Makeup Design
Hong Kong Film Critics Society Awards: Film of Merit
Golden Horse Awards (Taiwan): Won Best Cinematography; nominated for Best Director, Best Leading Actor (Leslie CHEUNG), Best Film Editing, Best Art Direction, and Best Sound Effects
Cannes Film Festival: Won Best Director
Color, 96 minutes

IN THE MOOD FOR LOVE (2000)
花樣年華 / HUA YANG NIAN HUA (THE AGE OF FLOWERS)
Hong Kong, France
Production companies: Block 2 Pictures, Paradis Films, Jet Tone
Director: **WONG Kar-wai**
Screenplay: **WONG Kar-wai**

Producer: **WONG Kar-wai**
Directors of photography: Christopher DOYLE, Mark LEE Ping-bing
Editor: William CHANG Suk-ping
Art director: William CHANG Suk-ping
Music: Michael GALASSO
Cast: Tony LEUNG Chiu-wai, Maggie CHEUNG, Rebecca PAN, SIU Ping-lam, CHAN Man-lui, CHIN Tsi-ang
Hong Kong Film Awards: Best Actor (Tony LEUNG Chiu-wai), Best Actress (Maggie CHEUNG), Best Film Editing, Best Art Direction, and Best Costume and Makeup Design; nominated for Best Film, Best Director, Best Screenplay, Best Supporting Actress (Rebecca PAN), Best New Performer (SIU Ping-lam), Best Cinematography, and Best Original Film Score
Hong Kong Film Critics Society Awards: Best Director and Film of Merit
Golden Horse Awards (Taiwan): Best Leading Actress (Maggie CHEUNG), Best Cinematography, and Best Makeup and Costume Design; nominated for Best Feature Film, Best Director, Best Leading Actor (Tony LEUNG Chiu-wai), Best Original Screenplay, Best Art Direction, and Best Original Film Score
Cannes Film Festival: Best Actor (Tony LEUNG Chiu-wai) and Technical Grand Prize (Christopher DOYLE, Mark LEE Ping-bing and William CHANG Suk-ping)
Color, 98 minutes

2046 (2004)
Hong Kong, France, Italy, China
Production companies: Block 2 Pictures, Jet Tone, Paradis Films, Orly Films Classic Srl, Shanghai Film Group
Director: **WONG Kar-wai**
Screenplay: **WONG Kar-wai**
Producer: **WONG Kar-wai**
Directors of photography: Christopher DOYLE, LAI Yiu-fai, KWAN Pun-leung
Editor: William CHANG Suk-ping
Art director: William CHANG Suk-ping
Music: Peer RABEN, Shigeru UMEBAYASHI
Cast: Tony LEUNG Chiu-wai, ZHANG Ziyi, GONG Li, Faye WONG, Takuya KIMURA, CHANG Chen, Carina LAU, Maggie CHEUNG, DONG Jie
Hong Kong Film Awards: Best Actor (Tony LEUNG Chiu-wai), Best Actress (ZHANG Ziyi), Best Cinematography, Best Art Direction, Best Costume and Makeup Design), and Best Original Film Score; nominated for Best Film, Best Director, Best Screenplay, Best Film Editing, Best Sound Design, and Best Visual Effects
Hong Kong Film Critics Society Awards: Best Actor (Tony LEUNG Chiu-wai), Best Actress (ZHANG Ziyi), and Film of Merit

Golden Horse Awards (Taiwan): Best Art Direction and Best Original Film Score; nominated for Best Feature Film, Best Leading Actor (Tony LEUNG Chiu-wai), Best Leading Actress (ZHANG Ziyi), Best Cinematography, Best Makeup and Costume Design, and Best Sound Effects
Color, 124 minutes

MY BLUEBERRY NIGHTS (2007)
藍莓之夜 / LAN MEI ZHI YE (THE NIGHT OF BLUEBERRY)
Hong Kong, USA, France
Production companies: Block 2 Pictures, Studio Canal, Jet Tone
Director: **WONG Kar-wai**
Screenplay: **WONG Kar-wai,** Lawrence BLOCK
Producers: **WONG Kar-wai,** Jacky PANG Yee-wah
Director of photography: Darius KHONDJI
Editor: William CHANG Suk-ping
Art director: Judy RHEE
Production designer: William CHANG Suk-ping
Costume designers: William CHANG Suk-ping, Sharon GLOBERSON
Music: Ry COODER
Cast: Jude LAW, Norah JONES, David STRATHAIRN, Rachel WEISZ, Natalie PORTMAN
Color, 95 minutes

ASHES OF TIME REDUX (2008)
東邪西毒終極版 / DONG XIE XI DU ZHONG JI BAN (THE ULTIMATE VERSION OF EASTERN HERETIC, WESTERN VENOM)
Hong Kong
Production companies: Scholar, Block 2 Pictures, Jet Tone
Director: **WONG Kar-wai**
Screenplay: **WONG Kar-wai**
Producers: **WONG Kar-wai**, Jacky PANG Yee-wah
Editor: William CHANG Suk-ping
Additional music: WU Tong
Color: 93 minutes

THE GRANDMASTER (2013)
一代宗師 / YI DAI ZONG SHI (THE MASTER OF THE GENERATION)
Hong Kong, China
Production companies: Block 2 Pictures, Jet Tone, Sil-Metropole
Director: **WONG Kar-wai**

Screenplay: **WONG Kar-wai,** ZOU Jingzhi, XU Haofeng
Producers: **WONG Kar-wai,** Jacky PANG Yee-wah
Director of photography: Philippe LE SOURD
Editor: William CHANG Suk-ping
Art directors: William CHANG Suk-ping, Alfred YAU Wai-ming
Martial arts director: YUEN Woo-ping
Music: Shigeru UMEBAYASHI, Nathaniel MECHALY
Cast: Tony LEUNG Chiu-wai, ZHANG Ziyi, Max ZHANG Jin, ZHAO Benshan, SONG Hye-kyo, CHANG Chen
Hong Kong Film Awards: Best Film, Best Director, Best Screenplay, Best Actress (ZHANG Ziyi), Best Supporting Actor (Max ZHANG Jin), Best Cinematography, Best Film Editing, Best Art Direction, Best Costume and Makeup Design, Best Action Choreography, Best Original Film Score, and Best Sound Design; nominated for Best Actor (Tony LEUNG Chiu-wai) and Best Visual Effects
Hong Kong Film Critics Society Awards: Best Film and Best Actress (ZHANG Ziyi)
Golden Horse Awards (Taiwan): Best Actress (ZHANG Ziyi), Best Cinematography, Best Visual Effects, Best Art Direction, Best Makeup and Costume Design, and Audience Choice Award; nominated for Best Feature Film, Best Director, Best Leading Actor (Tony LEUNG Chiu-wai), Best Action Choreography, Best Film Editing, and Best Sound Effects
Academy Awards: nominated for Best Cinematography and Best Costume Design
Color, 130 minutes (Hong Kong and China); 123 minutes (International); 108 minutes (USA); 111 minutes (3D version)

Anthology Films

THE HAND (2004)
《愛神》之〈手〉 / AI SHEN ZHI SHOU (THE HAND IN EROS)
One of the three segments in *Eros*
Hong Kong
Production companies: Block 2 Pictures, Jet Tone
Director: **WONG Kar-wai**
Screenplay: **WONG Kar-wai**
Producer: **WONG Kar-wai,** Jacky PANG Yee-wah
Director of photography: Christopher DOYLE
Editor: William CHANG Suk-ping
Art director: Alfred YAU Wai-ming
Production designer: William CHANG Suk-ping
Music: Peer RABEN
Cast: GONG Li, CHANG Chen, TIN Fung
Color, 48 minutes (in *Eros*); 60 minutes (screening at Hong Kong International Film Festival)

I TRAVELLED 9000 KM TO GIVE IT TO YOU (2007)
One of the thirty-four segments in *To Each His Own Cinema* for the sixtieth anniversary of the Cannes Film Festival
Production company: Block 2 Pictures
Director: **WONG Kar-wai**
Screenplay: **WONG Kar-wai**
Producers: **WONG Kar-wai,** Jacky PANG Yee-wah, Gilles CIMENT
Director of photography: KWAN Pun-leung
Editor: William CHANG Suk-ping
Production designer: William CHANG Suk-ping
Cast: FAN Chih-wei, Farini CHANG Yui-ling
Color, 3 minutes 49 seconds

Commercials and Other Short Films

TO MAKE YOU HAPPY (1992)
討你歡心 / TAO NI HUAN XIN (TO MAKE YOU HAPPY)
Music video for Tracy HUANG Ying-ying
Director: **WONG Kar-wa**i
Director of photography: Christopher DOYLE
Art director: William CHANG Suk-ping
Music: Johnny CHEN
Cast: Tracy HUANG Ying-ying, Tony LEUNG Kar-fai
Color, 4 minutes

WKW/TK/1996@7'55"HK.NET (1996)
For Takeo KIKUCHI
Director: **WONG Kar-wa**i
Director of photography: Christopher DOYLE
Cast: Tadanobu ASANO, Karen MOK
Color, 7 minutes 55 seconds

STARTAC (1997)
Commercial for Motorola
Director: **WONG Kar-wai**
Director of photography: Christopher DOYLE
Cast: Faye WONG, Tadanobu ASANO
Color, 3 minutes

IN THE MOOD FOR LOVE (2000)
花樣年華 / HUA YANG NIAN HUA (THE AGE OF FLOWERS)

Music video for Tony LEUNG Chiu-wai and Niki WU
Director: **WONG Kar-wai**
Editor: William CHANG Suk-ping
Music: Sandee CHAN
Cast: Tony LEUNG Chiu-Wai, Niki WU
Color, 4 minutes 15 seconds

HUA YANG DE NIAN HUA (2000)
花樣的年華 / HUA YANG DE NIAN HUA (THE AGE OF FLOWERS)
Montage of images from old Hong Kong films
Director: **WONG Kar-wai**
Archival footage selected by **WONG Kar-wai**
Editor: William CHANG Suk-ping
Music: "The Age of Flowers"(花樣的年華) (singer: ZHOU Xuan, composer: FAN
Yan-qiao, lyricist: LIN Mei)
Color, 2 minutes 28 seconds

UN MATIN PARTOUT DANS LE MONDE (2000)
(ONE MORNING EVERYWHERE IN THE WORLD)
Commercial for JC Decaux
WONG Kar-wai directing the Hong Kong part
Color, 1 minute

IN THE MOOD FOR LOVE 2001 (2001)
Short film shown at the Cannes Film Festival under the rubric "Leçon de Cinéma"
Director: **WONG Kar-wai**
Screenplay: **WONG Kar-wai**
Cast: Tony LEUNG Chiu-wai, Maggie CHEUNG

THE FOLLOW (2001)
Commercial for BMW
Director: **WONG Kar-wai**
Screenplay: Andrew Kevin WALKER
Director of photography: Harris SAVIDES
Editor: William CHANG Suk-ping
Art director: Artin WHIS
Production designer: William CHANG Suk-ping
Cast: Clive OWEN, Mickey ROURKE, Adriana LIMA
Color, 8 minutes

DANS LA VILLE (2002)
(IN THE TOWN)
Commercial for Orange S.A.
Director: **WONG Kar-wai**
Color, 41 seconds

LA RENCONTRE (2002)
(THE MEETING)
Commercial for Lacoste
Director: **WONG Kar-wai**
Director of photography: Eric GAUTIER
Music: Shigeru UMEBAYASHI
Cast: CHANG Chen, Diane DE MAC-MAHON
Color, 1 minute

SIX DAYS (2002)
Music video for DJ Shadow
Director: **WONG Kar-wai**
Director of photography: Christopher DOYLE
Music: DJ Shadow
Cast: CHANG Chen
Color, 3 minutes 41 seconds

THE CAPTURE TOTALE COMMERCIAL (2005)
Commercial for Christian Dior
Director: **WONG Kar-wai**
Cast: Sharon STONE
Color, 30 seconds

THE HYPNÔSE HOMME COMMERCIAL (2006)
Commercial for Lancôme Paris
Director: **WONG Kar-wai**
Cast: Clive OWEN, Daria WERBOWY
Color, 20 seconds

THE MIDNIGHT POISON COMMERCIAL (2007)
Commercial for Christian Dior
Director: **WONG Kar-wai**
Music: "Space Dementia" by Muse
Cast: Eva GREEN
Color, 1 minute

THERE'S ONLY ONE SUN (2007)
Commercial for Philips
Director: **WONG Kar-wai**
Screenplay: **WONG Kar-wai**
Director of photography: Philippe LE SOURD
Editor: William CHANG Suk-ping
Production and costume designer: William CHANG Suk-ping
Cast: Amélie DAURE, Gianpaolo LUPORI, Stefan MORAWIETZ
Color, 9 minutes

BUSINESS / WHITE / BLACK (2007)
Set of three commercials for Softbank
Director: **WONG Kar-wai**
Cast: Brad PITT
Color, 1 minute 30 seconds

NOTORIOUS (2008)
Commercial for Ralph Lauren
Director: **WONG Kar-wai**
Cast: Laetitia CASTA
B&W, 1 minute

BLUEBERRY DAYS (2008)
Commercial for Louis Vuitton
Director: **WONG Kar-wai**
Cast: Natalie PORTMAN
Color, 2 minutes 5 seconds

MASK (2011)
Commercial for Shu Uemura
Director: **WONG Kar-wai**
Cast: Sandrine PINNA
Color, 46 seconds

DÉJÀ VU (2012)
(ALREADY SEEN)
Set of two commercials for Chivas
Director: **WONG Kar-wai**
Screenplay: **WONG Kar-wai**
Director of photography: Philippe LE SOURD

Editor: Ronald ZEE, Marut SEELZACHAROEN
Cast: CHANG Chen, DU Juan
Music: Roel A. GARCIA
Color, 4 minutes

REGENERATION (2014)
再生 / ZAI SHEN (REGENERATION)
Commercial for Maysu
Director: **WONG Kar-wai**
Cast: SHU Qi
Color, 1 minute 30 seconds

AS SCRIPTWRITER

Feature Films

ONCE UPON A RAINBOW (1982)
彩雲曲 / CAI YUN QU (THE SONG OF RAINBOW)
Hong Kong
Production company: Cinema City
Director: Agnes NG Siu-wan
Screenplay: HO Hon-kiu, **WONG Kar-wai**, LO Man-sang, YEE Chung-man
Producer: Teddy Robin KWAN

JUST FOR FUN (1983)
空心大少爺 / KONG XIN DA SHAO YE (THE BROKE PLAYBOY)
Hong Kong
Production company: Always Good
Director: Frankie CHAN Fan-kei
Screenplay: Frankie CHAN Fan-kei, WU Ma, **WONG Kar-wai**
Producers: Frankie CHAN Fan-kei, Guy LAI Ying-chau

SILENT ROMANCE (1984)
伊人再見 / YI REN ZAI JIAN (GOODBYE FAIR LADY)
Hong Kong
Production company: Always Good
Director: Frankie CHAN Fan-kei
Screenplay: **WONG Kar-wai**, Barry WONG Ping-yiu
Producers: Frankie CHAN Fan-kei, Guy LAI Ying-chau

CHASE A FORTUNE (1985)
吉人天相 / Ji REN TIAN XIANG (GOOD FORTUNE FOR THE GOOD PEOPLE)
Hong Kong
Production company: Always Good
Director: LIU Wai-hung
Screenplay: **WONG Kar-wai**
Producer: Guy LAI Ying-chau

UNFORGETTABLE FANTASY (1985)
小狐仙 / XIAO HU XIAN (LITTLE FOX FAIRY)
Hong Kong
Production company: Always Good
Director: Frankie CHAN Fan-kei
Screenplay: **WONG Kar-wai**
Producer: Frankie CHAN Fan-kei

THE INTELLECTUAL TRIO (1985)
龍鳳智多星 / LONG FENG ZHI DUO XING (THE QUICK-WITTED TRIO)
Hong Kong
Production company: Always Good
Director: Guy LAI Ying-chau
Screenplay: **WONG Kar-wai**, Barry WONG Ping-yiu
Producer: Guy LAI Ying-chau

ROSA (1986)
神勇雙響炮續集 / SHEN YONG SHUANG XIANG PAO XU JI (THE BRAVE TWIN
CANNONS SEQUEL)
Hong Kong
Production company: Golden Harvest
Director: Joe CHEUNG Tung-cho
Screenplay: Barry WONG Ping-yiu, **WONG Kar-wai**
Producer: Sammo HUNG Kam-bo

SWEET SURRENDER (1986)
我要金龜婿 / WO YAO JIN GUI XU (I WANT A WEALTHY HUSBAND)
Hong Kong
Production company: Always Good
Director: Frankie CHAN Fan-kei
Screenplay: Frankie CHAN Fan-kei, **WONG Kar-wai**, Chan Fai-hung
Producer: Frankie CHAN Fan-kei

GOODBYE MY LOVE (1986)
惡男 / E NAN (NOTORIOUS MAN)
Hong Kong
Production company: Always Good
Director: Frankie CHAN Fan-kei
Screenplay: Frankie CHAN Fan-kei, **WONG Kar-wai**
Producer: Frankie CHAN Fan-kei

FINAL VICTORY (1987)
最後勝利 / ZUI HOU SHENG LI (FINAL VICTORY)
Hong Kong
Production company: D & B
Director: Patrick TAM Ka-ming
Screenplay: **WONG Kar-wai**
Producer: John SHAM Kin-fun

THE HAUNTED COP SHOP (1987)
猛鬼差館 / MENG GUI CAI GUAN (THE HAUNTED POLICE STATION)
Hong Kong
Production company: In-Gear
Director: Jeff LAU Chun-wai
Screenplay: **WONG Kar-wai**, Jeff LAU Chun-wai
Producer: Alan TANG Kwong-wing

THE FLAME BROTHERS (1987)
江湖龍虎鬥 / JIANG HU LONG HU DOU (THE BATTLE OF TRIADS)
Hong Kong
Production company: In-Gear
Director: Joe CHEUNG Tung-cho
Screenplay: **WONG Kar-wai**
Producer: Alan TANG Kwong-wing

WALK ON FIRE (1988)
獵鷹計劃 / LIE YING JI HUA (THE PLAN OF EAGLE-HUNTING)
Hong Kong
Production company: Seasonal
Director: Norman LAW Man
Screenplay: **WONG Kar-wai**
Producer: NG See-yuen

RETURN ENGAGEMENT (1990)
再戰江湖 / ZAI ZHAN JIANG HU (THE RETURN TO THE TRIAD)
Hong Kong
Production companies: In-Gear, Fu On
Director: Joe CHEUNG Tung-cho
Screenplay: Joe CHEUNG Tung-cho, **WONG Kar-wai**
Producer: Alan TANG Kwong-wing

SAVIOUR OF THE SOUL (1991)
九一神鵰俠侶 / JIU YI SHEN DIAO XIA LU (THE EAGLE-SHOOTING
HEROES 91)
Hong Kong
Production company: Team Work
Director: Corey YUEN Kwai, David LAI
Screenplay: **WONG Kar-wai**
Producers: David LAI, CHAN Pui-wah

AS PRODUCER

Feature Films

DONG CHENG XI JIU (1993)
射鵰英雄傳之東成西就 / SHE DIAO YING XIONG ZHUAN ZHI DONG CHENG
XI JIU (EASTERN SUCCESS WESTERN ACHIEVEMENT OF THE LEGEND OF
THE CONDOR HEROES)
Hong Kong
Production companies: Jet Tone, Scholars
Director: Jeff LAU Chun-wai
Screenplay: Jeff LAU Chun-wai
Producer: **WONG Kar-wai**

FIRST LOVE: THE LITTER ON THE BREEZE (1997)
初纏恋后的二人世界 / CHU CHAN LIAN HOU DE ER REN SHI JIE (ROMANCE
AFTER THE FIRST ENCOUNTER)
Hong Kong
Production companies: Block 2 Pictures, Amuse Group, Jet Tone
Director: Eric KOT Man-fai
Screenplay: Ocean CHAN Hoi-kei, Patrick KONG
Producers: **WONG Kar-wai**, Yokichi OSATO

CHINESE ODYSSEY 2002 (2002)
天下無雙 / TIAN XIA WU SHUANG (THE FIRST IN THE WORLD)
Hong Kong
Production companies: Block 2 Pictures, Hakuhodou, Jet Tone
Director: Jeff LAU Chun-wai
Screenplay: Jeff LAU Chun-wai
Producer: **WONG Kar-wai**

SEE YOU TOMORROW (2016)
擺渡人 / BAI DU REN (THE FERRYMAN)
Hong Kong, China
Production companies: Jet Tone, Alibaba Pictures
Director: ZHANG Jiajia
Screenplay:**WONG Kar-wai**, ZHANG Jiajia
Producers: **WONG Kar-wai**, Jacky PANG Yee-wah

Wong Kar-wai: Interviews

Wong Kar-wai on *As Tears Go By*

Lok Ching / 1988

From *City Entertainment* (Hong Kong). No. 241 (pp. 24-25). Interview conducted in Cantonese in 1988. Reprinted by permission of the publisher. Translated by Silver Wai-ming Lee from Chinese.

The test-screening room was almost full when I entered. The film had started before I settled down in the smoke-filled room. I had lots of questions when watching the film. After the screening, I sat down with director Wong Kar-wai and asked him some questions.

Wong is the screenwriter of *Once upon a Rainbow*. He met Patrick Tam after joining Always Good Film where he conceptualized *Final Victory* and *Sweet Surrender*. After overcoming some obstacles, he eventually directed his first film.

Lok Ching: Why is it titled *Mong Kok Carmen*?

Wong Kar-wai: *Mong Kok Carmen* is actually another story about a love story between a young police inspector and a dancehall girl. I set the story of Carmen in Mong Kok.[1] But some actors thought I was filming that story. When asked by journalists what they were making, the actors said it was "Mong Kok Carmen." I originally wanted to revise [the title], but everyone thought there was nothing wrong with it. So we just let it be.

LC: How did you come up with the idea of the film?

WKW: I had the story outline of *As Tears Go By* before writing *Final Victory*. It was inspired by a very short piece of news: two underage youngsters were instigated by the gang to kill someone. After getting paid and having a wild night of fun, they took action.

LC: Can you analyze the personalities of the three main characters?

WKW: They are all doing things that they ought not do. Maggie Cheung should not be staying together with Andy Lau. He is a temptation to her, but it *ends up* that she could never own him. Fly (played by Jacky Cheung) keeps on trying to do something of which he is incapable. Andy Lau should not have taken care of Jacky Cheung, but there is no other way out.

LC: Was this an idea that you had for a long time, or was it just a feeling towards these characters?

WKW: I do not make up my stories in a box. As a story develops, the personalities of the characters cannot be separated from your own preferences. The story can be developed in various ways, but it originates from you. It is like, based on my own understanding, I think these characters would react in such a way. My films are not about stories. I develop plots from the characters' personalities. I believe the story is not important, but the characters are.

LC: Would you talk about the relationship between *Final Victory* and *As Tears Go By*?

WKW: I would say the two films are a match. The two films have similar angles. I wrote both scripts with similar *themes* and characters so people feel the two films are alike. At that time we had three stories related to teenage characters. I was a bit tired of them. Characters continue to develop and stories might extend from this development. I have come to know these people during that particular period of time. So I portrayed them, thinking they were interesting. I don't believe in *research* because it is impossible to know someone's story just by chatting with them for a day or so. It takes time. I became friends with them, and we spent time together. I came to fathom how they lived. I couldn't start creating the story until I understood these people. There is a sense of distance if you write without being clear about something.

When writing about these kinds of people, screenwriters usually portray them in the gangster genre. But I do not want the characters to be too clear-cut, too "black and white." The characters have a lot of weaknesses. Like Andy Lau, you cannot say he is a positive character. This kind of portrayal might not be easily accepted by the audience. In *Final Victory*, the protagonists Tsui Hark and Eric Tsang have weaknesses too. But I think they are humans, and humans have weaknesses. The audience's acceptance of the characters depends on their portrayals. If they are vividly portrayed, the audience can feel it.

Final Victory is packaged by Patrick Tam. An audience from that social class of the protagonists may feel distant when watching the film. *As Tears Go By* may have the same problem too. But I believe if I made the film in a *raw* way, it would be quite innovative. My angle is to express my feelings within the main lines of the characters.

LC: Why are the relationships between the protagonists so special?

WKW: Some things are difficult to write about: why a man likes a woman, brotherhood, etc. These things are very subtle. But I want to raise the point that time is the most important factor. It's the contact between people. If I stay with you for a long time, it is like turning pages in a daily calendar and your marks can be found on every page. This kind of relationship is unconsciously built up. I did not know why I had to help you, but I just did. This is clearly stated in the last scene that takes place by the sea in *Final Victory*.

LC: Another example would be the relationship between Eric Tsang and Loletta Lee in *Final Victory* as well as that between Andy Lau and Maggie Cheung in *As Tears Go By*. Why would the relationships build up so groundlessly?

WKW: I feel the relationship between a man and a woman cannot be qualified by the length spent on them in the film, like the protagonists in *Waterloo Bridge*—they fall in love just after bumping into each other underground. In terms of the lightning during the scene at the pier, it is all a work of nature. It does not imply anything.

LC: The music in *As Tears Go By* starts so suddenly; is this your idea?

WKW: Some use of music is intended. Another reason is that we were in a hurry during postproduction. For example, we planned to insert a *love theme* in the sequences of "Take My Breath Away," but we gave up due to copyrights. Shooting was completed on the 27th and the film premiere was scheduled at midnight on the 4th,[2] so we used whatever music we had at hand. The theaters are screening the *C Copy* now. I hadn't watched the output myself until I went to the theater. I had to spend days and nights filming during the last month, so I asked William Chang to help me edit. He did well as he knew this film best. Patrick Tam edited two *action* scenes. O Sing-pui edited the scenes with Alex Man. Stanley Kwan helped with the dubbing. I made the *final cut*.

I am still working on some *mixing* to make the soundtrack better.

LC: Is anything cut out?

WKW: I changed the ending, deleting the scene at the jail. I let Andy Lau to die during the shootout. I don't want the scene in which Maggie Cheung remains speechless when seeing Andy Lau being mentally impaired.[3] The reason for the change is that the movie is too long. It is impossible to run 9,300 feet of film reel. Also, many people want Andy Lau's character to die because they cannot accept him as an idiot. Being mentally impaired is more unacceptable than death. I think it does not matter to end [note: WKW said *cut*] the movie at this point. I only want to express that they have some *energy* and how they release it. There isn't much difference in what the consequence is. This is an instinct. At that moment, they do it without considering the consequences. They have never made rational decisions.

LC: Is it that they plan rationally before taking action but are unusually emotional at the last minute?

WKW: Maybe they suppress themselves before taking action but finally do it. I know many people of this kind, and I have also witnessed their behavior in this way. When they reach a certain age, they become worldly and their *energy* fades away. They would feel miserable when they are *aware* that they could not do whatever comes to mind.

LC: Are you satisfied with this change in the ending?

WKW: The *ending* now is made in the most efficient way. And it is too simple to the general audience. There are not enough time and *tension* to bring the audience to the climax. I think this *ending* is *weak*, but acceptable.

LC: The action scenes are very special; are they improvisations? And do they intentionally represent different stages?

WKW: Actually I do not like formulated choreography. The real *violence* does not rest with movement, but with feeling. There should be one *point* in every fight scene, like in the scene at the open-air food stall. I shot it from the viewpoint of Andy Lau. When he wants to kill a guy, the camera focuses on that guy. Andy Lau stares at that guy and cannot see what happens around him. He is full of rage; he is as furious as the horrendous heat at the food stall. The only thing in his mind is that his rage will fade away after the killing.

The chase scene at the pool hall is a sudden event. The ending scene was shot from Jacky Cheung's viewpoint. At that very moment, he can hear very acutely, so you hear the noises from the police vehicles and people.

LC: How was the shaking effect made in the fight scenes?

WKW: I made it by 'adding frames' when shooting. I shot with the frame rate at twelve frames per second (usually a film is shot at twenty-four frames) and then printed every frame once more. This is how the effect was achieved.

LC: Is there any difficulty when shooting other scenes?

WKW: We shot a fight scene outside the Broadway Cinema on a weekend night. We wanted to film it in secrecy, but once we *set* the camera, people gathered around us. We stopped shooting every time the police arrived and continued after they left. Our crew took three hours and had good morale. Some of the crew members were worried that it would not work, but I was not scared at all. I believe there is nothing impossible to film. I think it was fun and challenging.

LC: Is there any special meaning about the interior of Andy Lau's home?
WKW: I want [his home] to reflect a sharp contrast between day and night. When night time arrives and the TV is on, these people become active. It marks the beginning of nightlife. During daytime, everything in the house is still. There are more camera movements and strange angles at night. One example is the shots of Andy Lau getting up and turning on the TV.

During the interview, Wong kept mentioning several things: his strict control over cinematography and lighting; his feeling towards *Mean Streets* (directed by Martin Scorsese); what if *As Tears Go By* was directed by Patrick Tam; his realization at a later stage of shooting that he should stay relaxed like Juzo Itami when he made films. Wong also reminded himself that making films is for fun. He explained this would make him ignore the difficulties while being on set and see the outcome as less important.

NOTES

1. The Chinese title of *As Tears Go By* can be literally translated as *Mong Kok Carmen*. Mong Kok is the most crowded place in Hong Kong where many gangster films are set. Carmen is drawn from *Carmen* the opera composed by Georges Bizet.
2. Midnight premieres were a common practice in the Hong Kong film industry from the 1980s to 1990s. Filmmakers would re-edit the film based on the audience reaction; therefore, the final cut could be different from the premiere/midnight cut.
3. The alternative ending of Andy Lau being mentally impaired is used in the Taiwanese version. Also, the Chinese title *Mong Kok Carmen* was changed to *Hot-blooded Boys*.

Wong Kar-wai Takes Charge

Cheuk Chi/ 1988

From *City Entertainment* (Hong Kong). No. 244 (p. 17). Interview conducted in Cantonese in 1988. Reprinted by permission of the publisher. . Translated by Silver Wai-ming Lee from Chinese.

Cheuk Chi: Among exceptional beginner screenwriters, Wong Kar-wai is considered to be both talented and lucky. He is thankful for the opportunity given by Kam Kwok-leung and has taken the opportunity to migrate from television to the silver screen. He has been keeping up with the good work since then.

Looking back at his individual screenplays, Wong is only happy with *Final Victory*. As Wong explained, he thinks director Patrick Tam is more capable of bringing the screenwriter's ideals into reality.

Wong Kar-wai: Every director with whom I have cooperated has his or her own strength. As a screenwriter, I certainly understand the importance of rapport and recognition between directing and scriptwriting, and this importance cannot be established in a meeting or two. This is the reason why I prefer working with directors with whom I am familiar and share a mutual understanding. It does not mean I am shy about working with others, but true communication can only happen after collaboration in two or more films. I believe many screenwriters have faced situations in which their scripts are altered; it is up to the individuals whether they accept the changes or not. For instance, the screenwriter might want to express a love scene with many lines, but the director could clearly express the scene in one or two shots. I can accept this kind of change, though; I believe this helps me gain experience. It is surely ideal if the director and the screenwriter are totally in sync, but this is impossible. In accordance, I tend to give what the director asks for, especially those whom I know well. I try to understand his or her way of directing without straying away from my original thought.

CC: Wong Kar-wai has worked for Cinema City and Always Good Film in the industry. He had another opportunity given by producer Alan Tang Kwong-wing.

These opportunities have not only led Wong to produce *Flaming Brothers* and *The Haunted Cop Shop*, but they have also led him to become the writer and director of *As Tears Go By*.

CC: It is undoubtedly ideal when the director is also the writer because writing and directing can be very subjective. There is less conflict. Would this total control become too extreme, particularly when the director wants to satisfy him/herself at the expense of budget?

WKW: Looking back at my screenwriting experience, I have come across many situations in which I had to compromise due to production budget. I believe a bigger budget does not guarantee a higher quality film; it does not even lead to a better box office. Although I sometimes insist to a certain extent—especially because I always emphasize aesthetics—this insistence may put pressure on the production department. I believe this applies to every director, but I usually stand more firmly on having a bigger budget when it comes to shooting on location and during postproduction. I personally think the production budget ought to be estimated when the screenplay is finalized. I ask to be informed of the expenses of certain scenes; this is the basic communication requirement between the director and the producer. For instance, if a scene is less than a minute but requires a lot of expenses, we certainly have to compromise. However, I will not accept the working method of arguing about the budget during the shooting. Or else, what is preproduction for? However, a reasonable case to eliminate an on-location shoot would be a conflict in the actors' schedules because the scene was scheduled to be filmed over three days.

Directors are supposed to work within the budget to express themselves. I usually inform the producer in advance about shooting and cost details, so we are well prepared if there need to be adjustments. I learned this from my experience as a film producer; I am thus confident in controlling production costs as a director.

However, the expense of *As Tears Go By* somehow exceeded the estimated budget. This was due to the lack of detailed planning, which in turn was due to conflicts in actors' schedules and some sudden script changes. During the shooting we discovered the plot was somewhat similar to a film that was in production by another company, so we had to make a quick decision to change the script. We suspended filming for a period of time. From the beginning to the end, five months were spent on production, but only the last month and a half were fully devoted to filming. The rewrite increased production cost, but this business decision could not have been avoided. Strictly speaking, there were flaws in handling the matter. However, from another perspective, it was understandable why the production cost went beyond budget. We were in a hurry because of the scheduled date to screen. We could not have avoided going over budget.

The experience has helped me learn new things about shooting, developing ideas, and executing. This might be helpful when I face a similar situation in the future as a director or in other positions.

CC: Wong is fond of trying different things to make films. He prefers topics that are realistic yet romantic; this taste might stem from his personality. The work of every filmmaker is inevitably influenced by his/her personality, liking and disliking. Everyone has his or her own strengths, and no one is capable of making films in every genre. In his working position, Wong hopes to try different things. According to him, filmmaking is a job that he likes—and he likes it almost madly. Therefore, every position challenges and intrigues him. Perhaps one day he would be the only person in the crew; this must give him an overwhelming sense of satisfaction. And hopefully when he is a producer, he will suppress all his romantic thoughts and become sensibly realistic.

The Days of Being Wild: Eight-day Location Shooting in the Philippines

Angel / 1989

From *City Entertainment* (Hong Kong). No. 306 (pp. 36–41). Interview conducted in Cantonese in 1989. Reprinted by permission of the publisher. Translated by Micky Lee from Chinese.

This interview, "The Days of Being Wild"—crazy days—documents a week of filming *Days of Being Wild* in the Philippines. As the film is going to be in theaters soon, Wong Kar-wai pressures the cast and crew to speed up shooting from dusk to dawn.

"Witnessing a historical event taking place is more important than sleeping," one crew member told me.

Another said: "Film people live an inhumane life."

I asked, "Flying people?" No wonder the film is called *Days of Being Wild*.[1]

Wong Kar-wai: The biggest reason for the long production time of *Days of Being Wild* is location. I don't have a studio to build sets, so I need to find a location that is the closest to my idea and then refine it. But it takes a long time to find such a location. At the beginning we were more optimistic, but afterwards we learned it was very difficult. Basically the slow progress at the beginning is my own style. The beginning is an experiment; therefore, there were the most NGs[2] because I needed to *tune* the actors to follow my path. It has taken a lot of time. Because the public is paying a lot of attention to *Days of Being Wild* and there are many rumors, the filming became a very serious affair. In reality it was not as bad as others imagined.

My *Days of Being Wild* has nothing to do with James Dean's *Rebel Without a Cause*.[3] But when we think of *Rebel Without a Cause*, we think of the 1950s and '60s. Because *Days of Being Wild* takes place in the same era, we used the title. It is a mere convenience. The inspiration of *Days of Being Wild* comes from my special feeling for 1960s Hong Kong. The story is about human relationships, including those between mother and son and between lovers; there is a misalignment of space.

I used to be able to make films in a relaxing way. There would only be criticism after the films were done, but the public started to notice me after *As Tears Go By*. Now when I make films, I attract a lot of bad attention and rumors; these rumors affect everyone's mood. I don't know if it is a good or bad thing.

I have not thought if I'd like to make an *art film*. When I was young, I would be very happy if I saw a good film. Others gave me this happiness. When I became a director, I hoped to give the audience the same feeling. My expectation for every film is the same: I hope it will be good, that it is not a waste of time. I have never thought of turning a new page in history. After I completed the producers' training at TVB [Television Broadcasts Limited] and did practicum for half a year, I left the television station to make films. I have worked for different studios for nine years. The greatest joy of my childhood was to watch movies. After working in the movie industry for a while, I wanted to make films. This is something natural . . . my experience comes from those days meeting more people. When I understand more, the films become more accurate. Everyone has to endure hardships. From an optimistic viewpoint, the experience of the past few years has been beneficial. I ask myself every time, "What do I want?" That's why you see me making changes at the last minute because I want to make sure I have paid my utmost effort. I can't have *regret* in the future.

Angel: How does the director see his actors?

WKW: I feel Andy Lau has made a lot of gangster films in recent years; his real self is not gangster-like. Although he does have some emotional times and can be sensitive, he is a very cheerful person. I asked him to give me a "blank page," to act in *Days of Being Wild* as if he had never acted before. It could be more insecure to an actor. He feels other actors' characters have much flair, but his has none. But I hope his character balances others—some characters are ordinary, others are more dramatic. This should be the way of doing things.

Leslie Cheung has a great performance because he is playing himself. A few things in *Days of Being Wild* closely resemble Leslie's real self. Leslie is not a simple person [note: WKW used the word *basic*]; he plays rebellious characters the best.

Carina Lau's character is very intuitive [note: WKW used the word *physical*]. She gets what she want; she is very direct. Her personality stands out a lot. Carina is a solid and calm actress, very resilient. In the beginning, her character in the original script has schizophrenia, but after the screenplay was revised many times, her character is the most direct in the film. She plays a character who feels everything is alright after a good night of sleep. The best quality of Carina is she is very natural. She does not have much acting experience, but it turned out to be a good thing. She does not act in a stereotypical way [note: WKW used the word *stereotype*]. This is the most precious quality of an actor.

Jacky Cheung plays a one hundred percent enthusiastic character. He has the warmth of northern Chinese, but this kind of person gets hurt the most easily. Actors will no longer be challenging after working too much with me because they will always play themselves. If Jacky played the villain in *Swordsman*, he may need to act more. But I don't like seeing actors acting; it is meaningless to me. I like reality.

Maggie Cheung's character in *Days of Being Wild* is an ordinary girl, like Andy Lau's character, which is very difficult to play. Maggie is very special because she is not suitable for doing ordinary acting. Her own body movement is very complicated; she is able to show complex emotions without any dialogue. Because of this quality, she does not perform well if she is told how to act in a scene.

Angel: How do the actors see their performances?

Leslie Cheung: In January 1989, associate producer Joseph Chan Wing-kwong introduced Wong Kar-wai to me to talk about the film. At the beginning I was supposed to be play a minor role, but we became more familiar with each other. Then I became the main male character. I am an arrogant person because I see myself as a *professional*. I see others as amateurs. If others are not in the same league as I am, I will ignore them. But after getting to know Wong Kar-wai, I realized he has many visions. I believe he is the most *promising* director in Hong Kong.

Working with an actor of my talent, many directors will accommodate me. They will accept whatever I do, but Wong won't. His requirements are very strict. When an expression crossed my face, he would suggest that I try another way to act, to try to think outside the box. I feel his working attitude creates sparks within me; it creates certain *chemistry* [note: LC used the word *chemicals*]. Wong is the director who asks me to NG the most. The record is forty-seven *takes*.

I have a special feeling for the 1960s. I only remember the bell bottoms of the '70s, but there were many major events in the '60s: Marilyn Monroe's death, John Kennedy's assassination. In addition, my own family was the most intact in the '60s; therefore, I have a special feeling for that era. William Chang was very successful at re-creating the '60s. When I was filming in Seymour Terrace in mid-level Central, I felt like I was at home; therefore, I was more into the role.

Andy Lau: I tried to forget all my past acting to be in *Days of Being Wild*. We can say I gave a piece of blank paper to Wong Kar-wai. I gave him a chance to write me a letter about Andy Lau. In *As Tears Go By*, I acted to perform my own perception of Andy Lau; therefore, in *As Tears Go By*, many dialogues, movements, and the character's thoughts are Andy Lau in first person. But it is not the same for *Days of*

Being Wild. This time Wong Kar-wai wants me to act like Andy Lau from his point of view: how he would present this character in this situation. The Andy Lau in *Days of Being Wild* is the Andy Lau from Wong Kar-wai's perspective.

This time I play a passive character. The camera rarely shows my eyes and face in contrast to other characters. They stand in the front of the camera while I stand in the back. After seeing *Days of Being Wild*, you would doubt whether this character exists or not. Wong Kar-wai has this arrangement because he thinks I have always caught the attention of the viewers, but he wanted to have a change. I was not accustomed to it in the beginning. Even though I was standing in the back, I am a key man in the film. The entire film hopes to *present* my character the best. If not for this character, this film would not become a film. This character continues into the sequel.[4] The director wants the audience to remember the relationship between Maggie Cheung's and my characters.

Carina Lau: At the beginning I was scared of Wong Kar-wai. This fear came from Tony Leung Chiu-wai. Tony Leung has worked with Wong Kar-wai, and Tony told me one day he had twenty-six NGs. He blamed himself for not knowing how to act. This instilled a fear in me—a feeling that this director is demanding. In addition, the performers in *Days of Being Wild* are all award-winning actors and actresses. Working with them make me feel a lot of pressure.

For every scene, every expression, and every movement, Wong Kar-wai would tell me a lot of information that makes me give a convincing performance: I am this woman; this is my background; this is what my mother is like. These details may not appear in the film, but this kind of information makes the actors dive into the acting. He suggested I watch *Betty Blue* since my character is similar to Betty. I also went on a diet to lose weight because I play a dancehall girl. Wong Kar-wai loaned me many movies with belly-dancing for preparation.

My acting is unlike Wong Kar-wai's style. He wants actors to be the most ordinary, the most natural, making him feel they are not acting. But I have been in television for many years, and I like acting. . . . After working with Wong Kar-wai, I feel my acting skills have improved a lot.

NOTES

1. In Cantonese the pronunciation of "nonhumane" is the same as "flying people." The Cantonese title of *Days of Being Wild* is pronounced as *Ah Fei Jing Juen.* "Fei" in the Chinese title is the character for "fly." The term "Ah Fei" was popular in 1960s and '70s. It refers to rebellious youth or young gangsters who do not conform to social norms or

abide by laws. The Chinese title of *Days of Being Wild* can be translated as "The story of a rebellious youth."

2. NG is used in the Hong Kong television and film industries to signal stop and retake. It means "No Good."

3. The Chinese titles for both *Days of Being Wild* and *Rebel Without a Cause* are identical.

4. The sequel was not made.

All about *Days of Being Wild*: A Dialogue with Wong Kar-wai

Jimmy Ngai / 1990

From *City Entertainment* (Hong Kong). No. 305 (pp. 38–40). Interview conducted in Cantonese in 1990. Translated by Silver Wai-ming Lee from Chinese. Reprinted by permission of the publisher.

Jimmy Ngai: We are all interested in the ins and outs of the *project*.

Wong Kar-wai: It is a bother if I have to talk about the *project* from the beginning to the end. It could take two to three hours.

JN: Let's try to begin with the story.

WKW: It was simple. The starting point was that I had to make a set of films—each having two installments. Conventional films focus on causal events. An experienced audience is able to predict the development of the story. A *sophisticated* audience can even go faster than the storyteller—they are used to this kind of storytelling. My thought was this: since people are aware of the structure of storytelling, I should make changes in the structure so that they cannot speculate what the next event will be. I think *surprise* is very important. After deciding on the length, I needed enough characters to *support* the film: A set of two films does not mean making a longer film but condensing three films into two. The structure is thus larger. It is either a large cross-section or the key element is time. You know, a two-part film is actually one film. It just lets me use more time to change the audience's habit of understanding storytelling.

JN: But eventually, the finalized work will be divided into two parts and shown separately.

WKW: It is just the theatrical release. I have many choices afterwards: I can re-edit it into a new version. It could be three or four hours long on VHS. VHS actually dominates the film market now. The VHS version of *Days of Being Wild* that will be released in the future is what I want to do the most.

JN: You mean we have to watch *Days of Being Wild* on VHS?
WKW: I think some theaters are still willing to show it.

JN: I heard that at the beginning you wanted to construct a story on a larger scale of time and space.
WKW: Originally the background was to be segmented into three parts: a fishing village, urban Kowloon, and the Philippines with the corresponding periods of the 1930s, 1960, and 1966. But at the end I gave up the parts that take place in the fishing village.

JN: And 1960 and '66?
WKW: I came to Hong Kong from Shanghai in 1963. In my memory, Hong Kong was . . . *memorable*, as if even the sun was brighter. Also the radio was in the air . . .

JN: It was probably the infrastructure of the city.
WKW: Indeed, but everything becomes better in memory. At that time everything was slow. Of course, I absolutely could not precisely represent the '60s; I only tried to portray the pictures in my subjective memory.

JN: Now we know about the time. What about the characters?
WKW: What is interesting is that originally in the '60s, the "lovers" suffer repercussions after many years: romance is a dreadful illness that inflicts long-lasting damage. In contemporary society everything is so fast that we don't have time to remember anyone. But after experiencing many changes, I realize that the things happening in the film can still happen in our daily life today. It only makes you feel distant because it was set in the '60s.

JN: Then the film is about lovers and their affairs?
WKW: Romance is the kind of relationship that most easily engages people. But what motivates the tangled affairs? For someone? For oneself? For a demand? Or in search of a suitable partner? It is fine if we do not *analyze*, but once we *analyze*, the hidden purposes can be discovered.

JN: This sounds *dramatic*.
WKW: The story is *dramatic*, but the details/techniques are not *dramatic* at all. It is most important to grasp the audience's curiosity so that they keep watching.

JN: The audience's curiosity . . . I am full of curiosity about the crazily big cast.
WKW: Those four men and two women?

JN: I would appreciate further details.
WKW: I started *casting* at the end of last year. I wanted those performers at the very beginning, so I met with them and tried to negotiate and schedule with them one by one. It started smoothly. It felt like everyone wanted to get it done.

JN: What is it? I suppose you didn't even have the outline of the story?
WKW: When talking about *Days of Being Wild*, everyone had his/her own imagination.

JN: With only your name and the title *Days of Being Wild*? Awesome!
WKW: It went smoothly after the actors and actresses were *committed*. I developed the story gradually based on their personalities and images. I kept revising once the shooting started.

JN: Till now?
WKW: Yes. I don't think a scriptwriter/director knows how the performers should act in the beginning. Every performer has his/her unique personalities. Getting along with each other and then developing the character based on his/her personality is the best way.

JN: How about the investors? Were they shocked after knowing the cast?
WKW: Not really. There is no free lunch. The bigger cast you use, the more money you can get by selling distribution rights overseas. It's just business.

JN: How long had you prepared before shooting?
WKW: Around three months. My original concept was much more complicated than the present one, but timing did not allow it to happen, nor did the budget. Our preparation was passive. As the actors and actresses had scheduled with us, we had to work against time. We had to start as scheduled; after the booked period, the actors were not available anymore. It is also exhausting to write and direct all by yourself.

JN: You don't need to be both the scriptwriter and director, right?
WKW: No scriptwriter would like to be stuck with a director for such a long time. They have to make a living!

JN: This is from your experience?
WKW: Correct.

JN: I am interested in the investors again. What about them?
WKW: They are very *supportive*. Of course, it is after all a business. They have pressures. Like the screening schedule, there aren't many peak seasons in a year. So we wanted to screen *Days of Being Wild* at Christmas. It would be better if I had more time. On the other hand, I have been working with them for a few years, and we have a mutual understanding. The drawback of this understanding is that I know their hardship all too well. I would *compromise* rather than be too persistent. Besides, there is too much *noise* from the public which has also affected filming.

JN: Such as?
WKW: For my filmmaking habit, I am used to doing *adjustments* after the filming starts. I need to have a look first, think about it, and then decide the next step. But there would be *noise* from the public: "Oh? Shooting has stopped? There must be problems!" This naturally caused panic when the investors heard that. Actually it is just like taking a short break for a few days. Nothing unusual.

JN: Speaking of *noise*, let's talk about the pressure from *As Tears Go By* on *Days of Being Wild*.
WKW: Actually I was also under great pressure for the first film. It is about my expectations for myself. This time the biggest pressure came from the *noise* that started before filming; but I do not think it was because of *As Tears Go By*. Rather, it was about the cast of *Days of Being Wild*—it is undoubtedly a big cast. People cannot help whispering to each other. Once the buzz started, it snowballed until people saw the film as a big thing. The result was that I not only felt the pressure, but the crew felt it too. I don't like that feeling.

JN: But you expected that the public would be alerted by the big cast, hadn't you?
WKW: When it happened, the pressure was much greater than I expected.

JN: You just mentioned the entire crew felt the pressure . . .
WKW: Like the actors and actresses. They all wanted to perform well; or what's more, wanted to do better than others. Other crew members had no choice but to do it perfectly.

JN: But shouldn't it be perfect every time?
WKW: I prefer leaving some space. But I couldn't do it this time. I hope to have some space in the future.

JN: To be honest, what's your expectation for *Days of Being Wild*? Perhaps you might say you don't have one—that *it's just another exercise.*

WKW: I won't say something like *"another exercise."* This is too easy for the future. Only I would know what I can get from *Days of Being Wild*—for example, a better understanding of myself. On the contrary, the public's reaction can never be controlled and is thus unimportant. I would be lying if I told you the good reception of *As Tears Go By* had no effect on me. At least, I feel people start to *take you seriously.* I do not feel I have changed. It is like I used to regard thirty as an old age before I reached it. I have passed thirty, but I feel no change.

JN: You are only aware of the world in films?

WKW: When I watched films at a younger age, the attraction was that I could immediately immerse myself in that world. I was happy about that. Speaking of being a master or the critics' comments, I really don't think they are important. If I make a film and the audience likes it, it will be fine—it is best when I can share with others what I have experienced.

The This and That of Wong Kar-wai

Yeung Wai-lan and Lau Chi-kwan / 1994

From *City Entertainment* (Hong Kong). No. 402 (pp. 40–46). Interview conducted in Cantonese in 1994. Reprinted by permission of the publisher. Translated by Micky Lee from Chinese.

Reactions to Wong Kar-wai's films are very extreme: some give high praise to the films, others heavily criticize them. When *Days of Being Wild* was released, half of the reviews were positive, the other half were negative. When *Chungking Express* was released, the cultural critics had a heated debate about it. No one would miss a chance to talk about the film. Wong Kar-wai has been much talked about, but he does not initiate talk about his feelings and opinions. Therefore, this interview focuses on the upcoming *Ashes of Time*, as well as this—his films—and that—his favorite directors.

At the end we discover Wong Kar-wai works in the industry not because he loves films, but only because he likes to search for and enjoy other worlds made possible in films. To him, he can abandon films.

Yeung and Lau: *Ashes of Time* is based on two characters, Eastern Heretic and Western Venom, in Louis Cha [Jin Yong]'s work, but we heard that the story has no connection to his fiction.

Wong Kar-wai: Not unconnected . . . At the beginning, *Ashes of Time* is about another story. I like the names Eastern Heretic and Western Venom, and they are envisioned as two women. When we sought copyrights, we discovered there is no difference between the rights to the names and the story *The Legend of Eagle-Shooting Heroes,*[1] so we felt why don't we make *The Legend*? I like reading *wuxia* novels,[2] so I wanted to make *The Legend*. The most interesting characters are Eastern Heretic and Western Venom. People think Eastern Heretic is very cool because he is not tied down and is very cynical. But I have a different opinion about him; I think he is selfish. As for Western Venom, I like him because he is very tragic.

At the beginning I wanted to get in touch with Louis Cha because when he created those characters, he must have thought of events that occurred in the characters' earlier lives but he did not lay them out in the book. But I could not get in touch with him, so I began to think about what might have happened in their earlier lives. This allowed me to have more creative space, so I started to *develop* another story. The ending of my story is the beginning of *The Legend*.

Y&L: Do you use the period film genre merely because the two characters are interesting?
WKW: First, the period film genre was popular at that time.

Y&L: Which was two years ago?
WKW: Yes. Second, I had not made a period film. I have always thought this genre is fun to make; you can be as imaginative as possible.

Y&L: Others who make period films have their motivations: some want to criticize the present by talking about the past, others want to make fight scenes. What are your motivations?
WKW: I am not that ambitious; I only wanted to try. Period films are actually very difficult to make; therefore, I adopted an *easy-way-out* attitude by using a contemporary perspective. Also, I don't emphasize class; period film is very *formalistic*, different classes have different rituals and lives. It is ridiculous to spend too much time on researching into their way of living because no matter what it is fake. What does it matter if we research into how they poured their tea and ate their meals? At the end, it is our guess.

When we were making *Ashes of Time*, we discovered we have missed one point. At the beginning, my idea was to have Leslie Chueng's character be the avenger. Later I read books about vengeance in China which state there were many rules of vengeance in ancient times. Therefore, I thought if one has to take revenge for his family, he has to spend ten years, twenty years to prepare for it. It is neglected in the books that in those days there were several areas of no man's land. After spending so much time and experiencing so much during the wait, the avenger does not remember how to talk to others, or he begins to talk to himself. The initial motivation becomes unclear. Period film does not emphasize the time spent on the journey.

Y&L: Why didn't you make a period road movie?
WKW: Originally, I wanted to trace the source of the Yellow River, to follow the river from Qinghai to Hukou Waterfall, but the difficulties were grave and we

could not afford it. In addition, there is no way to ask actors like Leslie Cheung and Brigitte Lin to make a road movie.

We were touched by [John Ford's] *The Searchers*; the main character spends so many years searching for a person, he truly realizes time is changing. During the search, he makes a living by selling things. This is a great film; it made me think about life and its horizon.

Y&L: Then it became the story of *Ashes of Time*?
WKW: The crew had to stay on location, so we *stay*.

Y&L: Is *Ashes of Time* mainly about love?
WKW: It is mainly about love. I have put my favorite stories in this film. This is a *Half a Lifetime Romance*[3] between Eastern Heretic, Western Venom, and a woman.

Y&L: Does *Ashes of Time* use the period film genre to talk about contemporary love relationships?
WKW: Some love is eternal. At the end I finally realized what *Ashes of Time* is about—also, how *Ashes of Time* relates to my previous films. In fact, all my films are about being rejected by others or the fear of being rejected. In *Days of Being Wild*, everyone is rejected. They are afraid of being rejected so they reject others first. It is also about the reactions after being rejected, such as how Maggie Cheung and Carina Lau overcome the problem. *Chungking Express* is the same, but I may have changed. The ending of the film is *open* for interpretation. The relationship between Faye Wong and Tony Leung is ambiguous, but they can accept each other. But *Ashes of Time* is the most severe [in terms of rejection] because it is the summation of the first three films. All the characters are afraid of being rejected, afraid of how they will spend their days after being rejected. For example, Brigitte Lin becomes a schizophrenic. She becomes two persons; she uses the alter ego to comfort herself and to give herself excuses. Tony Leung Chiu-wai uses death to reject all things, to give up himself. He cannot accept that he has to turn around, but he cannot not turn around because he loves his wife. At the same time he did not give himself a chance to forgive himself, so he uses a *destructive* way to solve the problem. Leslie Cheung is the same; he is hiding out in the desert because after he was rejected he could not be the one who takes the initiative. Tony Leung Kar-fai forgets about everything after drinking the wine, which is also a way to avoid rejection. At the end I realized the summation of all my films is to talk about "being rejected," "avoidance," and such. Some said my films are about time and space, which is wrong. Maybe the films only relate to me. The characters are all very introverted. They do not express themselves. They are afraid of *getting hurt*.

Y&L: Leslie Cheung in *Days of Being Wild* is a self-absorbed person, but he can influence others around him. He can even manipulate others' feelings. In *Ashes of Time*, how do you see Cheung's character?

WKW: At the beginning I asked Leslie Cheung to play Eastern Heretic but realized there wouldn't be any surprise because everyone *expects* him to be cool, like his image in *Days of Being Wild*. So I did not want him to play Eastern Heretic, but to be Western Venom instead. Western Venom is full of hatred because he has a lot of issues. He is also an orphan, so he knows how to protect himself. He knows the best way to avoid being rejected is to reject others first. That is his attitude in life. He will close himself up forever, not let others stand close. At the end he understands that this does not *work*. He understands that this attitude has made him miss many chances. This understanding mainly comes from the death of his enemies. Also, this understanding comes from Hong Qi (played by Jacky Cheung). This person does not feel bad about being rejected; he will do whatever he feels is right.

Y&L: In *Days of Being Wild*, Leslie Cheung is absorbed in his own world, and Andy Lau in *When Tears Go By* is too stubborn, like a dead end road. We feel *Chungking Express* is much more optimistic. There are *mismatches* between people and time, but at least at the end of *Chungking Express*, Leung and Wong have a *possibility* to develop . . .

WKW: I feel *Ashes of Time* will be broader. At the postproduction stage, I would compare it with *Chungking Express*, but the artistic weight of *Ashes of time* is heavier than *Chungking Express* because the depth and the width of *Ashes of Time* are *heavier* and more complex than *Chungking Express*.

Y&L: Your films have a lot of details in lighting and mood creation. How about *Ashes of Time*?

WKW: The main characters in *Ashes of Time* are actually the wide space; the biggest difficulty is we don't use candles. In ancient times, light came from candles, but we used lighting. Christopher Doyle avoided using candles because he could have more freedom with lighting. We did some postproduction on the master tape, which became what appears on the screen. The effect came out great, thanks to colorist Calmen Lui at Universe Laboratory.

Y&L: There are many characters in *Ashes of Time*. Are they connected through many stories?

WKW: Leslie Cheung connects all the stories. He is the central force. Everyone has to go through him, and from him there are stories.

Y&L: You have something new for the audience in every film. How about in *Ashes of Time*?

WKW: The new thing this time is I used many traditional elements. The film is not difficult to understand; it is very explicit. The most special thing in *Ashes of Time* is the heavy use of interior monologue. I listened to the radio when I first came into contact with *wuxia* fictions—the feeling is very intimate. This time I use many interior monologues to see if they can be used in films. Therefore the story is very explicit.

Y&L: Now there is a trend of using interior monologue in Hong Kong films. Will it become an abuse?

WKW: Interior monologue is one perspective to record events. It has to be used appropriately or else the story has to depend on interior monologue. Do I have to be like [Robert] Bresson who restrains himself? Bresson taught us not to spend unnecessary effort to make films but to use the most concerted effort. But if everyone is like him in this world, it will be very *dry*. Using concerted effort is like choosing vitamin pills that have the most concentrated dose, so there are many choices. Another example is the films of Satyajit Ray—one feels very moved. They belong to another kind of classic beauty. No director should adhere to the same school.

Y&L: In your films, the dialogues could concisely construct the personalities and emotions of the characters.

WKW: I personally feel they are not very good; the best dialogues are Godard's. Our dialogues are literary-like, but Godard's are *poetic*.

Y&L: A question that I have always wanted to ask: Why did the version of *Chungking Express* screened at the premiere have to be reedited for the regular screening? I actually like the premiere version much more. It is more mysterious when compared to the final cut. It is more *illogical* which suits the inexplainable actions of the characters.

WKW: Actually, the length of *Chungking Express* at the premiere exceeded the requirements of the theater, so we had to cut out fifteen minutes. A lot of people said the scenes with Brigitte Lin are boring, so we mainly cut her scenes out. The scenes with Faye Wong have not changed much.

Y&L: However in the final cut, the relationship between Tony Leung Chiu-wai and Faye Wong gradually develops, unlike the premiere version in which the relationship is more ambivalent.

WKW: In fact that was my original thought; the premiere cut resulted from the separate postproduction that I and William Chang did. I edited the scenes with Brigitte Lin, and he was responsible for Faye Wong's parts. We did not know the progress of each other. At the end, I felt many places could be refined; however, William Chang did not know the exact length, so he did not dare cut too much. He tried to keep some scenes. This working method may be *absurd*, but this *absurdity* is not intentional.

Y&L: We know you improvised *Chungking Express*. Some directors use this method to keep *real time*. What is your intention?
WKW: Like having a vacation, I was more relaxed. I needed to get reacquainted with my own *instinct* and intuition. In our daily lives, we have to consider every step very carefully. that's why things have to be arranged very meticulously and seriously. Gradually, we lose our intuition toward things; we lose our instinct. Making *Chungking Express* is like pushing you into the traffic. You can only use your instinct to *reenergize* yourself [note: WKW used the word *energy*].

Y&L: Why did you spend so much time on editing?
WKW: I usually find someone whom I trust to do the editing. Then I can use a more objective angle to analyze the result. In fact, *Days of Being Wild* had a short editing time. Patrick Tam only spent three weeks on it. For *Ashes of Time*, the editing took a lot of time because we did not figure out the story structure. There are many fragmented stories in *Ashes of Time*, and we wanted to know how they could become a coherent idea. This was an insolvable problem until recently. The editing time for *Chungking Express* was also short.

Y&L: But you are not pleased with the editing?
WKW: The biggest problem is my films are not developed from stories. If my films were developed from stories, then there would be more causal events. They have to be one scene after another. But my films are developed from characters, and that allows for more *possibilities*.

Y&L: Probably because of all these *possibilities* and the nonmainstream narrative structure, the characters make time a key question when others talk about your films.
WKW: Now when critics talk about films, they only use the films to talk about their *taste* and perspective. Their criticism has nothing to do with me. I have begun to feel I am an *object* that allows critics to talk about their perspective from this *object*.

Y&L: Is it because the public opinion places a great emphasis on you?

WKW: I don't think so. I and my films perhaps have become a *topic*. This is not a bad thing, but I feel the current trend is problematic. Sometimes I really want to say, "Hey, don't blame everything on me! It is only you who like overinterpreting my films!"

Y&L: But your films are indeed the focus of the cultural circle.

WKW: Maybe my films have many cues, which let critics *develop* their own theories.

Y&L: Your films don't have a conventional narrative story structure. The structure is loose, and the characters have a distance from one another. Therefore, some have said your films are about deconstructionism.

WKW: My films and deconstructionism have no relation. Perhaps one can find cues in them, but I have never started from there. I am not David Lynch.

Y&L: Some courses offered at the University of Hong Kong like to discuss your films—most of them are about postmodernism, Hong Kong culture, and nostalgia.

WKW: Young people should not listen to others' lectures; that will make them sound old. Young people should be more direct; watching more films is better than listening to others' lectures. When one puts theories in films, they stop enjoying films, and watching films becomes a *formula*. Actually, I was once at that stage. In the beginning, when you watch films, you read many film reviews. It feels like playing a game looking for cues and categorizing them. In fact I asked myself, "So what?" Some say this *form* should be this; the *structure* should be that. In the end, "So what?" I only want to ask, "What do you look for?"

Y&L: Do you resist theories?

WKW: I feel one will inevitably be at that stage, but one day you will jump out from there, will not be addicted to theories; otherwise, one would sound too old. If a young kid comes to me and tells me a bunch of theories, I will be bored and irritated. This problem is the most obvious in Taiwan; some teenagers sound like theorists. Why don't they experience more and create more?

Y&L: Some say *Chungking Express* gives viewers the same impression as Haruki Murakami's novels.

WKW: Maybe because of the similarities of using numbers and time. Of course, Murakami's work has influenced me. But I would rather say that I am influenced by Albert Camus than by Murakami. Why do people mention Murakami? Probably because they just use my films to talk about Murakami.

Y&L: Is it because you and Murakami both talk about fate in relationship?

WKW: The only similarity between Murakami and me is that we are affectionate men.

Y&L: Some say Brigitte Lin's character in *Chungking Express* does not have to be played by her because she wears a wig and dark glasses and just walks around anyway.

WKW: Sometimes I think: if this blonde woman was not played by Brigitte Lin, but by any actress, would the audience have the same feeling toward the character?

Y&L: I think the stars have already built up their images. Viewers have *expectations* for them. When they see the stars in films, they see an already-established image.

WKW: Just like some ask why Andy Lau the cop in *Days of Being Wild* does not fight or shoot. It is because if Andy Lau walks around he will have an *impact* on the audience. Viewers see an actor as a particular *image*. When he does not have that image in my films, viewers are surprised.

Y&L: Some say the *Chungking Express* scene in which Brigitte Lin and Faye Wong bump into each other is very sudden.

WKW: Viewers have not allowed for that space!

Y&L: Some feel there could have been some cues.

WKW: Many feel that the scene would be more realistic if there were some cues. In addition, the convention of Hong Kong films requires a cause and then an effect. Is it possible that the characters could have a cup of tea between the two events? No. However, the drinking-tea event is the only reality.

Y&L: That's why viewers cannot stand Kieslowski's films.

WKW: I disagree. I think many people can accept Kieslowski's films.

Y&L: I feel a bit because he is famous.

WKW: That's for sure.

Y&L: When *The Double Life of Veronique* was in the theater, half of the reviews were positive, half were negative. But in *Three Colors: Blue, White, Red*, all reviews were positive. Some scenes, such as the old woman picking up garbage, were not fully understood by viewers. They just said, "Very deep!"

WKW: That's right, *all because of Kieslowski*. But I don't think he is in the first tier.

Y&L: Which directors in recent years do you think belong to the first tier?

WKW: . . . no one. I feel all directors in recent years just follow those before them but won't go beyond them. Carax won't be better than Godard, but clearly he follows Godard's path.

Y&L: But their styles are very different.

WKW: That's exactly it. But many people have already praised Carax for being great. I think Gus Van Sant who made *My Own Private Idaho* is interesting. But is he first-tier? This does not seem possible. The only films that are must-see are those of Martin Scorsese.

Y&L: Even the quality of his films is declining.

WKW: Like when you watch *The Age of Innocence*, it is easy to find errors. You won't say, "Wow, I learned something today!" But his quality has stabilized; he won't bore you.

Y&L: Has the approach of '97 affected your work?[4]

WKW: We can't tell the effect of '97 yet, but '97 has affected many people's way of life. It has caused societal changes. At present, many people feel like they should speed up, and they are not looking ahead. They will stop whatever they are doing by '97. To me, I have not yet found many obvious changes, but there may be fast changes around me. Therefore, I always feel you can't immediately see something. Like the June Fourth Massacre, everyone was enthusiastic about doing something when it happened, but I feel we should not conclude anything at that *moment*. Instead, we should conclude it in ten year's time.

Y&L: But mainland China has increased *censorship* on mainland Chinese films. Will you be afraid that one day *censorship* will be imposed on Hong Kong films?

WKW: There is *censorship* in Hong Kong films!

Y&L: We feel Hong Kong *self-censors* itself!

WKW: The *censorship* in Hong Kong is not state *censorship*, but the audiences first *censor* you. The production companies first *censor* you.

Y&L: I think Hong Kong cinema is more horrendous because of *self-censorship*.

WKW: That's why no one in Hong Kong has made a truly *political* film because they have already *censored* themselves.

Y&L: In mainland China, some people made political films, so the state strengthened *censorship*. Hong Kong filmmakers surrender themselves first.

WKW: Another reason why the focus on mainland films is that political films will attract attention, but I have begun to feel this is deliberate. If filmmakers truly want to send a message, we ought to *respect* them.

Y&L: More and more Chinese films are exhibited overseas. We feel they are not Chinese films but only films that serve foreigners. Your films have begun to be exhibited overseas. *Ashes of Time* was submitted to Venice Film Festival in September. Are your films made to please certain audiences?
WKW: The critics said I don't care about the Hong Kong market. Would I please certain audiences? In reality, I also don't like those films. I feel those films are like the old star village,[5] which caters to certain audiences.

Y&L: Actually, they *sell* some very *stereotypical* images.
WKW: I feel Tarkovsky should be the most respected. He was exiled overseas, and he is making films that are very realistic. His films are very *deep*, like during the credits of *Nostalgia* he dedicated his work to his own son and homeland. You feel very touched because you feel he is an authentic person. He is not concerned about how the audience reacts.

Therefore some say I make films for festivals. Actually, I don't because my films are not suitable for film festivals. They do not suit their taste. For example, some asked me if *Ashes of Time* could be about '97. If so, then the judges would be very interested. But I feel, "So what?" How much do westerners[6] understand Hong Kong? They only see it as a topic, a common language.

Y&L: To conclude, I feel if you wanted to attract westerners, you would put in your films elements that interest foreigners.
WKW: Meaning you have to play according to their rules in their games, but I don't feel that is necessary.

Y&L: *The Blue Kite*, *To Live*, and *A City of Sadness* all look at history and politics from the view of the family.[7]
WKW: I have not seen *The Blue Kite* and *To Live*, but I have seen *A City of Sadness*. It is a very good film. It really wants to say what the older generation feels about the White Terror in Taiwan. I feel *The Puppetmaster*[8] is not as good. I used to dislike Hou Hsiao-hsien's films. I feel his earlier films are not original. Only since *Daughter of the Nile* have I felt his films are good. *Daughter of the Nile* is able to show the nightlife and way of life in Taipei. *The City of Sadness* is a mature film; it has a grand style. I have not seen *To Live*. After *Ju Dou,* the films of Zhang Yimou are not that good.

Y&L: Have you seen *Beijing Bastards*?⁹

WKW: I have. It is not good. *Beijing Bastards* was made to say deliberately, "I am very rebellious." But I can't see the *feeling* anywhere.

Y&L: When I saw *Beijing Bastards*, I felt they could not find their own expression in an established ideology, so they used different "rebellious" methods to release their frustration.

WKW: I think the filmmakers know what they want, but they can't express it properly—they can't be like Zhang Yimou. Zhang Yimou is very clear about what he wants.

Y&L: You always say you don't want to do things in a conventional way. Are you a rebel?

WKW: I will not rebel just because I want to. I only want my films to have something that is *unexpected*. When we see films, we are attracted by a certain *moment* because that is different from what you are accustomed to. When you see a film as a *routine*, the film may suddenly give you something unexpected. You will then be greatly impacted. It is like a very loud film suddenly becomes silent. You will remember that silence. I want my films to have that impact, using different methods to express that feeling. This completely depends on planning.

However, it is very difficult to make experimental films in Hong Kong. The audience in Hong Kong needs continuous sensory stimulation. The need may be influenced by Hollywood where audiences are willing to have their emotions manipulated. The Hong Kong audience is lazy—understandably so because everyone is too tired, too busy. When I watched *Speed* (1994), I thought it was good. But it is good only if films are like that once in a while. If every film is *Speed*, then it is not that good. If you want to do better, you have to *take risk*. I feel in the end I cannot not do better.

Y&L: Do you have a goal when making films?

WKW: My goal is not to make films that I will regret later. I always remember that I have made four films, and I don't regret making them. My biggest *nightmare* is to make a film that I don't want in my filmography.

Y&L: Are you thinking of what kinds of films you will make later?

WKW: There are many, but these are not concrete plans yet because I discovered there has been a change—I like shooting during the day and shooting something *bright*.

Y&L: That is, you don't want to make more dark films like *As Tears Go By*?

WKW: Yes, because I feel I have made enough of them. I feel I should turn to another place to make films.

Y&L: Is it because you are more optimistic?

WKW: Sure. Perhaps it is because of my age. I used to think some issues had to be expressed positively. At a certain age, I thought, they don't have to be that positive. For instance, loneliness is in fact not that sorrowful; you can be happy while being lonely.

Y&L: The stubbornness of the protagonists in *Days of Being Wild* and *As Tears Go By* cost them their lives. But in *Chungking Express*, there exists a possibility of communication.

WKW: Because you become more receptive when you reach a certain stage and realize that you have been closing others off, which is no way to live. When you pay attention to other people around you, you realize many things can be positive; therefore, I feel I gradually became more *open*.

Y&L: People wait to see if your new films are like *Days of Being Wild*.

WKW: If people keep thinking about *Days of Being Wild* without watching the new films carefully, they will always see *Days of Being Wild*. *Days of Being Wild* has not influenced me much. It is only a transition, a stage. It is how I saw things when I was small.

Y&L: Are you nostalgic?

WKW: I used to be. Now I am not. I have stopped being nostalgic since *Chungking Express*. *Ashes of Time* and the first two films were a stage. *Chungking Express* is a new stage. *Ashes of Time* is, in fact, very wide. I always wanted to learn how to make a film in which nothing happens in the beginning, and then everything happens at the end where there is a *climax*—surprising the audience because they did not expect that. *Ashes of Time* does this at the end when Leslie Cheung *goes through* the entire process before leaving his home.

Y&L: I see you spend a lot of time *editing* your films. Do you feel the important step is *directing* on site or *editing*?

WKW: Every step is important. It depends on what kind of director you are. If you are Hitchcock, it does not matter because he was clear about what he wanted when he shot. That's why no one knew how to edit his films—only he could do it. Now when I shoot, I mostly have a concept, but I am not completely sure about the sequence of shots. I know what is needed, and then I choose the best way to illustrate the concept during editing.

Y&L: Can you talk about your working relationship with Patrick Tam?

WKW: I met Patrick Tam when we worked on *Final Victory* seven or eight years ago. We have been working together since then. We have a good working relationship; I learn a lot from him, in particular filming techniques and set management. I remember the first day when we shot *As Tears Go By*, I was disorganized so I asked him how to shoot. That was the day for the scene in which Andy Lau was in the outdoor food stall. Tam reminded me: "Why don't you think of this as a 'blood road,' and you have to run into it to kill?"[10] He is not someone who is good at creating theatrical scenes, but he can easily tell you how it feels, if you can catch what he means. He has an opinion on everything. For example, he said: "When you shoot the scene of Maggie Cheung in the phone booth, it is actually a deep hole; later how can she find a way to climb out from it?" But I was not thinking in the same way. After he told me what he thinks, I would feel there is another possibility.

Y&L: There are only fives words to describe your films: "Good Reviews Bad Box Offices." "Good Reviews Bad Box Offices" may mean your films are very difficult to understand—the audience could not stand them. That leaves the films to the cultural critics to discuss. The general audience is not willing to buy tickets. Do you think this is true?

WKW: I think it is true because people think this person's films are not obvious; they are very elusive. When the audience sees *Days of Being Wild*, they *expect* to see *As Tears Go By*. When they see *Ashes of Time*, they *expect* to see a *wuxia* film. That's why I have to keep letting audiences know and accept "that's how he makes films." Whether they buy the tickets or not are up to the audience.

In fact, both *Days of Being Wild* and *Chungking Express* are experiments for me to try out different ways to tell stories. *Ashes of Time* is more mature. When I *reach* a certain level of expression, things will be *okay*.

I don't agree with people who arbitrarily label my films as art films. Are there anything called art films? From the beginning, there has only been the art of cinema, not art films. If one could find one's position, that's already good enough.

Y&L: What is your distribution overseas?

WKW: They are better since *Days of Being Wild*. *Chungking Express* and *Ashes of Time* were sold to the French and Japanese markets. In fact, I have always emphasized that I need to understand the audience, then I will do something I like within the expectation of that audience. I should not force myself. For example, I had a heavy burden when I made *Ashes of Time* because I knew the sales of distribution rights would be good. If the rights are sold at a high price, the distributors will *expect* something *for mass audience*. So I have to use certain elements to face a broader audience. But I was much more relaxed when making *Chungking Express* because I only had to work within the *budget* and to please those audience members who have already accepted me. If I could plan, I would be more relaxed when making films. When you *test* a market until people know what kinds of films Wong Kar-wai makes, then there will be no more walking out, no more chair cutting, no more cursing.[11]The good point comes when people know this is what you make, the audience accepts it; then I will be relaxed; and no one will lose money.

Y&L: Do you face a lot of pressure when making films?

WKW: I think the pressure is not *fair* to me. Why are there so many complaints? Everyone is making films! Those complaints made the work progress difficult. Sometimes there are a lot of ungrounded rumors. But the media's attitude is that they will spread the rumors first, then they will clarify them with you. I feel this has affected my work.

Y&L: What is your purpose of making films?

WKW: No purpose.

Y&L: Because you love films?

WKW: No. First, making films is my job. Other than that, the greatest fun of films is you can live many lives; you can create a world in which you can put many characters. To say it inarticulately, it is like *playing God*—like in Greek myths, you put characters in them and see how the characters run and walk. In fact, you can jump into the characters to experience many lives.

Y&L: Which directors do you like?

WKW: Too many, can't count. In fact, I like different directors at different stages. In my early days, I liked Westerns; then Japanese films, which are cool. Then I liked European films, which are cool too. But good films are always in my heart. I remember joking with Patrick Tam: If there was a fire at home, which films would you take away with you? Your *list* will change, but at that time you would know which films are the most important. However, if there was a fire, you'd rather bring your *passport*, not VHSs and VCDs, because in the end, you can abandon films.

NOTES

1. *The Legend of Eagle-shooting Heroes* (aka *The Legend of the Condor Heroes*) is a novel written by Louis Cha (aka Jin Yong). Louis Cha is well-known for writing many *wuxia* novels which have been widely read in the Chinese-speaking world.
2. *Wuxia,* which literally means martial hero, is a literary genre about martial arts. Unlike *kung fu*, the story of *wuxia* usually takes place in the ancient past. In *wuxia* films, heroes usually fight with weapons, not bare fists like in *kung fu*. Special effects (such as wire work) are used in *wuxia* films.
3. *Half a Lifetime Romance* is an Eileen Chang's novel first published in Shanghai, 1950–1951.
4. 1997 was the year Hong Kong returned to the People's Republic of China (PRC) and became the Hong Kong Special Administrative Region of the PRC.
5. Star village is a tourist attraction in which artisans demonstrated long-lost Chinese arts and crafts, such as making figurines with flour dough.
6. Wong Kar-wai used the term *gweilo*. Gweilo used to be a derogatory term for British. But it has been so commonly used that it is a term to refer to all white people by Hong Kong Chinese.
7. *The Blue Kite* (dir: Tian Zhuangzhuang, 1993); *To Live* (dir: Zhang Yimou, 1994); *A City of Sadness* (dir: Hou Hsiao-hsien, 1989).
8. *The Puppetmaster* (dir: Hou Hsiao-hsien, 1993).
9. *Beijing Bastards* (dir: Zhang Yuan, 1993).
10. *Speed* (dir: Jan de Bont, 1994).
11. The audience was frustrated and annoyed while watching Wong's *Days of Being Wild* so they vandalized the theaters during the screening.

Working like a Jam Session

Michel Ciment / 1994

From *Positif* (France). no. 410 pp. 39–45. Interview conducted in English and Chinese in Venice on September 11, 1994. The interviewer thanks Norman Wong for his translation from the Chinese. Reprinted by permission of the publisher. Translated from French into English by M. A. Salvodon © 2015.

Michel Ciment: You were born in Shanghai in 1958, and at five years old you left for Hong Kong.

Wong Kar-wai: Yes, but it wasn't easy! We left in 1963, just before the Cultural Revolution. My father was a hotel manager, and my mother was a homemaker. I was the youngest of three children and my mother brought me with her to Hong Kong. The idea was for her to return to Shanghai and bring back my brother and sister. But a month later, the Cultural Revolution exploded, the border was even more hermetically sealed, and she was not able to go get them. Everyone was afraid to return to China and not be able to leave once there.

MC: What studies did you pursue?

WKW: After high school, I went to a polytechnic school[1] in graphic arts because it was the only place that offered classes in photography, a field that interested me a great deal. On the other hand, I was not really interested in drawing. When I was young I remember my father always buying books, especially Chinese literature, and I spent the most of my childhood reading. Later, the only way to communicate with my brother and sister was through writing letters. In their letters, they talked about French, English, or Russian classic works from the eighteenth and nineteenth centuries, the old editions of which were still available in China. In order to share ideas about books with my siblings, I got the same works in Hong Kong. I therefore read a great deal as an adolescent.

MC: Did you practice photography a great deal?

WKW: Yes, but unprofessionally, though I had some talent in this field. During my second year in my polytechnic, I dropped photography to take a production course at the TVB (Television Broadcasts Limited), a TV station in Hong Kong. TVB wanted to train directors, and this was the first time they set up this type of curriculum. I was nineteen years old, and, since then, I have attended my graphic arts course. Afterwards, for a year and a half, I was an assistant director in television before becoming a freelancer and writing screenplays.

MC: What did these years of study give you?

WKW: I must say that I wasn't a model student. During my time at the polytechnic, I always had a camera with me which I was constantly taking out to take pictures. I went to the library a lot as well because it had an abundance of art and photography books. It was a great opportunity for me to gain knowledge that was different from what high school had taught me. My mother was crazy about movies. My father worked all day. When I came home from school around 1 p.m. in the afternoon, I was free, and my mother would take me to see movies. She especially liked westerns, like films with John Wayne, Errol Flynn, Clark Gable, but also with Alain Delon! Later, at the graphic arts school, I discovered another cinema, the films by Bertolucci, Godard, Bresson, and the Japanese masters like Ozu or Kurosawa.

MC: When you started to write screenplays, did you already think that you were going to make films?

WKW: I believe I always had the feeling that I would become a filmmaker someday. Still, both seemed to me, then and now, to be totally different. When I write a screenplay, I tend not to specify anything having to do with the visual realm; I don't think people would understand [it]. To me, words can't express a vision. So dialogue matters a great deal to me, as well as the descriptions of certain situations and actions. I often receive screenplays from young writers that are full of visual cues. I always tell them that these are useless because the tempo and images are the director's responsibility.

MC: How many screenplays have you written?

WKW: About fifty, though my name appears in the credits of only a dozen films. The others came from brainstorming sessions. In Hong Kong at that time, six or seven young scriptwriters would be gathered in a room for days, talking and pitching ideas. And the oldest one would write the script . . . I worked like this as a scriptwriter for seven years. Among us was a very experienced scriptwriter, Wong Ping-yiu (working under his English name Barry Wong), who was in a way my *mentor*. We worked in the same company, and I think that he was responsible for 70 percent of the important films made in Hong Kong during that period.

Even though Barry was very quick at writing scripts, he didn't have much time and would pass some off to me. His name appeared in the credits, but we split the money. Our company was called Always Good but it subcontracted as well to major studios like Golden Harvest or Cinema City.[2]

MC: What genres did you write?

WKW: All kinds: comedies, action movies, kung fu movies, and even porn movies. At first, I didn't hang out with the directors I wrote for because I was very shy. I would meet them, pitch an idea, and when they agreed to it, I went back home to write alone. I was very slow, and I remember that one time, I took a year to finish a script, which drove everyone crazy. Later when I had gained more self-confidence, I would have daily meetings with the director and would write each scene with him.

MC: Among the ten films whose scripts are credited to you, which ones are your favorites?

WKW: They were all made by different filmmakers. I like *Final Victory* by Patrick Tam in particular. It's about failed gangsters from a working class background, whose heroes were having affairs with the wives and mistresses of the protagonist—a senior member in a gang. I think that Patrick, who isn't making films now, was an important filmmaker at the time—the most talented of the Hong Kong New Wave.[3] He also introduced me to the films of Rohmer, Antonioni, and Godard. We became close friends, and later I asked him to work on the editing for my second film, *Days of Being Wild*, as well as *Ashes of Time*. We know each other so well!

MC: Did you become a filmmaker because you weren't satisfied with what was made from your screenplays?

WKW: I don't think so. I'm not on any kind of power trip and wasn't jealous of the filmmakers for whom I wrote. Neither did I have much reason to complain. However, I remember some visits to a set when I wanted to say, "Action!," because I had different ideas on the camera angle and I wanted something other than what I was seeing. When someone asked me if I was ready to direct, I said yes.

MC: How did that happen?

WKW: Alan Tang, a famous actor from the 1960s with almost two hundred roles to his credit became a producer. I had worked with him on two screenplays. He liked giving a chance to young directors. After many discussions together, he deemed that—with the full weight of his professional acting experience—my explanations on the characters and the plot were very convincing. He thought that I could become a good director. That's how he gave me my break.

MC: That break was *As Tears Go By* in 1988.

WKW: The idea was that this first film would be part of a trilogy. The first part of the trilogy has not (yet) been made. The third part is *Final Victory*, directed by Patrick Tam, which is about a gangster in his thirties who comes to term with his failure. In *As Tears Go By*, the second part, he is twenty-something. In the first part, *Hero for a Day*, the gangster is an adolescent.

MC: *Mean Streets* inspired your films. How do you view the relationship between this Scorsese film and Hong Kong society?

WKW: I think Italians have much in common with the Chinese: their values, their sense of friendship, their mafia, their pasta, and their mothers. When I saw *Mean Streets* for the first time, it was a shock to me because I had the impression that the story could have happened in Hong Kong. In fact, I only borrowed the character played by Robert De Niro. The other characters come from my own experience. When I was a scriptwriter, I had a close friend who was a stuntman in films and who had been something of a gangster. We would spend the entire nights together until five o'clock in the morning in the seediest bars in Hong Kong. From there I gleaned loads of details that can be found in *As Tears Go By*. We knew a guy who didn't know any English, but who had a British girlfriend, a bartender: she kept leaving him and going back to him. They were a strange couple who didn't communicate at all. This inspired a character in the film. This is how I spent three or four years of my youth—drinking, fighting, and driving fast cars.

MC: How do you work with your chief cameraman?

WKW: In all, I had two cinematographers for my four films. Andrew Lau Wai-keung, who photographed *As Tears Go By*, was only on his second film.[4] He also worked with the second team of *Days of Being Wild* and *Ashes of Time*, and he had set the lights on the first part of *Chungking Express*. The second cinematographer is Christopher Doyle. Andrew Lau is very energetic, the best out there for hand-held camera work. He knows everything, and we communicate well with each other. His only weakness is that he lacks the subtlety for very sensitive lighting. Today he is a director,[5] but I think that he could become a talented visual artist. For Doyle, he's a master of lighting, and we get along well. Though we don't speak the same language, we share the same references from films and paintings. He has a great sense of aesthetics, but he is less technical in his use of the camera. At first, he was a sailor; then he did photography. This gave him his artistic talent that pleased Hou Hsiao-hsien and Edward Yang, for whom Doyle had worked in Taiwan. I needed someone like him for *Ashes of Time*.

MC: It's surprising that the cinematography is uniform in *Chungking Express* despite the presence of two different cinematographers.
WKW: I'm the one who assured the continuity, and I told them that we were going to work like we were in a *jam session*. Neither knew the story. I contacted Doyle in Japan where he was working on the postproduction of a film. Three days later, he joined me in Hong Kong to finish the film in two weeks. We filmed like madmen. I told him that this time we wouldn't have to adjust the lighting so much (other than those in the apartment) because it was being made like a *road movie*, without a fixed setting. We didn't have the time to set up a tripod or to use a camera dolly: I wanted us to make it as if we were doing a documentary, with a hand-held camera. And Doyle accepted this challenge, taking photographs of everything very quickly while making an image of high quality. But for *Ashes of Time*, he took a really long time refining the shots. Every day he would tell me, "It's death in Yulin," from the name of the place in the north of China[6] where we were making the film!

MC: Is it your success with *As Tears Go By* that allowed you to get all these famous actors for *Days of Being Wild*?
WKW: The film had not been successful in Hong Kong, but it did extremely well in Korea and Taiwan. It nevertheless received nine nominations for the Hong Kong Oscars,[7] which is unusual for a first film. My producer then proposed to direct the second film with actors I chose. I directed *As Tears Go By* at twenty-nine, and I was thirty-one years old when I made *Days of Being Wild*. Thirty is a big deal; we feel like we're getting old! I wanted to evoke in the second film things I was afraid of forgetting later. As a child, shortly after my arrival in Hong Kong, I felt very lonely since I did not speak Cantonese. My mother and I were in this little apartment during the day, and we listened to the radio that I did not understand. The only theme tune I still remember is the BBC news bulletin. One night, my parents went out dancing. In the middle of the night, I woke up and got scared. I turned on the radio, and I heard the latest BBC news bulletin, which reassured me. This is the period I evoked in *Days of Being Wild* that begins in 1960 and ends in 1966. I love its story, which took me two years to structure. In it, I evoke two families through the first postwar generation. One family is Cantonese and originally from Hong Kong, and the other one—Leslie Cheung's family—is from Shanghai. They are separated by language; and in the second part, they end up getting to know each other. Unfortunately, I never made the second half of the script. The film came out at Christmas and had set up great expectations because of its stars. The public was convinced that they were going to see a new *As Tears Go By* with a lot of action scenes. Yet *Days of Being Wild* didn't have much of that, neither did it have much of a plot, technically speaking. It was a total failure; in Korea, the viewers even

threw things at the screen. So the producer refused to finance the second part. The aesthetic of the two films differed greatly. The first one had a fast editing and a lot of music. The second had a rather slow tempo that corresponded to my idea of the 1960s. I attempted to divide the film into four movements. The first one was very Bresson-like, with many close-up shots. The second one looked like a B-movie with complicated movements of the camera and sequence-shots. The third one was filmed with a depth of field. The fourth one resembled the second one more with quite a bit of movement. The story went equally from one character to another, which made the division into several movements even more obvious.

MC: Have you evolved in your manner of directing comedies?

WKW: Since I am constantly changing the screenplays, I don't let the actors read them, and I don't rehearse them. I always have a general idea of each scene, and I arrive on the set three or four hours before filming. That's when I imagine the situations and the movements of the camera. Then I tell my actors the lines from the dialogue that they must say. Of course, I've already talked with them a great deal about their characters. What matters for me is to communicate the reasons for their gestures and actions: Why is he sitting there? Why is he smoking a cigarette? Why is she sleeping there? Why is she crying so loudly? When one knows a character well, everything goes without saying, and one can easily understand his motivation. At the beginning of filming, I made a lot of takes, enough so that my actors and I found a common rhythm. Then I am much more efficient with the number of takes.

MC: For *Ashes of Time*, you were inspired by a contemporary martial arts novel, *The Legend of Eagle-shooting Heroes*, by Jin Yong (Louis Cha).

WKW: First, I was attracted to two characters, Eastern Heretic and Western Venom; the first name means "the eccentric East" and the second "the bad West." At the beginning of the 1990s, martial arts films became very popular again and a producer invited me to make one. I agreed because I have always loved this genre. I had never made a film with period costumes and that appealed to me. I was then very broadly inspired by the original novel, a very long novel with two appealing characters in their sixties. I had to invent their past. The stories of chivalry—*wuxia* in Chinese—belong to Chinese literature like Luo Guanzhong's classic *Romance of the Three Kingdoms*. But the contemporary stories by Jin Yong—who is very prolific (he has written a dozen of them)—in fact belong to *pulp fiction*. They are extremely popular and everyone was waiting to trap me! They didn't know that I was going to do something different. My approach differed from the films that I was used to seeing.

MC: Your martial arts choreographer for the fight scenes, Sammo Hung, collaborated with King Hu on *The Fate of Lee Khan* (1973) and *The Valiant Ones* (1976). Have you seen the films of this great director?

WKW: I discovered them when I was a child, but I didn't really understand them because of their philosophical content and their association with Zen Buddhism. Sammo Hung, apart from his skills in adjusting fight scenes, is also the best Hong Kong director of action sequences for twenty years. He was trained at the Peking Opera School. He is the one who choreographs that kind of scene.

MC: You tend to stylize these sequences, to use ellipses to the point of making the action itself becomes secondary to the structure of the film.

WKW: The traditional martial arts film has the goal of stimulating the viewer's senses. I wanted the senses to also be a means for expressing the characters' feelings. For example, when Brigitte Lin is playing with the sword, it's a dance. When I filmed Tony Leung Chiu-wai, the blind warrior, in slow motion, I showed his fatigue as he faces his life, which is symbolized by the weight of the sword. Jacky Cheung, on the other hand, is filmed in ten images per second to suggest that he is emerging, that he is rising in contrast to Tony Leung Chiu-wai, who is heading towards death. Certain sequences were made [on the set], others like those with Jacky Cheung were basically made in the lab.

Tsui Hark took up the tradition of martial arts on screen, so well-illustrated beforehand by King Hu with extraordinary ballets in the air, since the actors were suspended from wires. But he was imitated by others so much that this style became sterile, which led to an impasse. When I decided to make *Ashes of Time*, I was resolved to not follow this trend because it seemed dead to me. With the exception of Brigitte Lin, whose actions are exaggerated, I wanted the other actors to fight on the ground so that their duels gave an impression of an actual duel, not artificial ones.

MC: The structure of the screenplay, with their labyrinthine flashbacks and the voice-over narration, make one think more of the American film noirs than period films.

WKW: During the period I was writing screenplays for other directors, they always asked me for simple and direct stories and that is what I wrote. My first film, *As Tears Go By*, was part of this tendency. After having finished it, I read *Chronicle of a Death Foretold* by Gabriel García Márquez; I was very impressed by his way of telling a story. I began to read many Latin American novelists, and the one who most influenced me is Manuel Puig—the author of *Kiss of the Spider Woman*—with his narrative divided into a series of fragments that shunned chronology. In the end, the feelings transmitted to us are so much stronger for having come through in this fragmented form. This technique influenced *Days of Being Wild* and *Ashes of Time*.

MC: The theme of betrayal dominates *Ashes of Time*.

WKW: For me, the theme is more about being rejected, of not belonging. This is what Leslie Cheung says in his narration when he speaks of himself as an orphan. In order not to be rejected, he rejects others first. Because of Brigitte Lin's rejection by Tony Leung Kar-fai, she invents an older brother. Betrayal is, therefore, merely a consequence. Tony Leung Chiu-wai plays the role of a man who is rejected by his spouse, who cheated on him with his best friend. Since he still loves her, the only solution for him is self-destruction. In Tony Leung Kar-fai's case, he plays a character who loves Maggie Cheung, while she is taken with Leslie Cheung. Since he doesn't want to be rejected, he never admits to his feelings, and as a sort of compensation, he makes himself loved by others in order to experience the feeling. It's another way to experience rejection to which he is a victim and is different from Tony Leung-Chiu-wai's way. There are two characters that stand out: Jacky Cheung and Charlie Young. The former isn't afraid of rejection. As for Charlie, since she is sure that someone will come to her aid, she waits patiently. Both will have a happy ending, and they influence Leslie Cheung in his decision to leave the desert, [as shown] in the last scenes of the film.

As I talk about it, I realize that it's a thread that runs through all of my films, this idea of rejection. All the characters from *Days of Being Wild* experience this feeling. I suppose there is an evolution in *Chungking Express* because in the end, Tony Leung Chiu-wai and the woman [Faye Wong's character] are not afraid of being rejected by others.

MC: How did you find the different action locations for *Ashes of Time*?

WKW: Due to budgetary limitations, China was the only place we could film. I scouted the country in search of landscape close to the ones in the book that had inspired my film. After trips from the north to the south without any success, someone showed me a photograph of the place where Leslie Cheung['s character] retired to. I sent William Chang, my art director, so that he could scope out places, and he returned to tell me that it was likely a suitable background for the film.

MC: How was the decision about the actors made?

WKW: I had already worked with all of the actors except for Brigitte Lin and Tony Leung Kar-fai. I like to know the people whom I am going to direct. For me the biggest challenge the film posed was Brigitte because the public was used to seeing her cross-dressed in [Tsui Hark's] martial arts films. She intrigued me a great deal, and I thought she could interpret a schizophrenic personality. As for

Tony Leung Kar-fai, he is short. Yet our imaginations push us to see these ancient warriors as very virile, with a tall bearing. Tony Leung [Kar-fai] was able to make it conceivable.

MC: Is the time of the action imaginary, or are you referring to a time specific to Chinese history?
WKW: The original novel occurs during the Song Dynasty, more than eight centuries ago. Jin Yong's talent is clear in his ability to create legendary fictions and to know how to integrate them in the official Chinese history. When I first looked at the material, I decided not to do research like King Hu in order to get to a historically authentic image. My only criterion was not to integrate elements that appeared later than the time period of the story. But objects, clothing, and architectural features that preceded the Song period could be used. I also didn't want the language to be too slangy or modern in the dialogue, without consciously searching for an ancient, stylized language.

MC: Why did you stop working on *Ashes of Times* to work on *Chungking Express*?
WKW: We had a break of two months while we waited for some film equipment to arrive to redo the sound; it had been taped in the desert and was of poor quality. Since I had nothing to do, I followed my instincts and decided to direct *Chungking Express*.

MC: The two police officers in *Chungking Express*, with parallel destinies, mirror the characters of Ouyang [played by Leslie Cheung] and Huang [played by Tony Leung Kar-fai] in *Ashes of Time*. They are presented like reflections of each other, the two sides of a coin. Both are abandoned by their girlfriends.
WKW: I chose two cops for *Chungking Express*, but I wanted the first cop not to be in uniform. Brigitte Lin, with her cold appearance and her blond wig is also, in my view, in a kind of uniform. In the beginning, I wanted to do a film in parts. One would take place in Hong Kong Island, the other in Kowloon; the action in one film would happen during the day, the other at night. And despite the difference, it would be the same story. After the more serious and intentional approach in *Ashes of Time*, I wanted to do a lighter, more contemporary film, but one in which the characters dealt with the same problems.

MC: What interested you the most about this Hong Kong neighborhood near Chungking Mansion?
WKW: It's a very famous building in Hong Kong. Research shows that about five thousand tourists visit it every day. With two hundred inns, it's a mixture of very different cultures. Even for the people in the surrounding neighborhood, it's a

legendary place where the relationships between people are very complex. It's also a place of concern for the Hong Kong police with all the illicit trafficking going on there. This overpopulated and hyperactive place is a good metaphor for the city itself.

MC: Brigitte Lin and Tony Leung Chiu-wai also appear in *Ashes of Time*. Were you interested in further exploring their personalities?

WKW: First of all, I was fascinated by the other actor, [Faye] Wong, who plays the waitress in the second part of the film. In the scene in which she runs into Brigitte Lin, for me, they are the same woman, ten years apart. Tony Leung [Chiu-wai] was perfect for the role because he really looks like a police officer.

MC: In all your films, there is an elliptical manner in which you tell the story, a way of jumping quickly from one shot to the next.

WKW: It's maybe the influence of Godard and Bresson. I decided to direct *Chungking Express* in a short time period. For me, it was like a *road movie*. I had come up with two short stories several years ago, without being able to make a film of them. So I then got the idea to bring the stories together in one single screenplay. When I started to film, I hadn't yet written it completely. I filmed it chronologically. The first part took place at night. I then wrote the rest of the story during the day! Thanks to a brief interruption because of new year celebrations, I had a little more time to finish the rest of the script.

MC: Do the numbers that you attribute to the two police officers to identify them have a particular meaning?

WKW: Since I am rather lazy at coming up with names for my characters, I thought of using numbers, which gave a certain flavor. After all, Kafka called all of his protagonists K.! When I read the nineteenth century Russian novelists, I have such a hard time orienting myself with all the names and nicknames that I am happy to return to the simplicity of names in Kafka!

MC: What is your relationship with the Fifth Generation Chinese directors and with the ones of the Taiwan New Wave?[8]

WKW: In the People's Republic of China, the directors come from a long tradition, but it's a tradition very much shut down to the outside world. In Hong Kong, there is a lot more mixture, and we are influenced by the West. Since 1945, there are many Chinese people who have emigrated to Hong Kong. They used to speak Mandarin, not Cantonese, and participated in the development of the film industry, often dealing in their films with the past rather than the present. This was also the case in Taiwan. But for the past fifteen years, the new directors have become interested in today's problems. They've broken away from the propaganda films that were numerous in the 1950s and 1960s, like the ones from the mainland, of course, even if their goals were different. In Hong Kong, we are more inclined toward entertainment, and I imagine that one day this will be the preoccupation of all three Chinese cinema traditions (Hong Kong, Chinese, Taiwanese) that will become one!

MC: From a cinematographic standpoint, which Chinese films—wherever they come from—left you with the greatest mark in the last ten years?
WKW: *A City of Sadness* by Hou Hsiao-hsien.

NOTES

1. Hong Kong Polytechnic, later became Hong Kong Polytechnic University.
2. Two major studios in the 1980s. They have ceased operating now.
3. The Hong Kong New Wave began in the late 1970s with a group of directors such as Ann Hui, Tsui Hark, and Patrick Tam. They are believed to have established a new style of Cantonese films that were very different from those prior to the late 1970s.
4. Before *As Tears Go By*, Andrew Lau Wai-keung had been the cinematographer of several films like *Where's Officer Tuba* (1986), *City On Fire* (1987) and *The Thirty Million Rush* (1987).
5. Andrew Lau Wai-keung has been directing since 1990. His most notable films are the *Young and Dangerous* series (1996–1998) and the *Infernal Affairs* trilogy (codirected with Alan Mak Siu-fai, 2002–2003).
6. Yulin is a city in Shannxi Province bordering Inner Mongolia to the north.
7. *As Tears Go By* received ten nominations in total and won two awards in the Hong Kong Film Awards.
8. Taiwan New Wave, or Taiwan New Cinema, refers to the work produced by a group of new directors in 1980s. These films often address social issues with elements of realism. Prominent figures include Edward Yang (*That Day, on the Beach*, 1983) and Hou Hsiao-hsien (*A Time to Live, a Time to Die*, 1985).

The Northern Beggar and Southern Emperor in a Pleasant Forest: Dialogue with Wong Kar-wai

Lin Yao-teh / 1994

From *United Literature* (Taiwan). No. 120 (pp. 130–37). Interview conducted in Mandarin Chinese on September 21, 1994. Reprinted by permission of Lucy Chen. Translated by Silver Wai-ming Lee and Maurice Leung from Chinese.

Lin Yao-teh: You have always been good at writing about metropolises.

Wong Kar-wai: The Fifth Generation of Chinese directors[1] and the Taiwanese director Hou Hsiao-Hsien have their eyes set on the countryside; I am more into metropolitan cultures.

LYT: Basically, reality means metropolitan cultures to our generation.

WKW: The Cantonese and Taiwanese movies that I watched when I was a kid were unrealistic. They unrealistically set the past in present contexts. At that time, Japanese and French movies were also introduced into the Hong Kong market, so cultures blended into a mixture. Under such an informational cosmopolitan context, I started paying attention to matters related to people in a metropolis.

LYT: You must have a clear self-consciousness about your experiences growing up and your life as a creator.

WKW: As I analyze my own work, I would consider *As Tears Go By*, *Days of Being Wild*, and *Ashes of Time* belonging to the same stage. *Chungking Express* marks another stage of my work.

LYT: From a business perspective, *Ashes of Time* should be screened prior to *Chungking Express*.[2] Now the media have all fixed their eyes on *Ashes of Time*; *Chungking Express* is totally ignored. But according to your wish, the films were released sequentially; the open and imaginative ending of *Chungking Express* has become even more meaningful.

WKW: *Days of Being Wild* is often interpreted as a story about time and memories, but haven't you noticed these are actually only a part of the movie? The main characters of the first three movies are all fearful of being rejected. This has been a major problem of modern metropolitans. The most common injury we face in our daily lives is being rejected. This has something to do with my background.

LYT: With your experience of immigration.

WKW: I moved from Shanghai to Hong Kong at the age of five. With the language barrier and the fact that I don't have many relatives in Hong Kong, I was alienated during my school life. My mother was a movie enthusiast. She had fallen in love with movies imported from the West back when we were in Shanghai. After moving to Hong Kong, she always took me to the movies in the afternoon after school. We watched two or three films a day, mostly westerns and those set in ancient Rome, and fantasy films. It was later when we started watching Mandarin movies.

LYT: There must be some particular movies that left an impression. Like, I always remember the monsters in *Seventh Voyage of Sinbad*.

WKW: To me, *The Mysterious Box of Lunar Palace*[3] stirred my imagination.

LYT: The relationship between you and your mother must have been very special.

WKW: My father and I had a distant relationship. He was seldom home, always abroad. I spent most of the time with my mother. Most of the female characters I have written were based on my mother and my wife.

LYT: I bet there are strong images in your memories with your mother.

WKW: It was winter in Shanghai. She was off duty. The children were sleeping on the same bed. My brother, sister, and I were all underneath a quilt. My mother had a good relationship with the unit comrade at a dairy company, so we had milk every morning. There was sunlight in the winter morning, giving me a warm and secure feeling. Like Albert Camus, who has also written a lot about mother and son, the son wanted to live his own life at the age of twenty. But since his mother was ill, he was stressed out every time he went out because he knew his mother needed him. As the sentiment rotted, the stress became hatred. In Camus's *The Stranger* [*L'Étranger*], I feel like I have lived through many scenes. This work resonates with me a lot.

LYT: Talking about Camus, I am also curious about your reading experience as an adolescent.

WKW: My father had a weird belief that one should read all the classic literature during childhood and adolescence.

LYT: I have been through similar hardship. I lost my reciting ability after I had to recite the whole book of *Analects of Confucius*.

WKW: My first book was *Romance of the Three Kingdoms*, then *Water Margin*, and *Dream of the Red Chamber*.[4] [Because] my elder siblings were stranded in mainland China, the books they read at that time mostly came from the Soviet Union, except those old editions from French romanticism and realism of the eighteenth and nineteenth centuries. This contributes to another unusual reading background of mine—my father insisted that I write to my siblings, and, for the sake of common topics, I spent most of my time in the library of my secondary school reading world literature.

LYT: I suppose you hadn't read them with another level of interpretation, all the between the lines?

WKW: There are more or less some impressions left when you really read a lot, especially [the work of] Honoré de Balzac.

LYT: *La Comédie Humaine*?

WKW: Yes. And I read a lot of American novels after that.

LYT: Who are your favorite American novelists?

WKW: John Steinbeck and Ernest Hemingway. As I grew older I started to read some Japanese literature too. First came Yasunari Kawabata. I love his *Snow Country* and *The House of the Sleeping Beauties*.

LYT: What about Kobo Abe? He has his unique expression of metropolitan time-space perspectives.

WKW: Yes, *The Woman in the Dunes* is exactly what you mean. But Abe isn't the one who has influenced me the most. Let me elaborate. I don't care much for Yukio Mishima either. But after reading work of *Buraiha* [the Decadent School] and neo-sensualism, I became a big fan of Osamu Dazai.

LYT: Dazai's work is full of hopes and nothingness. His last novel before his suicide was *No Longer Human*. What about Riichi Yokomitsu? In his *Head and Belly*, he wrote about an express train skipping minor stations en route like a stone. It was really movie-like.

WKW: Oh, Yokomitsu is my second favorite Japanese writer after Dazai. And it was in the year of 1989 when I came to read Haruki Murakami's work.

LYT: Murakami's work has gone downhill recently.

WKW: I was interested in Murakami from the beginning, but his novels have not varied that much these years. My then favorite was *Pinball, 1973*. As a whole, Kawabata, Dazai, and Yokomitsu have influenced me more.

LYT: What about Latin American literature? Jorge Luis Borges is at the top of my list.

WKW: I started reading South American novels after the Márquez mania, like those by Borges as you've just mentioned. Márquez's *One Hundred Years of Solitude* is a significant novel; another is *Chronicle of a Death Foretold*. I had begun screenwriting when I was reading *Chronicle of a Death Foretold*, yet I had never thought of telling stories with events in a reverse chronology. [Márquez] made me to think about that. Among South American writers, it is the author of *Kiss of the Spider Woman* who has influenced me the most.

LYT: Manuel Puig.

WKW: By far it is he who has influenced me the most in making films.

LYT: Which do you like better, the movie or the novel?

WKW: The original novel is the best. But *Kiss of the Spider Woman* isn't his best piece. His best novel is *Heartbreak Tango*, a real significant piece. I haven't read anything great after that. I'm recently looking for books to read, and I'm reading *Zizhi Tongjian*[5] at the moment.

LYT: I suggest that you read *Book of Jin*. The poignant history of the uprising of the five barbarians is full of magic. More worth noticing is the beautifully written Tang-styled texts. *Book of Jin*, written during the Tang dynasty, is actually a brand new revisit to the history of the Jin dynasty from the perspectives of Tang civilization.

The most interesting vengeful character in *Book of Jin* is Fu Deng, the distant grandnephew of Fu Jian. His great uncle's empire was scattered after the Battle of Fei River, himself [Fu Jian] killed by Yao Chang, a renegade subordinate. Fu Deng gathered his troops and chased Yao from east to west, eating the corpses of their enemies on the way. The ancestral tablet of Fu Jian was carried all along. And "revenge till death" was carved on every armor . . .

WKW: When I was filming *Ashes of Time*, I was reading a book about ancient revenge. Not until then did I know there were many rules when it comes to revenge in ancient China. Revenge planning took a lot of time, five years, ten years, even decades. My original idea was Ouyang Feng [Western Venom, played by Leslie Cheung] seeking revenge on Huang Yaoshi [Eastern Heretic, played by Tony Leung

Kar-fai] but with Feng gradually losing his ability to speak since there were all uninhabited areas on his way. Because of this he has lived in his imagination and is unclear about his vengeful motive. *The Searchers* (1956) by the American director John Ford is also a story about searching for someone. It expresses the idea that it is no longer important whether that someone is found. The valuable thing is the discovery of the meaning of time and life during the search.

LYT: Yes, we haven't talked about modern Chinese literature yet.
WKW: I've read a lot of Lu Xun's work.

LYT: Lu's *Dawn Blossoms Plucked at Dusk* is a gem, but it is often neglected.
WKW: Yes, it's wonderfully written.

LYT: Any contemporary work worth mentioning?
WKW: I haven't found any work worth reading. There has not emerged any school [of writing]. I still prefer modern literature by Lu Xun and Zhou Zuoren. I also enjoy Lao She. Recently I've also become interested in "Hai Pai" [Shanghai style] novels.

LYT: You mean the work of neo-sensualism by writers in Shanghai like Shi Zhecun, Mu Shiying, and Liu Na'ou?
WKW: Mu is the best among them. I would like to make a film about him. Some of his work is about fallen things such as nightlife, rogues, and prostitutes, yet other work talks about the lives of the lower class. I think his personal history is also quite legendary. Also, I proposed a visit to Shi Zhecun last time I went to Shanghai.

LYT: I visit him every time I'm in Shanghai.
WKW: Once a Japanese producer invited me to make a short film. I proposed to make an adaptation of a Shi novel.

LYT: *The General's Head* would be a nice pick.
WKW: But I prefer *Spring Sun*. It is very suitable for a movie adaptation. "Hai Pai" writers position their viewpoint in the city. They all love watching films; therefore, you may sense movies in their work.

LYT: Mu's *A Platinum Statue of the Female Body* and *Major Kuga* should provide plenty of imagination if you are to turn them into film art.
WKW: There is so much wonderful stuff in Mu's books. I would take the chance to make a film on Mu's novels.

LYT: You could connect several of Mu's short stories, making a collage—just like how you did for the stories of the four characters in *Days of Being Wild*.
WKW: Basically, Mu's stories can be easily put together.

LYT: In fact, writers like Mu are associated with the Japanese writer Yokomitsu, whom you like. Shanghai-style neo-sensualism was founded only four years after the Japanese neo-sensualism (1924). The "Hai Pai" writers were largely influenced by Japanese literature at that time. You could still find many settings for location shooting in Shanghai, which allow you to reconstruct the 1920s and 1930s.
WKW: I passed by Kaifeng [in Henan province] when filming *Ashes of Time*. People said the city was well preserved. I didn't think so; there were too many modern things. I would rather shoot in Taiyuan and Datong in Shanxi Province, where you can still sometimes find original ancient temples and shrines.

LYT: Chinese architecture depends largely on wood structures. You cannot expect them to be as well preserved as stone structures in Greece and Rome.
WKW: What really matters is the Chinese people's lacking sense to preserve heritage sites.

LYT: Márquez of Colombia and Graham Greene of England were so different in their personalities, genres, and behaviors, yet they became close friends. They also had a common friend, the Panamanian military leader Omar Torrijos. So, who are your good friends throughout these years?
WKW: I don't have many friends. I am not good at socializing. Talking about my friends . . . I have Jeff Lau, who is very different from me. Another is William Chang, my art director.

LYT: We've talked about Puig. His novels, such as *Betrayed by Rita Hayworth* and *Heartbreak Tango*, were not only published as serials in the traditional way but were also widely distributed via radio, television dramas, and booklets. And, of course, *Kiss of the Spider Woman* became a film in 1976. I think you could write novels too. Take the scene played by Tony Leung and Faye Wong in *Chungking Express* as an example: the narration [monologue], the whole structure, and tempo—except the film language expressed by the camera—are already a delicate short story. Perhaps you should try expressing your ideas using texts, comics, or other means. Like, David Lynch's *Twin Peaks* was fun.
WKW: I am thinking about this.

LYT: Narrations from *Chungking Express* and *Ashes of Time* are both literary.
WKW: I first came across *wuxia* novels as radio dramas. There were times in Hong

Kong when it was popular to broadcast novels as radio dramas. I read the novels only after that and finally watched the films adapted from them. That was why I wanted to try mixing the characteristics of these media into a single piece of work when I made *Ashes of Time*.

LYT: You mean imitating a radio drama using a narration, increasing the literary interest between the monologue and the dialogue, and combining them with the movie?

WKW: Yes. In addition, the first *wuxia* novels I read were by Louis Cha [Jin Yong]. After that, I started reading Gu Long.[6]

LYT: You have hidden Gu Long–style delights underneath the skin of Jin Yong's characters—even though the characters' nicknames are Jin's.

WKW: True, true. And let's talk about the fight scenes. Every fight scene in *Ashes of Time* is designed to represent an era of *wuxia* films. Tony Leung's scene represents the style with a solemn and tragic hero like Chang Cheh's characters.[7] Jacky Cheung's scene is more like a Japanese *jidaigeki* [period films]; winning or losing is on a single slash. Brigitte Lin's scene is obviously the Tsui Hark–style flying stuff [wire work]. I tried to put everything in this movie.

LYT: You have included every element of postmodern cinema in *Ashes of Time*—the music, the editing, and the non-monolithic expression. From a certain viewpoint, you have secretly changed the form and nature of genre films; you have slightly revised the essence of genre films.

WKW: This is true for *As Tears Go By* and *Ashes of Time*. *Days of Being Wild* is more complicated.

LYT: *Days of Being Wild* is a mixture of several conflicting styles.

WKW: I have personally found four: the first is the postmodern style, which you know well; the second is seen in the scenes with Leslie Cheung and Carina Lau, which resembles the flirting scenes from '50s Hollywood movies; the third is a road movie, mainly comprising the part filmed in the Philippines; . . .

LYT: What about the fourth?

WKW: It's hard to describe . . . I feel like it could be described as film noir.

LYT: So you mean the dark, violent horror films.

WKW: Yes. *Days of Being Wild* is divided into four units. On the other hand, *Ashes of Time* is a large platter. Everything composing a *wuxia* movie is put into it, when the main idea is nothing about *wuxia*. It expresses an entirely different value system.

LYT: The fixed roles of heroes in traditional *wuxia* novels and films have been now totally nullified by you.

There is actually something very different between you and Steven Spielberg.
WKW: Of course, there is. His films have great box office appeal.

LYT: The premise of my statement is that there is something similar between you and him; you both try to combine some traditional elements and create new visual and psychological effects by patching and merging them.
WKW: And what's different?

LYT: Spielberg does it smoothly, while you always leave meta trails intentionally.
WKW: We all have the impulse to re-create what we saw and experienced when we were young. . . . . My movies before *Ashes of Time* were heavier. When I made *Chungking Express* I was already brighter. You know the problem of the world. You inevitably have to face everything as you live in the modern society. At the end you have no choice but to amuse yourself in order not to feel miserable. *Chungking Express* is a movie to teach you how to "entertain" yourself—you are isolated, you live by yourself, but there are many ways for you to have fun. I started to believe that my weight comes from not being mature enough. And now I am good at letting go.

LYT: Authors should be aware of the broad space for invention, for playfulness. Suppression and burdens are not everything. In your movies, we could almost see a complete miniature of the transition from existentialism to postmodernism. Do you have any strange habit that is worthwhile to exchange for a secret of others?
WKW: No.

LYT: How is your relationship with your wife? It sounds like a boring question asked by entertainment news reporters.
WKW: Normal.

NOTES

1. The Fifth Generation of Chinese directors refers to a group of filmmakers emerging in the 1980s. Most of them graduated from the Beijing Film Academy (which was forced to close down during the Cultural Revolution) in 1982. Prominent figures include Chen Kaige (*Yellow Earth*, 1982); Zhang Yimou (*Red Sorghum*, 1987); and Tian Zhuangzhuang (*The Horse Thief*, 1986).

2. *Chungking Express* was released in July and *Ashes of Time* was released in September.

3. The editors cannot find a foreign film shown in Hong Kong with the same translated title because the interviewer and publication are from Taiwan where film titles are sometimes different. It probably refers to *The Thief of Bagdad* (directors: Michael Powell, Ludwig Burger, Tim Whelan, 1940)

4. *Romance of the Three Kingdoms*, *Water Margin*, and *Dream of the Red Chamber* are regarded as three of the Four Great Classical Novels in China.

5. *Zizhi Tongjian*, literally "Comprehensive Mirror in Aid of Governance," is a chronological narrative of the history of China. It was mainly written by Sima Guang and published in 1048 AD.

6. Gu Long (1938–1985) was famous for writing *wuxia* novels widely published in the Chinese-speaking world. Some were adapted into films directed by Chor Yuen, like *Killer Clans* (1976, based on the novel *Meteor, Butterfly, Sword*) and *Clans of Intrigue* (1977, based on the *Chu Liuxiang Series*).

7. Chang Cheh (1923–2002) was famous for directing many kungfu and *wuxia* films such as *One-armed Swordsman* (1967) and *The Blood Brothers* (1973).

A Coin of Wong Kar-wai

Gary / 1995

From *City Entertainment* (Hong Kong). No. 427 (pp. 33–35). Interview conducted in Cantonese in 1995. Reprinted by permission of the publisher. Translated by Micky Lee from Chinese.

Love relationships in today's cities may no longer be about love at first sight or long-lasting love. With some fate and chance, people from different worlds may be brought together. Even a coin will do.

Images are primary in Wong Kar-wai's films: not only are the visuals on the screen important, but so are the images evoked by dialogue. Images depicting year, month, day, hour, and minute [in *Days of Being Wild*] or mackerel, bolognese, and cling wrap [in *Chungking Express*], though not shown on the screen, appear in the audience's minds. Dialogue conjures the richness of images.

Wong Kar-wai is very sensitive to time, number, space, and things. Through their existence (or lack thereof) on the screen, [he] shows the emotions of city dwellers. Through image and dialogue, the emotions of the characters, the director, and the audiences are brought together.

This interview recorded the director's views on time, number, space, and things.

Gary: Your films are very creative, such as the improvisational style of *Chungking Express* and the fragmented, yet coherent, narrative style of *Ashes of Time*. What kinds of breakthroughs do you have for *Fallen Angels*?

Wong Kar-wai: The starting point of *Fallen Angels* is the three stories in *Chungking Express*. Due to time constraint, I only shot two stories, not the third one. Therefore, I developed the [third] story. Hence, *Fallen Angels* is similar to *Chungking Express* in some ways. But of course, I don't want to remake *Chungking Express* as *Fallen Angels*. The style this time is somewhat different. For instance, we have used a handheld lantern, making it more colorful. The most important [difference] is the use of ultrawide angle lens, using 9.8mm as the *standard lens*, making the distance between the characters looks far, but in fact the characters are very close.

G: Is this feeling of being close, yet far away the message of *Fallen Angels*? An emotional relationship of city dwellers?

WKW: I think it is. Of course when you live in such a (small) city, the relationship between people seems to be very close, but the psychological distance is very far.

G: I remember you mentioned in an interview that when you were making *Ashes of Time*, you concluded a stage of filmmaking. You have finished expressing the depressing, pessimistic feelings in *As Tears Go By* and *Days of Being Wild*. The tone in *Chungking Express* is clearly more positive and optimistic. Does *Fallen Angels* have a positive tone, or do you return to the previous heavy tone?

WKW: I think the tone of *Fallen Angels* is positive, even though it is about having fallen. But one who is willing to fall has one's own fun. The characters in the film are in search for this kind of fun.

G: You use a lot of night scenes in *Fallen Angels*; is there any purpose other than the story requires them?

WKW: Actually many things can happen at night. When we were filming, we could hide many things in the night scenes. This is particularly the case now because finding a location is getting more and more difficult. We have used up most possible locations. Using night scenes could hide many ugly things, giving it a pass.

G: Speaking of location, in addition to night scenes, your choice of locations is also very special. You usually use places that reflect and symbolize Hong Kong, such as Mong Kok in *As Tears Go By*,[1] Tsim Sha Tsui, Chungking Mansion, and Lan Kwai Fong in *Chungking Express*.[2] This time in *Fallen Angels*, you use the Hong Kong Stadium, Shanghai 369 Restaurant [in Wanchai],[3] and so on. Did you have any intentions when you were choosing the locations?

WKW: This is quite interesting; I hadn't noticed this tendency. I only discovered I used a lot of places in Wan Chai when I made *Fallen Angels*. Wan Chai has two worlds that are separated by the tram track. The one close to the harbor is the world of Suzie Wong; many people have used that location. On the other side is Queen's Road East, where there are many old things. When I was looking for locations, I gradually realized these places have been lived in and experienced by Hong Kong people—restaurants, old newspaper booths, and grocery stores more or less reflect the way of life in Hong Kong. In the very near future, I believe those places will disappear. Like, when we watch old Cantonese films at night, many old locations are no longer here, but they are preserved by those old films.[4] Therefore I ask myself, "Why can't we do the same?" Therefore, this time many stories take place in the old Wan Chai district. I was not conscious [of this], but it was a fact.

Many old things in *Days of Being Wild* are no longer here. The residence of Leslie Cheung became a luxury residential building; Queen's Cafe was relocated . . . that's why this time I am conscious [of shooting in old districts]. I feel I should follow this direction, to preserve old things.

G: That's like a function of cinema, which is to preserve time, to stop the course of history.
WKW: That's right; that's a magical thing about cinema.

G: Because of this, your films are quite nostalgic.
WKW: I don't think they are nostalgic, only that I will miss things after they disappear. I think now I only want to preserve, to stop time, to fix things on the reel. Later when the audience sees this film, they may not like the story, but they learn something about events that happened in the past.

G: Just now you mentioned *Fallen Angels* is a bit like *Chungking Express* in terms of the positive tone, but some would say *Fallen Angels* is a hybrid between *As Tears Go By* and *Chungking Express*. What do you think?
WKW: If this is the way of thinking, then is the style of every film a hybrid of previous films? Not just one or two? Because I direct every film, I more or less build up the experiences. In addition, some characters have to be played by certain actors. I can't randomly mix up the films. For example, the characters of Andy Lau and Jacky Cheung in *As Tears Go By* can't be played by Leon Lai [in *Fallen Angels*], and Andy Lau may not be suitable for *Fallen Angels*. Every actor has his or her unique aura.

G: This time the cast of *Fallen Angels* is all new and young. Is there any special meaning? Are they as innocent as angels?
WKW: I chose them, first, because of film budget; many first-tier actors are too expensive, [using them] will make the film become a big budget one. At this point I don't want to make big budget films. A budget like *Chungking Express* gave me a more comfortable space, making the process more relaxing, and the outcome is not bad.

Also, now in Hong Kong there aren't too many new actors; there are only a few of them. In order to give the audience a fresh feeling, I want to use more new faces. Takeshi Kaneshiro, Faye Wong, and Valerie Chow were well received in *Chungking Express*. If this was the case, then why not use new actors?

G: Your films are always about the love relationship of city dwellers, but often it is about being in a wrong place and being lost. What do you think?

WKW: I feel the biggest problem with city dwellers is that they love themselves more than others; that's why their loved ones are not that important. What is important is whether they have fun or not during this process. Now everyone knows how to protect him/herself; everyone understands loving someone can often hurt. But some could find fun in the process of being hurt because most city dwellers love themselves more, [and] they are reserved toward others.

G: I recently came across an interview in which you talked about how filmmakers are only repackaging "old canned food." To you, do you have any new ways that make repackaging more creative?

WKW: This is not about whether the repackaging can be more creative or not, but I rearrange existing things. The rearranging process is actually another type of creation. In actuality, the subject matters and genres of many films have been used, but [I] only rearrange, making these things more modern in style. Because now we are experiencing a habit, just like seeing films is a habit. When you reverse the order of events in a narrative, you may feel surprised. Afterwards when you are used to this, you don't see the problem anymore. This is how we live.

G: What is special about the soundtrack this time? Do you have popular songs like *California Dreaming* in *Chungking Express*?

WKW: This time we have Taiwanese songs; they are related to the plot . . . actually the songs in the films are usually what I listen to; the only exception is *Ashes of Time*. Because this film needs a consistent soundtrack, I thought I'd use dramatic music like that of Morricone. Because the soundtrack of westerns and *wuxia* is dramatic, I wanted to create that effect.

G: Some time ago I heard that you wanted to make a film from a screenplay written by your father. Will this be the next project after *Fallen Angels*?

WKW: I don't think I could afford it yet because this film will be very expensive. It is about China in 1949. At that time Chinese were exiled from Shanghai to Guangzhou, and from Guangzhou to Hong Kong. The story is about how five women faced historical changes. Because the entire story touches upon a few decades, the budget is going to be big. That's why I set it aside until it is the right time to make it.

G: The two stories in *Chungking Express* are linked together when Takeshi Kaneshiro and Faye Wong meet. Is there anything about fate and chance [in *Fallen Angels*]?

WKW: This time everything starts with a coin. Just like that, it really begins . . .

G: But how does this coin make the story begin?

(The director refused to answer this question. It looks like this coin is extremely important for us to understand the plot: it links the stories between Leon Lai/ Michele Reis and Takeshi Kaneshiro/Charlie Young.)

NOTES

1. The Chinese title of *As Tears Go By* is *Mong Kok Carmen*. Mong Kok is a densely populated area in Kowloon with a mix of residential and commercial areas. It is a place where gangsters have their bases.
2. Tsim Sha Tsui in Kowloon is a commercial area. Chungking Mansion is located in Tsim Sha Tsui. Lan Kwai Fong in Central is populated with bars, restaurants, and nightclubs. It is highly popular with expatriates, trendy Hong Kong youngsters, and the middle class.
3. Wan Chai is a district in Hong Kong Island where old neighborhoods are gradually gentrified into new commercial areas. Skyscrapers are built upon landfills in Victoria Harbour.
4. Local television stations used to play old Cantonese films produced by various Hong Kong studios after midnight to fill airtime.

The Film Supermarket of Wong Kar-wai

Gary Mak / 1995

From *City Entertainment* (Hong Kong). No. 428 (pp. 24–27). Interview conducted in Cantonese in 1995. Reprinted by permission of the publisher. Translated by Micky Lee from Chinese.

Wong Kar-wai is an oddity in Hong Kong cinema, he may even be a miracle. His films have been heatedly debated among film critics; the way he makes films is also a subject of debate inside and outside the film industry. His films receive positive and negative reviews equally. To Wong, making films is like producing merchandise for a supermarket: there are different kinds of goods as well as different ways to produce them.

Gary Mak: This time you use ultra-wide angle lens to shoot *Fallen Angels*, which distorted the sense of space. Why did you have such a concept? Is it related to the expression of the contents?

Wong Kar-wai: Because the space in Hong Kong has become smaller (laugh) . . . therefore, we often have to use *wide angle*. If we are already using *wide angle*, why don't we try something more extreme? So we tried the *widest* lens. We rely on *wide angle* to make a four hundred-square-feet room in Hong Kong look spacious, to make the spaces in Hong Kong become slightly larger.

GM: But in terms of content, would that help to express the relations between the characters?

WKW: After a while, the use of wide angle cannot be separated from the plot. At first, because of the small space, we used a wide angle. We found the outcome to be not so bad, so we continued using it. On the other hand, ultra-wide angle lens would distort the *perspective* seen through the lens. The distance between the characters looks far away, but in fact they are very close. This fits well with the relations between the characters.

GM: If we look at it more carefully, this [way of shooting] distorts the distance between the characters and the audience: it looks like [the characters and the audience are] very close, but in fact it is very far away. Does this echo the theme of "too close, yet too far" between the characters? Or did you try to involve the audience in the film?

WKW: I reserve the answer for you critics to write about.

GM: So, when you were creating this film, did you think of using this film language to express some *messages*?

WKW: I never think about *message* when I make films. I merely rely on intuition: if intuition tells me this is the way to do it, then I will go ahead and do it.

GM: And the intuition comes to you on the set?

WKW: Not necessarily. Sometimes I feel the outcome is not as good as I thought, but sometimes it is better than I thought. Sometimes I don't have to be on the set [to have the intuition]. I only think of the image for tomorrow's shooting. All these are intuitions.

GM: When it comes to the *stage* of script, how prepared are you?

WKW: I leave many cues; I understand the relationships between the characters. I mostly know how the plot would develop. But we cannot control time; we cannot spend much time working on the screenplay, then do casting after refining the screenplay. From the point of view of an independent production, very often we have the casting first; then we find distributors; then we negotiate the deadline to turn in the final cut.

GM: If we neglect all these objective limits, would you personally prefer to have a complete screenplay, or would you start shooting without a screenplay?

WKW: Both are fine because the outcome is the same. Even if we have a complete screenplay, very often it does not work out because of the actors' work schedule or the lack of spark between the actors. Regardless of having a complete screenplay or not, you keep on making changes during the shooting. But of course, when making the changes, you need to know clearly what you want to happen, and you need to control the story development.

GM: So, was the use of ultra-wide angle lens an *idea* that you had on the set? Was it your idea or Christopher Doyle's?

WKW: The first one was my idea because I got to decide what kinds of lenses and angles are used during the shooting. But this time I gave Christopher Doyle a lot of trouble because using wide angle lens to shoot in a short distance left the camera's shadow on the characters' faces. This also gave me many troubles. Therefore we had many NGs.[1]

GM: How did you create the five characters in *Fallen Angels*?

WKW: First, the hit man played by Leon Lai originally came from the third story of *Chungking Express*. At that time because of the length, we did not make that story. That killer character was created long ago. Last time Takeshi Kaneshiro played a cop; this time we wanted to make a change. He speaks Mandarin Chinese, so I thought I'd make him a mute who likes to trespass on others' shops to do business at night. At the end he encounters Charlie Young, and they develop a relationship. For Karen Mok's character, she is someone *picked up* by Leon Lai one day. Leon hopes to spend a night with her, but in fact he had courted her a long time ago.

GM: In fact, last time in *Chungking Express*, we have seen the characters bumping into each other in the film, but they did not recognize each other. Is there something similar in *Fallen Angels*?

WKW: This time there will be more chances for unacquainted characters to meet. After they meet, there will be dialogues. Takeshi Kaneshiro and Michele Reis will have more chances to meet because they live in the same building.

GM: This arrangement reminds me of Kieslowski's films.

WKW: In fact many people make films like this; there is no relation between his films and mine.

GM: I remember one time when I was visiting the set, Michele Reis was in a scene spending her time in the laundry room. She was doing nothing important: picking up the telephone, picking up a towel, sitting around idly, etc. You spend quite a lot of time shooting scenes of mundane events. Do you worry you'll bore the audience?

WKW: I don't think so. Last time Faye Wong had a scene like this in *Chungking Express*. The audience accepted it, and it is not non-commercialized. These scenes may appear to be irrelevant to the plot but are in fact very important, especially when you are interested in someone—his/her behavior becomes very important. Because of one's bias towards others, sometimes words can deceive, but behavior can't.

GM: But are you worried there aren't enough commercial elements?

WKW: *Fallen Angels* is, in fact, quite commercialized, same for *Chungking Express*. I think the average person has a rather narrow definition of what commercialized films are. But one thing is clear, film is one kind of commercial activity. Therefore there should be different packaging and targeting, [the film industry] should be more like a *supermarket* that can accept different business models, merchandise; [one] should not *comment* that this shop has a problematic way of doing business, that shop has too much low-end merchandise . . . the market needs different things and ways of operation. If you look around at today's films, there are many non-commercialized films that are visually stunning, but they do not make money.

GM: Just now when we mentioned the scene where Michele Reis does mundane things, I could also associate that scene with the style of 1950s Italian filmmakers such as De Sica. They liked to show the daily lives in real time. Were you influenced by their films? William Chang once said he was influenced by 1960s French New Wave films.

WKW: There must be some influence because that was the time when we first saw films. We were naturally influenced by all those [film] movements. In addition, we did not study films, we grew up in movie theaters. In those days, we would see Cantonese films, Japanese films, Hollywood films—they became our entire film education. But that does not mean we would make films because of their influences, and we would not be influenced by a particular type of film. On the other hand, I have to consider if film forces you to think in a certain way or if it gives you some thinking space? If one does not like a careful calculation in every *drama*, if one does not like manipulating the audience's reaction, then why not give the audience more space?

GM: Recently there is a book on Hong Kong popular culture[2] that uses your characters to illustrate the sentiments of city dwellers at the fin de siècle. Do you agree with this viewpoint?

WKW: I think this author has not been paying attention [to my films] because every film of mine is very optimistic, and the characters survive and live on at the end. This is unrelated to fin de siècle. Now many people like abusing terms (with an annoyed tone): what fin de siècle, what decadence culture, what postmodernism, and so on. I think these things (relations between characters) could happen in any time period; they have no relation to the end of the century. In fact every day is the end of the century.

May be [the book author] thinks the characters have to bear the challenge of love, but in fact they all prevail. For example, all six characters in *Days of Being Wild* live on, the same to those in *Ashes of Time*. But they have to wait till they are in their thirties or forties to overcome [the challenges].

GM: Your films are mostly about love relations of city dwellers.
WKW: In fact, to young people in their twenties, thirties. Life is more than that;

there are many things outside love relationships. That's why there are many other elements in *Fallen Angels*. I am very interested in family relations, but the audience wants those in *wuxia* films, cop-and-thief films. That's why I use family relations as much as space allows.

GM: Do you please the audience by adding action scenes in every film?

WKW: In fact many people ask me why I used cops in *Chungking Express*. My first response is because I like their uniforms; the second is because Hong Kong films have to have action scenes. In today's society, gangsters and cops usually have fights. Then I chose a hit man for *Fallen Angels*. But the question is not whether there are action or non-action scenes because action is only a way to express emotions, a kind of behavior and activity.

GM: In your films, the acting is very shallow. Even if the characters break up or change lovers, they do not change much. This is the case for Tony Leung Chiu-wai and Takeshi Kaneshiro [in *Chungking Express*]. In fact, does this way of acting respond to city dwellers' ambiguous attitudes toward love relations? Or are there other purposes?

WKW: This is only my preference. Perhaps it is because I am like that. I feel this is an appropriate way to express emotions.

GM: Will you refuse dramatic acting?

WKW: No, but the dramatic acting has to be good. Sometimes it has to depend on the story. I would accept a character who grows up in a rural village to be highly dramatic.

GM: From your perspective, what is exceptional acting? For the concept of acting, is it about being another character and playing that character well, or is it about not thinking about acting but playing oneself?

WKW: Basically, if one could see the acting, it is already not good. Most times good acting cannot be described. Although many say playing oneself is the best kind of acting, one never knows the real self. The talk of playing oneself is actually a kind of acting. I think the most important thing about acting is it has to be convincing; it has to get the audience absorbed [in the film].

GM: Although the process of making films is difficult and there are many difficulties to overcome, some directors enjoy this process because during the filming process they could look back and be introspective. Also, the product stimulates thoughts for the audience. What do you think about filmmaking?

WKW: There are two parts: a director may ask oneself during the filmmaking process, "Why is making films so difficult? Is it possible not to make films?" Making films is like a life sentence. Looking back, though, one would enjoy that time because what is worth remembering is a thing of the past. Film is the same. The duration of enjoyment may be three minutes, but that of pain may be two years.

GM: Your films have always been the spotlight for film critics, and there are many criticisms of your films. Are there any occasions of misreadings?

WKW: I think this is not important because once you make a film there will be someone writing about it. In addition, everyone has his or her own view, so I absolutely won't interfere in others' thoughts. I could not control [how others think] anyway. However, many people's views are not about a film but about how their views of this film are different from others, so they are debating their different viewpoints and stances, not about the film. A film should give others a space to think.

Nevertheless, the only thing that irritates me is some make mistakes on descriptive information, such as the shooting locations, the shooting duration. If I saw [the wrong information], I would not be too *happy*. I won't speculate on their motivations. But as media workers, they should first carefully do fact-checking before writing about the details. That should be their work ethic.

GM: I think your dialogues are very special, in particular the interior monologues of the characters. Besides their expressing cosmopolitan sentiments, they also have poetically irrational logic. The dialogues provide much space for the audience to interpret.

WKW: During the writing process, I only thought this character should talk like this, merely from the point of view of the characters.

GM: You studied graphic design; why would you attempt to be a director? Were you influenced by films that you had watched so you wanted to be a director?

WKW: At the beginning, I only wanted to find a job after graduation. At that time TVB[3] had training for directors, and they paid a stipend. I thought, why not? I could study and make money at the same time. Then someone asked me to direct, so I began this kind of lifestyle. At that time I liked films very much, but not enough to want to be a director. I accepted the job [to direct] when others gave me one.

GM: After studying graphic design, do you feel this helps you to be a director, with things like screen composition?

WKW: Completely unrelated. Those who study *design* are not particularly creative. It was just by chance that I studied *design*. At the beginning I did not want to do that much homework. I wanted to have more time to think. I found out it was not like that afterwards.

GM: Do you like a particular film genre?

WKW: Everything that is good, . . . the kind that is touching for the audience.

GM: So when you are making films, do you want them to be touching for the audience or for yourself?

WKW: If the film is touching, the first one to be touched has to be the director him/herself. Sometimes it does not have to be a weepie. You can be touched by seeing a worker mending the sidewalk. [It is touching] as long as one is authentic, when one has good *intentions*. And my standard of making films is that I don't allow myself to have a chance to regret later.

GM: When you were making films, did you think of making the audience feel touched?

WKW: Yes, films should be communicative at the end, but I hope to *present* some ways [to communicate], to illustrate this is also an acceptable way to communicate. I could accept many things at the beginning, but I should not stop trying because others do not accept it. It is like you could only walk along Nathan Road in Tsim Sha Tsui.[4]

GM: Do you worry about repeating yourself when you were making attempts in the process?

WKW: Of course, I can't repeat [myself]. If today I remade *As Tears Go By*, I think the audience might not like it. Actually when the director communicates with the audience, it is a kind of attempt. Because after every attempt, I would know the distance between myself and the audience. If there is a problem I would try again. If there is still a problem I would try again until the gap between the audience and me is reduced. Of course, all these should be done within the premise of not losing my way of doing things.

GM: Your films are always associated with "good film reviews, bad box office." What is your thought on this?

WKW: Looking for new revenue and reducing costs—this has always been my way. If you are the kind of director who wants to make your own films, you have to find a space to survive. In particular in the past few years, I gradually have felt I need to tell others that I can only make this kind of film, not other kinds. If you like this kind, I welcome your business; if not, then it does not bother me. At the end I think if I constantly have to accommodate the overseas market, then I could not please both parties. I could not please everyone; more [importantly], I could not do what I want to do.

GM: You have made five films. Do you see any improvements?

WKW: I don't think of it as a question of improvements but how people change because of time. The so-called improvement is nothing but a change.

GM: How about other Hong Kong directors?

WKW: Each master has his/her own way; everyone is producing merchandise in this supermarket. I only hope to make better products, to make the audience buy tickets.

GM: But as a whole, is it like what people outside the industry say: Hong Kong directors are regressing?

WKW: Not regressing, but in recent years there are only a few directors who are prominent, such as Wong Jing,[5] who makes many films in a year. He has given a livelihood to many people. There aren't too many emerging filmmakers because Hong Kong does not nurture talent; people are not farsighted enough. If there is any crisis, people would only cut the resources and time to train new talent. Taiwan also has to face the same problem.

In addition there is no big studio that will come out to support other independents. They also have to face the pressure of the overseas market, but the market asks for those films that are commercialized. As a result, the products are all the same. If there is a big studio, it may have enough capital to invest in different film genres.

GM: Now Hollywood tends to make big productions with special effects. Do you worry they will monopolize the market?

WKW: Not necessarily. At the same time [Hollywood] could accommodate many genres, like the audience who is used to *Judge Dredd* could also like *Forrest Gump*. In this *supermarket* there have to be different products. Advanced technology naturally will be integrated into films; this is the trend. Therefore, the PRC government and the Taiwanese government ought to send students to the US to learn digital arts.

But would the market demand of all these [commercial] films kill others? I don't think so because the original purposes are not the same. Because of capital shortage, there would be plans to make films that do not require big budgets. That's why non-mainstream films have their space to survive, in particular now that words are replaced by images. With the advancements in technology, non-mainstream films will have their own markets.

GM: You have once said your films are old wine in new bottles, like repackaging old canned food, but I personally think Wong Jing's films also *recycle* others', or perhaps his own *idea*. Both are essentially the same thing, but the reactions outside the industry are very extreme: one side is full of praises, another side is full of insults, what do you think?

WKW: I think everyone has different purpose. I have not seen Wong Jing's films for a long time, so I found it hard to critique them. But I personally think while many describe his films as low-taste, *cheap*, this is very superficial. I had seen his films before. Wong Jing is an excellent storyteller; the audience only needs to spend three minutes to know how the story develops. This is not an easy thing to do. Many directors spend half a day, and the audience still doesn't know what the story is. That's why Wong Jing has the talent to succeed.

GM: What is the meaning of films for the audience?

WKW: Personally, I hope to do what I had wanted to do when I was small, which is to bring sorrow, joy, and a sense of loss to the audience. Film is only a channel: whether it is one between the director and the audience or one between the director and the actors or one between the audience members, at the end it is communication between humans.

NOTES

1. NG is commonly used in Hong Kong television and film industries. It means "no good" and therefore a retake is needed.
2. It may refer to the Chinese book written by Natalia Chan. See Natalia Chan, *Decadent City: Hong Kong Popular Culture* (Hong Kong: Oxford University Press, 1995).
3. TVB stands for Television Broadcasts Limited. It is the dominant TV station of the two providing free-to-air channels in the 1980s. Production is usually done in-house.
4. Tsim Sha Tsui is a shopping/commercial area in the Kowloon Peninsula. Nathan Road is the main street. Chungking Mansion—a shooting location in *Chungking Express*—is located on Nathan Road.
5. Wong Jing is a prolific film director and producer who made a lot of comedies that are seen as "low taste" by film critics but they have excellent box offices.

Open Communication: Wong Kar-wai

Yik Ming / 1997

From *City Entertainment* (Hong Kong). No. 485 (pp. 15–18). Interview conducted in Cantonese in 1997. Reprinted by permission of the publisher. Translated by Silver Wai-ming Lee from Chinese.

Wong Kar-wai's Motorola commercial, like his filmmaking process, attracted a lot of media attention. The news coverage is always about the budget, the image design, and the prolonged production schedule. The commercial received media attention before it was even finished; however, no one talks about what the final product—the advertisement—is like. Every time I watch a new film by Wong, I want to know what tricks he is going to play. This is especially the case when recent mobile phone commercials have imaginative storylines, extravagant action, wonderful special effects, and fascinating visuals. I wonder what new tricks Wong can use to make the commercial unique.

Therefore, when we see Faye Wong with an afro hairdo and broken alleys with graffiti on the wall, we know Wong has succeeded again. Other commercials have gorgeous costumes and beautiful sceneries, but they are all rejected by Wong. He makes commercials the way he makes movies—wild and passionate. This is indeed eye-opening.

Why did Motorola choose Wong? "Our corporate value is creativity enriched by inner strength. When we look at the entertainment business, there is no one like Wong Kar-wai and Faye Wong who can reflect our value. The former is also the sole leader of the industry; this is another similarity between us," a Motorola marketing representative told me.

The theme of this Motorola commercial is oddly simple: communication between people. The slogan is "Open the sky of communication." This is nothing new (other commercials have used "Communication is X."), but Wong has returned to the basics and developed his piece from a basic idea. This attitude exemplifies a proverb in the West: "The most sophisticated is simplicity," and the commercial opens up the sky of art for Motorola.

The good thing about Wong's films is not only the new technique, but also the genuine emotion. *Days of Being Wild* is plain and simple, but the emotions of the actors are naturally and genuinely expressed, unlike those embarrassing [emotional] exaggerations in Hong Kong films. That is why [*Days*] is persuasive as is this Motorola commercial. No matter how blinding the special effects other commercials have, Wong wins the audience's heart by the rich emotions in this Motorola ad. Therefore, the commercial is not just a commercial, but it is also a film. I regard it as a short film directed by Wong, and wonder how the future film *Summer in Beijing*[1] would be. (Isn't it a story between a Japanese guy and a Beijing girl?)

Yik Ming: How do you describe your relationship with mobile phones?
Wong Kar-wai: I don't use them often.

YM: What is your expectation for this commercial?
WKW: Motorola expects a commercial different from others, so do I.

YM: What atmosphere does the art director, William Chang, want to create? How does he style the protagonists? Do they look good?
WKW: There is a common misunderstanding that an art director is responsible for helping the stars' make-up. But this is not the responsibility of an art director. An art director is in charge of the visual presentation. I think William Chang is a responsible art director. We mostly use primary and monotonous colors and avoid a riot of colors.

YM: The commercial runs for three minutes. Does it mean you condense a feature film into a three-minute one?
WKW: It is different. In terms of form, a three-minute short film isn't equal to one-thirtieth of a ninety-minute film. A three-minute short film requires another form. For example, a feature film is like a novel, a three-minute short film may be like prose or something short.

YM: There is a thirty-second version of this commercial. What are some difficulties when you tell a story in thirty seconds?
WKW: That's why I didn't try to present a story because of the time limit. I present a message instead. As the commercial is about the *communication* function of a mobile phone, it *serves the purpose* once the commercial associates itself with communication.

YM: What is the theme of this commercial?
WKW: Communication.

YM: What is the main difference in techniques between making a commercial and a film?

WKW: You have a lot of resources when making a movie. You may develop your ideas one by one. But when you film a thirty-second commercial, you have to get straight to the point as you count to three.

YM: Is the Faye Wong in the short film more like her true self, a model in the commercial, or a character in your feature films?

WKW: I think she is the mixture of all three. I can't see Faye Wong herself in the short film. But as Faye Wong plays the character called "Faye Wong" in this commercial, the public perception of Faye fits into who Faye is [as a character in the commercial]. And this is a Motorola commercial, so these three [images] can coexist.

YM: How many characters are there in the commercial?

WKW: Just two: a man and a woman. I think two is enough as the theme is communication between people.

YM: Which scene in the commercial is the most difficult to make?

WKW: The scene with the pinball machine. The venue made it difficult. We had planned to shoot [this scene] for a long time, but the venue did not give permission. We had to move to another location and decorate it again, so we were in a hurry. I think this was the most difficult case.

YM: You have chosen some special locations like "Tong Lau" [old residential buildings], "fruit wholesale market," and "night club." Is there any special meaning about these venues?

WKW: I think these locations are suitable for shooting. Actually, daily lives mainly take place at home, in public places, and in crowded venues.

YM: From which social class are the male and female protagonists? What are their personalities like?

WKW: I don't think they represent a particular class. They represent themselves. They could be anybody from any class.

YM: What is the difference between using a male and a female as the protagonist in the mobile phone commercial?

WKW: I am not sexist. I think they are the same.

YM: You have collaborated with William Chang and Christopher Doyle many times. Do you have a good working relationship with them?
WKW: Yes, we do not need to explain much to each other. I did not mention what kind of images and lighting I expected, but we got the anticipated effects naturally when it came to shooting.

YM: Do you think art means creating something new?
WKW: Not necessarily. I think one cannot make art when one is being conscious. Art is something natural.

YM: Do you have any unforgettable moments or new thoughts during the process from planning, shooting, to editing?
WKW: Every shooting is just a process. It is like when you go swimming in the winter; you consider it for a long time. Then you feel bone-chilled, so you walk back and forth. You eventually jump into the water, getting back to the shore after a quick lap. The advantage of shooting this commercial is it only took me a short period of time. It is like you do not need to swim for that long.

YM: In your opinion, is there any kind of special spark between Faye Wong and Tadanobu Asano in the commercial?
WKW: I don't think they are like a couple in the commercial. They are like kids instead. Many adults have their inner child. In the act, they are like two kids.

YM: What is the relationship between the two protagonists? During the shooting or the recess, did they have good communication?
WMW: From my point of view, during the shooting or the recess, they were curious about each other, but they found it difficult to chat. Just like [the characters] in the commercial, they are clueless about how to chat with each other. Behind the scene, the language barrier might make their communication difficult.

YM: In your opinion, why did Motorola invite you to direct the commercial?
WKW: As per Motorola, the reason of picking me and Faye for the commercial is because they believe Motorola, Faye, and I are a "perfect combination." Faye is a pop diva in Asia, and Motorola is the leader in mobile devices. They hope I will use an innovative way to illustrate the theme of "Open the sky of communication."

YM: There are many special scenes, like playing pinball and snowing. What do they signify?
WKW: I wanted to experiment filming them.

YM: Have you experimented with anything you haven't had [in your films] in this commercial?

WKW: It is like a stutterer who tries to tell a story without a pause—telling a ninety-minute story in half a minute.

YM: How did you feel after the last shot?

WKW: I wanted to go home and sleep as soon as possible.

YM: Does Faye's performance fulfill your requirement?

WKW: There isn't much difference [between her performance in this commercial and that in the film]. She is just as eccentric as usual. The main difference is she used to be quiet, but she is talkative now.

YM: Why did you choose Asano as the male character?

WKW: Because he meets the requirement of the character, not because we are old friends.

YM: How is Asano's performance? Do you want to work with him again in the future?

WKW: At first we did not fully understand each other due to the language barrier. But he worked very hard, and we now trust each other. If there is an opportunity, we will work with each other again.

YM: How do you feel working with Faye again? Do you want to work with her again in the future?

WKW: I haven't worked with Faye for two or three years. This opportunity gave us a chance to be together again. When the shooting started, we needed time to warm up. If timing allows, we will work with each other again.

YM: Your previous work is artistic while the advertisement is commercial. Do you think they are in conflict?

WKW: Anything is *OK* as long as it has good quality.

YM: Do you think this commercial maintains your artistic style? Would you describe this as a piece of art?

WKW: I am very thankful that Motorola has given me great freedom to film this advertisement. I am satisfied with the outcome. It is the audience who has the right to decide if it is a piece of art or not. I think this commercial aligns with my style.

YM: Is there any insufficiency?

WKW: There are always limitations in filming, like timing, budget, and space. I can only do the best within the limitations.

YM: As per the advertising agency of Motorola, this commercial is a perfect combination of the three of you. What do you think?

WKW: I feel this has been a happy process. Motorola's trust in me and the ad agency's effort have made it a good collaborative experience.

NOTE

1. *Summer in Beijing* is supposedly a feature film by Wong but was never finished or released.

Each Film Has Its Own Ounce of Luck

Michel Ciment and Hubert Niogret / 1997

From *Positif* (France). No. 442 (pp. 8–14). Interview conducted in English. Reprinted by permission of the publisher. Translated from French by M. A. Salvodon © 2015.

Michel Ciment and Hubert Niogret: A double originality marks the film [*Happy Together*] from the beginning: a Hong Kong director decides to make a film in Buenos Aires with the tango as a musical leitmotiv, and he begins a homosexual relationship in the most direct manner, without any "aesthetization" or bad taste.
Wong Kar-wai: Before making the film, I thought that since the story was taking place in Buenos Aires, it would also be a film about this city. Upon arriving, I realized that this was not the case. And neither is it a *gay* film. I wanted to tell a love story between two men. After *Chungking Express* and *Fallen Angels*, many people copied these two films in Asia. A few days ago, in the office of a Korean distributor, I discovered a trailer of a film, it seems, is a hit in its country of origin. Yet everything, the music, the camera movement, the montage are all taken from my two films. They nicknamed the director the "Korean Wong Kar-wai!" That was a warning for me: I had to go forward. I then told my chief cinematographer that this time we should do something different. This was another reason I made *Happy Together* because after *Fallen Angels*, everyone asked me if I was going to make a film on Hong Kong 1997, which is to say, the return of my city to China. Since I didn't know anything about it, I thought that the best way to avoid answering the question was to go make a movie abroad. I am a fan of Manuel Puig's novels, and one of them is called *The Buenos Aires Affair*. I liked the title, and [it] gave me the idea to go film in this city that was somewhat the antithesis of Hong Kong. Then little by little, as I was making *Happy Together*, I distanced myself a little from the initial project, and, finally, it was as if I had re-created Hong Kong in Buenos Aires.

MC&HN: The film owes nothing to Manuel Puig.
WKW: No, it isn't an adaptation of any of his novels, but I did want to pay homage to my favorite novelist. Then I became aware that the title, *The Buenos Aires Affair*,

would be on the wrong track because it would focus too much on the importance of the city, so I preferred calling it *Happy Together*.

MC&HN: Yet the film offers a very original perspective on Buenos Aires, which is far from the touristic stereotypes and close to a certain reality.

WKW: This may be true for you, but I think that Argentinian viewers would criticize me for not showing their city enough. But that wasn't my goal: I wanted to depict the world in which these two young men belong, and, in some way, they are reduced to the room they inhabit. The person who scouted for locations with me was often surprised by my choice of locations, but I was guided by the smells, the lights of the places I visited. I made the film in the La Boca neighborhood, which is one of the most dangerous in Buenos Aires. Everyone was a little afraid, including the actors. I don't know why, but I thought that these places evoked Kowloon, this Hong Kong district that I identify with so easily. The hotel where we made the movie was very cheap: a room costs five dollars a night. And the place was full of suspicious people, including gangsters who were hanging out nearby. Some who were clearly dangerous demanded that we give them money. But I know these types, and I was glad to be filming there. This neighborhood brought me closer to my world because other parts of Buenos Aires seemed very unfamiliar. The ambience was completely foreign to me, and, clearly, the city is more of a European city than a South American one. It's somewhat the opposite of Hong Kong as I show it in the film. I also wanted to film at a faster speed because Buenos Aires has a rhythm that's too slow for me!

MC&HN: You are not the first heterosexual filmmaker to approach the topic of homosexuality. But like Stephen Frears, you avoid both sentimentalism and explicit provocation that we often find in gay films. In the end, you film the homosexual couple in the way that you would film a heterosexual couple.

WKW: That's the reason I open the film with a lovemaking sequence. I approach it directly, very explicitly, to show that this is a part of their lives, like sharing a meal or washing clothes. Romanticism did not interest me. I like the idea of a viewer arriving late and, having missed this first sequence, he could think that this is a story about two brothers. During filming, I would often ask Christopher Doyle, my chief cinematographer, and William Chang, my editor: "Is my film *gay*?" But once the film was done, I understood that it was simply a love story.

MC&HN: What importance do you give to improvisation in a film like *Happy Together*?

WKW: It's a rather funny story. Before leaving for Buenos Aires, I had a two-page synopsis, and I was convinced that this was the first time that I had felt so sure about my story. Before beginning a film, Lai Yiu-fai (Tony Leung Chiu-wai) was leaving for Buenos Aires because his father had been killed there without any apparent reason. Then he realized that he was looking for someone he [the father] loved in Buenos Aires. At the end, he realized that this person was a man, Ho Po-wing (Leslie Cheung). I was sure I had a dramatic story. But I then realized that this synopsis had too many different stories: the search, Tony's problems in Hong Kong, his father's life, his relationship with his male lover from ten years ago. This seemed very complicated to me, especially since I only had one month of filming because Leslie had to return to Hong Kong for a concert. On top of this, we were in the middle of a worker's strike, and we were having problems with production. Time was flying by, and I decided to write the simplest narrative, a *road movie*, once again with the new encounter of these two men from Hong Kong, who meet in Buenos Aires without knowing why.

MC&HN: It's a *road movie*, possibly, but in a room!

WKW: And even in a kitchen! Still, by radically changing the story, I was left without a script to speak of. At the beginning, I had a few pages, but I did write some scenes the night before filming, and even on the set, just before filming.

MC&HN: During the three months that you were scouting for locations in the city, what did you learn?

WKW: At first, I tried to understand Buenos Aires and its inhabitants. But quickly, I realized that I didn't have time to open myself to the outside world and that instead I needed to focus because I have the tendency to get distracted by a thousand pervading details. If I see an ashtray, I want to shoot it. This would have been dangerous for me to spread myself out like that, and I wanted to turn all of my attention to the scenes we needed to film. Moreover, I'm the scriptwriter, the director, and the producer, and having brought over a team of thirty people from Hong Kong with me, it was an expensive undertaking. These are people I have worked with for years, and they realized that I was having problems with the production and the story. If I had filmed it in Hong Kong, it would have been different because at the end of the day, everyone goes back home, and this way one can relax. But here we were all lodged in the same place, and, in the morning, we looked at each other, said nothing, but knew that you're worried. It's as if every day, we found each other in a room with multiple screens under constant surveillance, and this creates a certain tension! Every time there was a Chinese holiday, the desire to go back to Hong Kong returned, especially since our stay—which was supposed to last two months—was extended to four months because of all the hassle.

MC&HN: Was the theme of the Iguazu Falls planned from the very beginning of the story as you were restructuring your project?

WKW: I must tell you that our main problem was finding lodging for the two protagonists. With my art director, William Chang (who is also my editor), we were lucky because we quickly found where they would be living. So, he and his collaborators got to work on transforming the apartment, finding the wallpaper, et cetera. They discovered the San Elmo flea markets, which is an Italian neighborhood in Buenos Aires, and a lamp with a lampshade that had an imprint of the Fall. In fact, they bought similar lamps, and one was in my room. Looking at the imprint, I saw two guys looking at a waterfall. This seemed a beautiful story to include in my film: the idea of a man who wants to share his happiness with another man by going to look at a waterfall. This gave them a common goal and helped us to structure the narrative.

MC&HN: Your way of filming with rapid movements of the camera, as if in a state of emergency, makes your relationship to Christopher Doyle particularly important.

WKW: This assumes an intimate collaboration, of course, especially in this particular case when, because of Leslie Cheung's other commitments, in ten days we had to film all the scenes he is in. We even worked three days straight, basically with no interruption, and everyone got a little crazy. But I always thought the style of filming came from the way of filming, and, in this case, it could not have been faster. Normally, I choreograph the actors' movements and tell them where to move. Then I tell Christopher how the camera is going to move, and he works on setting up the lights. Of course, we had no problems communicating with each other because together we've made five of the six films I directed. We don't talk about lighting or about the setting or the angle because starting with our first collaboration I was very clear about my instructions, and he knows what I want. For example, we don't see eye to eye on close-ups. He wants them less close together, while my taste veers more toward the close-up. He knows this and gives me what I want. So our working relationship is very good, and when he moves the camera, I don't even have to look at the video screen because in following his movement I know what his take will be like. In general, on the set, we talk about anything and everything, but very rarely about photography. I prefer to ask him, for instance, what the meaning of the Tropic of Capricorn is because for me the story of these two young men begins when they pass the line of the Tropics.

MC&HN: Before beginning to film, did you have a particular relationship with tango music and with Astor Piazzolla's work?

WKW: Not at all. In fact, my first contact with Piazzola was at the Amsterdam airport where I bought his CDs on my way to Argentina! For me, it's more than tango. It's rhythm and passion. The music gave my film its rhythm, as well as giving rhythm to the city in which we filmed. Music is a part of sound, and the sounds of Buenos Aires are dominated by music, on one hand, yet the city is also about the sounds of radio and television, like the broadcasts of soccer games that you can hear wherever you are.

MC&HN: What is surprising in your purchase of Piazzolla's CD is that you stumbled upon a well-known melody of his arranged by Kip Hanrahan.

WKW: I believe a great deal in chance. In fact, my films are made up of the addition of small parts. At the end, I discover the whole. It seems to me to be a very Chinese way of thinking. One day, I was filming in La Boca, and I didn't know why I was doing such or such a shot. It was purely accidental. It's when we were editing that I realized that it was going to play a very important role. In other words, it's like a puzzle whose order I wouldn't know, but whose pieces would assemble themselves little by little. In my view, every film has its own bit of luck. For example, when we were filming *Days of Being Wild*, one sequence was supposed to occur during a sunny day, but it was raining nonstop. We, therefore, changed the script, but when we were about to film, the sun came out again. That time, luck was not on the side of the film. For the waterfall scene in *Happy Together*, we were very worried because rain had been pouring for a week, and we had very little time. But on the day of filming, the sun returned, and we took advantage of the abundant waterfalls that made for a spectacular background. There, on the other hand, we were lucky!

MC&HN: Do you film using a lot of film [negative] compared to what you will keep during the editing?

WKW: I work in segments, which I number without really knowing ahead of time the connections between them, nor do I know their order in the narrative. At the point of editing, I try a number of combinations. For *Happy Together*, we used Avid, a system of virtual editing. But I originally did my first editing on the Steenbeck,[1] and it lasted three hours because I like to work at the table. But the advantage of Avid was that it helped to tighten the film. It was, therefore, more of a process of elimination than of addition. I was still in the process of discarding what didn't seem necessary two weeks before the Cannes Film Festival because it seemed to me that this story didn't merit a long film. Obviously, by working this way, I use a lot of film. But there's another reason for this. We don't do any retakes, and I use my camera in a very mobile way to capture moments of truth, a little like in a documentary. For *Happy Together*, I was always in need of negatives, and we had to ask for help. I was able to get from Kodak a type of film that is usually not used in fictional films. It's a very old model with very little in stock. At the end of filming, the film had not arrived, and I asked Christopher Doyle to bring his camera to photograph the scene, image by image. This didn't bother me because in the end time stopped, and we were able to make the film with fixed images. But I also decided to shorten this scene as well. Like you see, all methods are good in the making of a film!

MC&HN: What was the contribution of Leslie Cheung and Tony Leung in the making of a film in which improvisation plays an important part?

WKW: I never ask my actors to play a character other than who they are. I borrow a great deal from their personality. During the first days, we work slowly since we have to find the right path. Little by little, when they feel confident, I let them improvise especially during the sex scenes! Tony and Leslie know each other well, in fact for a long time, so it's fun to watch them improvise in this way in front of the camera. Tony would ask me questions about his affair with Chang [Chen], the other man. In fact, I presented the situation to them; then they improvised while the camera filmed. They didn't stop, and it was really funny to see them participate in the movement of the scene without me saying, "Cut!," at any moment. They were waiting for me to stop them, but they had to keep going!

MC&HN: You have made four films with Tony Leung and three films with Leslie Cheung. How do you define their personality since you've admitted to borrowing some of their traits to construct their characters?

WKW: For me, Leslie Cheung's behavior in the film is very close to the Leslie I know in real life. He was, therefore, very at ease with his role. Tony, on the other hand, is very different. He is not so sure of himself and doesn't take the risk of doing crazy things in front of the camera. He is a very subtle and focused actor. This is why I wanted to make a change in him—to destabilize him—because I wanted to pull from him different accents. At first, he thought that my idea of making him Leslie's lover a joke. The first day of filming, he had to perform in the love scene. He was so shocked that he refused right away, and, at any rate, he wanted to keep his underwear on. During the next three days, he was so shaken that he sat in a corner doing nothing by himself; he was completely speechless. He wondered how he could explain it all to his mother. He was very tense last night [at Cannes] during the screening of the film in the large room of the palace because it was the first time he was seeing it, and he was dreading the film's release in Hong Kong in a month's time. I told him that I would bring his mother, but he refused. It would be him or no one! Leslie's reaction was very different. He said to me, "You want to tell a love story between two men, and I'm going to see just how far you will go." From this standpoint, I believe he helped Tony a great deal, and he kept telling him that it was only a film! Leslie can give the impression of being more fragile, but, in fact, he is someone with great determination. His status as a star singer and his acting profession are equally important for him, and he considers them one and the same.

MC&HN: How did you choose Chang Chen?

WKW: I had seen him in *A Brighter Summer Day* (1991) by Edward Yang, while he was still a child [actor]. Last year, when I saw him in *Mahjong* (1996) by Edward Yang at the Berlin Film Festival, I realized that it was the same actor, and he had changed very much. I think he's a remarkable actor. Up until then he had only done films with Edward Yang, whose methods are very different from mine. They have a kind of teacher-apprentice relationship, and Edward spends a lot of time discussing his role with him and practicing, which is not my way of doing things. This disturbed him a lot at the beginning, especially since I had asked my assistant to take Chang Chen to a gym and to have him take boxing lessons. I found him too fragile, too tender, too slow, and I wanted him to be more active, stronger, with better coordination of his physical movements. Even at the end of the film, I think he still had not understood it all, after believing that he was going to act in an action film!

MC&HN: With *Fallen Angels*, you went all the way with a kind of formalism. Isn't *Happy Together* a kind of return to a cinema in which the characters have more consistency?

WKW: For me, *Fallen Angels* was treated like a comic book in which the four protagonists were one-dimensional. The only character, in the strongest sense of the word, was the father of one of the young people [note: the mute played by Takeshi Kaneshiro]. In this way, the film reflected the enormous influence of comics on Hong Kong cinema. The viewing public is led to contrast real characters with heroes from comics. The experience with *Happy Together* is very different, of course. At the beginning of filming, I told Christopher Doyle and William Chang that it would be a simple and straightforward film about normal people who speak in slang. Why they came to Buenos Aires remains a mystery. I remember one of my friends, a member of the crew, had arrived in Buenos Aires a week before the rest of us. He told me that he wanted to go to the Canadian Embassy to try to get a passport because the quotas in Buenos Aires were more flexible than in Hong Kong and that it would cost only a few thousand American dollars. Basically, it's possibly one of the reasons why Leslie and Tony left Hong Kong for Argentina!

MC&HN: You like non-realistic cinematographic tricks, like an accelerated frame rate.

WKW: It's undoubtedly because of my impatience and that I wanted to do a film as fast as possible in order to return to Hong Kong! But seriously, I believe that it's like the Chinese expression which states that "time goes by like a fast current of water." In fact, in this film and in life, there is no progression. There is a routine aspect to their lives, while on the outside, the world is in constant movement. That's the contrast.

MC&HN: Did you always want this mixture of color with black and white?
WKW: I like its texture. I also wanted to separate the film in three parts. The past, for the viewers, is often associated with black and white. The second part is when the two men decide to start to live together again. And the third part is when Leslie leaves Tony. The story then becomes more intimate. They no longer see each other; they no longer speak to other people and only speak to themselves. I often remember the first sentence in Godard's *Little Soldier*: "For me, the time of action has passed. I've aged. The time for reflection has just begun." And this is somewhat what happens in the third part of *Happy Together*. Another reason why I filmed the first part in black and white (in fact, it was made in color but treated in black and white) is that it occurs during the summer in Argentina, which is very cold. The black and white seemed to restore this ambience.

MC&HN: It's rare for the editor and the set designer [William Chang] to be the same person in a film.
WKW: He wouldn't hesitate to cut a frame if it seems necessary to him, even if the décor had taken a lot of effort and time! In fact, William Chang is very rigorous with the film, himself, and me. We have been working together since my first film, and he understands my work well. But it is also his work. I don't give him orders, and he can be brutal in his decisions. His judgement is very good, and he knows my rhythm—so much so that the result is very close to what I think and what I feel. With him, the set designer and the editor are one. He thinks about dramaturgy. We don't talk about colors or texture, but he always asks questions on the way in which I'm going to begin a sequence, and depending on my answer, he is going to think about the costume and the settings. I think he himself could be a very good filmmaker because he knows cinema thoroughly.

MC&HN: Do you think the group you've formed with your collaborators for so many years is of a particular kind?
WKW: I often think of us as a jazz ensemble. Christopher and William are in high demand in Hong Kong, but when I put them together, I'm a little bit like a team leader. I suggest we have *jam sessions* on a new project. So we discuss the film intensively among the three of us. Christopher will ask me what kind of music

I'm going to use because that will inspire his movements of the camera and his style of photography. Tango was not his kind of music, but he had to admit that Piazzolla is amazing!

NOTE

1. Steenbeck is an editing suite that only deals with analogue film. Editing on this system requires manual cutting.

Interview with Wong Kar-wai:
In the Mood for Love

Michel Ciment and Hubert Niogret / 2000

From *Positif* (France). No. 477 (pp. 76–80). Interview conducted in English. Reprinted by permission of the publisher. [Editors' note: Wong's answers in English were transcribed from the interview included in *In the Mood for Love* DVD (Criterion edition). The questions were translated from French by Micky Lee.]

Michel Ciment and Hubert Niogret: You seem to have blended the preproduction and filming of the films 2046 and *In the Mood for Love*.

Wong Kar-wai: We tried to finish the production of this film [*In the Mood for Love*] in August last year (1999), but obviously we were too slow. Because we also had the economic crisis [due to SARS] in Asia, all the investors of this film *In the Mood for Love* withdrew. We had to stop production and find other investors. By that time we had already started to make the film 2046 so that meant we had two films mixed together to schedule, and the whole process was very painful because it's like loving two persons at the same time! When we were scouting locations for 2046, we thought this probably should go to *In Mood for Love* and vice versa. So in the end we decided the two films should be one film. So maybe in the future when you see *In the Mood for Love* and 2046, you will see something of 2046 in *In the Mood for Love*; and in *In the Mood for Love* you have some things from 2046.

MC&HN: Why did you decide to situate *In the Mood for Love* in 1962 and 1966? The story of *Days of Being Wild* took place in the same era, and you did not see *In the Mood of Love* as the second part of *Days of Being Wild?*

WKW: I'm very fond of that period in Hong Kong because it was a special period. The people whom we describe in the film: the landlady and all these Shanghainese communities were actually very special. They were people coming from China to Hong Kong after '49 when the Communists took over China. They were living by themselves; they didn't have any contact with the local Cantonese. They had their own language. They had their own food. They had their own cinema. In Hong Kong there was Mandarin cinema which was mainly for those people, and they had their own rituals. That's why I wanted to put the film in this environment because I came from this background. As a kid, I heard the gossips, and I knew our neighbors. I want to re-create this part of Hong Kong in the film. Only five at the time, [I] had an overall impression of that time, so some of the details in the film are more beautiful or nicer than they actually were. But in memories everything is fine.

MC&HN: Is the story between Maggie Cheung and Tony Leung the second part of *Days of Being Wild*?

WKW: Over the years people kept asking me, "Are you going to make a part two?" I thought to myself, "If I have a chance to make this film, will it be the same story or not?" I know I've changed. The way I see things has changed too, so for me I think the biggest difference is that in this film, we are describing people who are married. It's not like *Days of Being Wild* where they are single.

MC&HN: Your last film, *Happy Together*, is about a homosexual couple with explicit sexual expression. In *In the Mood for Love*, there is no sex scene.

WKW: The time is different in the '60s. One thing I am trying is to create a mood in which everything is covered, hidden.

MC&HN: In *In the Mood for Love*, is the story about the deteriorating relationship of a couple because of external pressure? You never see the interference, the little pressure exerted indirectly by distant elements. But this is the consequence: they are no longer together.

WKW: The point of this story is: I'm not trying to tell a story about an affair. I'm trying to tell a certain attitude in a certain period of time in the history of Hong Kong—how people treated these things. I think to make a story about affairs would be very boring because there are so many films about affairs. And there will be no winner in an affair, so I try to find another angle. The whole thing is about the time, the period, and also how people treated this affair over the years by keeping it a secret. Secret will be the main point of the story.

MC&HN: You chose not to show the other couple [the respective spouses of Tony Leung and Maggie Chueng] but imply them through Tony Leung the husband, and Maggie Cheung the wife. At the end, the two couples are the same.

WKW: At the very beginning I hated the idea to show the husband and the wife because that would be boring. You have to make comments about who's right and who's wrong. That is not the point of the story. I'd rather have these two actors going through both sides of an affair. There was a big argument between me, Maggie, and Tony: how did they portray the other half? Because they have an excuse saying, "How did this affair happen?" So they wanted to pretend to be the husband and wife. They tried to act like different people. But I said I want you to play yourselves because this will give another layer to the film, because maybe there's a dark side in Maggie or a dark side in Tony. They need an excuse to release it. So actually, they are not only portraying the husband and the wife, they are trying to show themselves.

MC&HN: You express time by changing the costumes and accessories, notably those of Maggie Cheung. How did you develop this idea?

WKW: I want to show the changes through not having changes. The film tries to repeat all the things: the music is repeating all the time, and the way we see certain space like the office, the clock, the corridors—they're always the same. We are trying to show the changes through minor things such as the clothes of Maggie or the relationship. Unfortunately, for a non-local audience, they would not know some details about the food. Because in the Shanghainese community, specific food is consumed in certain seasons. So actually the food is telling you it is May or March or June. The amah keeps on asking Maggie to stay and eat with them. She is making wonton which is made with certain vegetables. But we don't put [these details] in the subtitles because that would be too much. Those vegetables are only available in June and July so that means we know the characters are now in June and July 1962.

MC&HN: You have a filming method to show a permanent change in a scene. What were cut out and added?

WKW: When we started the project, we called it *A Story about Food*, and it had three stories. And so the extra story we see in *In the Mood for Love* is actually only thirty minutes. It only takes place in the restaurants, in the noodle shop, in the staircase after they buy noodles pretending to have an affair. After I started this part, the main reason for me to make that project is I like this story, so I forgot about the other two stories which weren't made. I just expanded the whole thing. So the most difficult part is: we started a quick lunch, but it became a big feast at the end. We started from 1962 until 1972—ten years. The reason why we wanted to end in '72 is because Hong Kong in the 1970s looked totally different—the people, the behaviors: how they dressed, how they looked, how they ate, and how they lived were extremely different from 1962. But at the end I decided to stop in 1966 because that would be an epic; there would be too much. It'd involve too many skills. We tried one or two scenes in 1972. But I think we need a lot to put in that part, so I don't think it is financially or physically feasible. So we stopped in

1966, which was a very interesting moment in Hong Kong history because of the Cultural Revolution in China. We had riots in Hong Kong, so a lot of people moved away from Hong Kong [to overseas]. It was the beginning of all this [second wave] immigration that happened afterward.

MC&HN: What are the two other stories?

WKW: There are two other stories: one is about a fast food shop owner and his customers; the other one is about a kidnapper and the person being kidnapped.

MC&HN: Is the ending scene in Angkor Wat part of the project, or was it added later?

WKW: We looked for a place to end the film because we think the last scene should provide something like a distance from the incidents. We can look at the whole thing from a distance to provide another dimension. So we looked for all these things in Thailand because we were shooting in Bangkok. We were trying to find some temples. Our production manager said, "Okay, why don't you shoot it in Angkor Wat because we have good connections in Cambodia," and I said, "Why not?" Years ago I saw a documentary on Angkor Wat, and I'm impressed by the place. It's like a museum of jealousy, passion, love, so I think we should end the story there. Because of that, we had to find a reason for Tony to be here and to be in Angkor Wat. We went through all these news reels, and around that time the big event was Charles De Gaulle visiting Cambodia. So we went through this documentary which I like because it is not only about the events, but it also has an effect like waking up somebody. The whole thing is like a fiction; it's like a dream, but there's a certain element which is true, which is factual.

MC&HN: Aren't the architecture and the arts also giving the sentiment and the permanence of things like this love that remains, like some old monuments?

WKW: It is like the remains of these things, and we can see all these rocks. We see there're thousands of stories like this over the years, and these form a history.

MC&HN: What is the legend that you talk about, the one that tells the rocks a secret?

WKW: It's a legend from an old book. I will use this legend in *2046* and *In the Mood for Love* at the same time. We are trying to explore how people keep their secrets in different ways.

MG&HN: At the end Tony Leung looks at a child and he smiles. This is quite mysterious. Is this a scene you added during the filming?

WKW: That's in the script. I'd like to have some ambiguity. That's perhaps his son, . . . the age matches; but that proves nothing. One never knows.

MC&HN: Like in all your films, the visual aspect is great. The work on the colors, the movement, the accessories, is very elaborate. Do you think the present Hong Kong cinema has a better quality, or do you think you are a rare case?
WKW: I think overall in Asia the film quality has improved a lot, and the quality is very close to western films. But I think there's no filmmaker like the old filmmakers, like Ozu or Kurosawa; they could create details that are extremely beautiful, extremely precise. Overall we are better, but there's no exceptionally good [filmmaker]. There're so many films made in Hong Kong and in Asia about Shanghainese in recent years, but we Shanghainese don't like them because we think they are not accurate. This is my intention, to make something that is accurate. I want to show people what these Shanghainese communities were really like. So we know all these details by heart; we didn't have to do a lot of research.

MC&HN: Is Maggie Cheung very different from herself in other films, or in real life?
WKW: One of the reasons why we have Maggie in this film is because she has a certain air, a certain quality, which definitely belongs to that period. The look, the air, the moves: she's got everything. And the Chinese title of this film is *The Age of Flowers*. Usually it applies to women at their best, at their prime, but I think the Chinese title of this film can in fact be applied to that period; it's the age of flowers of Hong Kong.

MC&HN: Two cameramen worked on the film: Christopher Doyle, who made less than one-third; and Mark Lee Ping-bing. However, there was a continuity.
WKW: Mark Li Ping-bing is the cameraman of Hou Hsiao-Hsien [a renowned Taiwanese filmmaker]. We once worked on the project *Fallen Angels* because Chris [Doyle] was away as usual. And this time, Chris had only finished one part of the film, so it was a new experience to me because in the past I could be a little bit lazy because I could rely on Chris on the framing, on the lighting. I didn't have to pay too much attention to those because I know he knows what I want. And now because I'm working with Li Ping-bing on this project, it's not a film that looks like my previous films. I have to control all the things, and I'm more involved in the framing and the lighting. It's a creative process which I can get more control of, and the look of the film is in more accordance with the content.

MC&HN: Why did you film in Bangkok?
WKW: It's so difficult to find locations in Hong Kong that look like old Hong Kong.

We shot the Singapore part in Bangkok because Singapore has the same problems. While I was shooting 2046 in Bangkok, I went around Chinatown and thought, "Wow, we should make the film here" because this is how Hong Kong looked [in the '60s]. All the exteriors were shot in Bangkok. The office [where Maggie works] was shot in Bangkok, the newspapers [which Tony works for] was shot in Bangkok because they have the old buildings. They've looked the same for the past fifty years. We shot all of the interior—the apartment—in Hong Kong.

MC&HN: In your filming method, what is the contribution of Maggie Cheung and Tony Leung?

WKW: It is exceptional for two Hong Kong actors to spend a year on one project trying different things with us. For me, the biggest challenge for Tony and Maggie is: I told them, "This film is not going to be verbal; you are not going to express yourself through dialogue. You have to express yourself through the body, your small gestures, your glances." With Tony, it is very hard because normally, in my previous films, Tony would be the narrator; he has a lot of inner monologues. He can express himself, but this time he becomes mute. He cannot provide any inner monologues; there is no point of view. He can only express himself through his body. I think it is a big challenge, and they did a very good job.

MC&HN: The score in the film has American artists (Nat King Cole), South Americans, like a reference to Argentina and *Happy Together*, and there is also some original music.

WKW: The Latin music is a reference of that time because in the '60s Latin American music was very popular in Hong Kong; most of the musicians in Hong Kong came from the Philippines. So the Spanish influence, or the Latin American music influence, was very strong. As a kid, when we went to a restaurant, the music was everywhere. So I want to keep that music in the film, not only as restaurant music, but also as a reference of that period. We also have some original music, which creates the tempo of the film and describes it. Like the music at the end of the film, it is a poem in itself. I would like to especially mention the one we use all the time, the waltz. It is not original music. It is music used in a Seijun Suzuki's film called *Yumeji.* and I know the composer. He gave me the tape, and I listened to the music before I started shooting this film. And that music became the reference of this film because I know the film should be like a waltz. It is two people dancing together slowly. At the end, I said, "Can I use this music in the film?" because we want to show the waltz influence, and I said this is the tempo of the film.

MC&HN: Nat King Cole, that's a point of view of South American glamor?

WKW: Nobody knows about Nat King Cole's Spanish songs or Latin American songs, and also we never knew there are some hit songs [of his] coming from Latin America. People only have the American versions.

MC&HN: When you filmed, did you put the music on the set to create an ambience?

WKW: I had the music in my mind already, but sometimes I would play the music to the actors or to the cameramen to let them know the rhythm. So, like the track shot, they had to know the speed of the tracking; they had to know the tempo of the film.

MC&HN: The mise en scène of this film is calmer, with fewer and shorter movements. Isn't this a change?

WKW: The biggest challenge is we always want to keep the audience as one of the [characters'] neighbors, so the way we see these two persons is always behind something: it makes the movement of these actors limited to a certain space, to certain environments, so it is very challenging to do. Because it's all about suspense, and we learned from [Robert] Bresson that we can only see the close-ups; we cannot see the whole thing. There is so much imagination outside the frame.

MC&HN: Where did you find the citation you used in the film? And why?

WKW: The text and the captions in the film came from a novel written by a Hong Kong writer Liu Yichang. I wanted to include that in the film because I think it describes how people thought at that time. And the writers in Hong Kong at that time have never been treated as serious writers. They were educated people or journalists coming from China after '49. They could not find a living in Hong Kong; they could only make a living by writing for the newspapers. They wrote columns, articles about food, horse racing, football games, medical advice, a lot of things. And they had to write huge volume every day. Liu Yichang was very famous at that time, and he wrote a huge number of articles. This novel is a very good documentation about life in Hong Kong in the '60s.

MC&HN: Similar to films that are distant, and in a very different style, one can consider your film is like a modern equivalent of Leo McCarey, like *Elle et Lui* (*Love Affair* and *An Affair to Remember*). What is your relation with the classic theme of secret, in the America melodramas or in the New Wave cinema, like François Truffaut's *Le Peau Douce*?

WKW: The film of McCarey is more romantic than mine. It gives a happy ending. In the process of making this film, there were so many things coming up. When we were shooting on the street in Bangkok, at the corner of the street there is actually a fire department. The streets remind me of some Italian films. It reminds me of

Michelangelo Antonioni. So we were shooting something like Antonioni; it is like a homage to all these people. When we were shooting in the office [where Maggie works], we could only have one angle because that place is too small, so we had to use a lot of close-ups and that reminds me of Robert Bresson's films.

MC&HN: What's your relation with the melodrama genre that was quite important in the Shanghainese cinema?

WKW: The second generation [of Shanghainese immigrants] merged with the local people, and there was no Shanghainese or Cantonese—everybody was a Hong Kong citizen. At that period of time, in 1962, we knew whether you are a Cantonese or a Shanghainese. Sometimes we hated each other; we didn't talk with each other—the Shanghainese mother didn't like the daughter going out with a Cantonese boy. It was very strict. Even the way we were shooting the Shanghainese community in this film (like Rebecca Pan [who plays the landlady], she's Shanghainese), we knew we were not in the tradition of the Shanghainese in mainland China. Even the Shanghainese now, they don't know or understand this community. It is like the Russians after the Russian Revolution. They lived in Hong Kong; they lived in Shanghai. They were a special type of people in exile. The whole experience of this community was like a dream; it's lost and it's gone.

MC&HN: In this film, you also use a lot of slow motions which are less often used in other films. Does this mean there was a problem with the pace?

WKW: This film is not verbal. Everything is expressed through the body, through the people—how they walk, how they talk and move—and there're some details I want to show in slow motion. I think most of the slow motion is not carrying the action, but the environments are like slow motion: in the pressroom and when Maggie hangs around during the mahjong games [in the living room]. It is all about a certain space, a certain mood, and I want to capture that in slow motion.

MC&HN: You talked about the film production lasting for one year. Did you film, stop, edit, film, mix, film?

WKW: We produce our films. We have to take the risks ourselves; we have no one standing behind our backs saying, "That's okay; you have to wrap up this film." So that's one of the reasons why we wanted to present a film here in Cannes because we can make this film forever. We had to find a way to stop this production. We needed a deadline, so I said, "Okay, we can go to Cannes." Then now we knew we have to stop all the things, and it's time to say goodbye to the project.

MC&HN: What's the link between what you filmed and what you edited?

WKW: We have filmed thirty times the length of the negative [of the final cut].

We have materials for more than two hours, and then we only kept ninety-two minutes. We edited it scene by scene [after the filming] because it is the way we work. At the end I just figured out the structure. And it is a process; it's not building up things. It's just taking things that we don't want out of the film and keeping what's essential and what we think is precise. I filmed in a chronological order. And during the production of *In the Mood for Love*, I filmed almost half of *2046* with other actresses: Faye Wong, Carina Lau. Sometimes we stopped working on *In the Mood for Love* because Maggie Cheung needed to go to Paris [where she lives with her French husband]. Sometimes I went with another group of actors to film in Bangkok. But I have not started editing *2046*. We will resume filming in September in South Korea because an authority in Busan [in Korea] wants to finance the production of a new film.

MC&HN: You have a French co-producer for *In the Mood for Love*, has there been any problem for them?
WKW: No, I like the way that Paradis Film does its features. They understand well our way of working, and they never intervene.

Muse of Music: Interview with Wong Kar-wai

Tony Lan Tsu-wei / 2000

From *Blue Dreams of Film* [http://4bluestones.biz/mtblog/] (Taiwan). October 2, 2004.
Interview conducted in Mandarin in 2000. Reprinted by permission of the writer.
Translated by Silver Wai-ming Lee from Chinese.

Tony Lan's note: Wong Kar-wai's films are like a dazzling pearl with multiple dimensions: some of the audience are fascinated by its visual image, some like its romance and philosophy, and some are infatuated by its music and sound.

Wong's *In the Mood for Love* won the Best Actor and the Technical Grand Prize in the 2000 Cannes Film Festival, which acknowledged the actor's performance and achievement in cinematography and art direction. But the film achieves more than these. Wong's idea of music constitutes the dazzling dimensions of the film.

This interview with Wong Kar-wai was conducted when he came to Taiwan to promote *In the Mood for Love* in 2000. This afternoon I am going to talk to Wong again about his thoughts regarding the music achievement in *2046*.[1] Therefore, I have reorganized some old interviews here from which you may find out more about Wong's taste and idea about music.

Tony Lan: Many people know that Frankie Chan is an actor as well as a director but have no idea that he is responsible for the music in *Chungking Express* and *Ashes of Time*. What is your relationship with him?

Wong Kar-wai: When I was working as a screenwriter for Always Good Film Company, he was the boss. Actually, he is the best witness of Hong Kong film score as he is the apprentice of Wang Fuling, the master in Hong Kong music. (He composed memorable scores for many films like *Love Without End* [1961].) He composed scores for most films in 1970s. He was already very wealthy at that time, while Jackie Chan was still a stuntman. He bought many cars and lent them to Jackie Chan.

Nowadays young people edit music on a computer. It is not accurate enough. Previously, you had to do the editing by controlling two sets of machines—one for forwarding and pausing at a particular frame, the other for rewinding. This brought high accuracy. But now this technique has been lost.

Chan is good at film editing as well as film scoring. After he knows what you are shooting, he will do the music on his own and seldom communicate with others. But he has a *sense* in music and the scores are always suitable for the films. But his idea of the music sequence may not be the same as mine, so I would rearrange the sequence. We argued about it every time.

TL: Why would you still ask him to score when you two always argue?

WKW: Film scoring is a very special task. As the director, I want someone who can give me the music as precise as possible so that I do not need to guess what kind of music it is and what effect it produces. If I had to communicate with a composer, a classically-trained musician, it would be a very difficult task. Therefore, if there is any suitable ready-made music, I will use it in my films.

It is difficult for a director to talk about music with a composer because the feeling and the language they use are different. For example, what is happy or sad? Everyone has his/her own definition of a particular word. I believe I have a relatively strong sense of music, but it is still difficult to express in language. Besides, it is about the visual image. I have found that many composers' music does not have any link to the film. Some music is pleasant to listen to but not suitable for a film score. The composer does not have a sense of the visual, so he/she does not know the chemistry of image and music.

Perhaps Frankie Chan may not be an outstanding musician, but he is definitely an excellent film composer as he knows the relationship between music and film and knows how to coordinate one with the other.

TL: You love music. Do you listen to it every day?

WKW: Not necessarily. I listen to music because I have to make films. I listen to every kind of music, but my criterion is whether the music could work with the image and give you a visual shock.

Some music is not special and doesn't grab your attention at the first hearing. But I know there will be *chemistry* if the music coordinates with a particular image.

TL: So it is only about your own intuition but not anything logical?

WKW: Right. You can't follow any formula. You can't tell the reason anyway, but you just know the feeling is right. But you may also create chemistry because of the history of a particular music. In *Chungking Express*, I put in a '70s song, like "California Dreaming" by the Mamas & the Papas. It is a contemporary story, but after adding the song, it creates a '70s atmosphere. Film scoring can be fun like that. There is another implication in the song, of course. Faye Wong's character wants to go to California. It's her dream so she keeps on playing that song in the fast food shop. It's fun to include a song with various implications.

TL: Do you have any preference of music?

WKW: No, I listen to all kinds of music. Recently I am listening to the music of a female singer banned in Iran, and the music of a popular female singer in South Korea. I don't have any reason but to just listen to it. The difference between me and other people is that I have a large database. When I listen to the right music, some images will arise in my mind. I know how to deal with that music and will use it at a suitable time.

TL: You spend a lot of time listening to music. Is the music chosen before you shoot the film?

WKW: In some cases. Like the repeating music in *In the Mood for Love*; it was chosen when I started shooting. There are two important elements when I deal with sound: first, it has to work with the *rhythm* of the film; second, one is about the *time reference* of a specific era.

As *In the Mood for Love* is set in Hong Kong in the 1960s, I wanted the image and costume to present the atmosphere of that era. I was born in Shanghai but grew up in Hong Kong. The most memorable thing was the different kinds of sound from the surroundings. It was the so-called *radio days*.

I listened to the radio when I was young. What I listened to created the atmosphere in the film: Pingju from [northern] China, Cantonese opera, Huangmei opera and popular songs (western music),[2] etc. (TL's note: The old music used in *In the Mood for Love* also includes: "Silang Visits His Mother" [*Silang Tanwu*] and "Leaving a Son in the Mulberry Garden" [*Sanyuan Jizi*] performed by Tan Xinpei—the master in Peking Opera—and songs like "The Age of Blossoms" [*Huayang Nianhua*] performed by Zhou Xuan. He also invites a sixties singer Rebecca Pan to make a guest appearance as well as perform her famous song "Bengawan Solo." That's why I made an effort to find old dubbing artists for recording, to re-create the feeling of that era. Therefore, basically the soundtrack in the film is to rebuild the radio sounds of that time. When I made *In the Mood for Love*, I wanted the audience to not only see, but also hear, that era.

TL: It is said that Rebecca Pan is your music consultant?

WKW: I should say she is one of the people who enlightened me in music. She was a famous singer in '60s, and I grew up with many of her songs. Her performance is the most significant part in *Days of Being Wild*. At first I wanted to mix her old performance with her new one, to do a remix. However, it did not work well as her pitch and range changed. I had to give up that idea. Besides, she knows '60s music very well and has a rich collection. I can directly consult her if I have any questions.

TL: Besides rebuilding the sound and atmosphere, you also found a composer to write the music?

WKW: Right. At the ending scene at Angkor Wat in *In the Mood for Love*, the music is composed by Michael Galasso, who worked with me in *Chungking Express*. He composed the opening theme in *Chungking Express*.

First, I confirmed that I would use the "Yumeji's Theme" composed by Shigeru Umebayashi in 1991 for the film *Yumeji* that was directed by Seijun Suzuki and starred Kenji Sawada. Then I told Michael Galasso that there should be a similar piece of music at the end of the theme, as a hallmark of the entire film and as an epilogue. Then he composed it.

TL: How is your cooperation with Michael Galasso?

WKW: First, I let him listen to the theme music composed by Umebayashi for *Yumeji*. I told him a similar kind of music would appear often in the film [*In the Mood for Love*]. I hoped he could give me a set of variations on this theme; but he could also have his own thoughts. Two weeks later he gave me the master tape. I was in a hurry to go to Cannes at that time. He composed many good tracks, but I only used one. Others were put in the original soundtrack.[3]

TL: How about you and Umebayashi?

WKW: Umebayashi is my old friend as he has composed for many Hong Kong movies and let me listen to his previous work, like [the soundtrack of] *And Then* (1985), directed by Yoshimitsu Morita and starring Yusaku Matsuda. After listening to the theme song of *Yumeji*, I thought it matched the rhythm of *In the Mood for Love*, so I told him I would use this piece of music.

As this is a piece of waltz in triple time, it requires the interaction between a man and a woman. It is kind of *rondo*; it keeps repeating itself. It is just like the relationship between Tony Leung Chiu-wai and Maggie Cheung in the film.

TL: But the theme melody is played repeatedly for a disproportionate amount of time. Why?

WKW: Not only is the music repetitive, but also the shots. This is what I intended to achieve. For example, each character in the film has his/her own way of life, its regularity, but when we concentrate on their apparently repetitive actions, we can observe the subtle changes. These changes are the dim truth of life.

Therefore, through the same music and scenes, we can see how time changes the protagonists' attitudes and minds: some changed, others remained the same. This kind of subtle depiction is the interesting part of the film.

TL: You put three Nat King Cole's pieces together. Why?

WKW: My mother liked Nat King Cole's music very much. It represents the music of 1960s. Many people ask me why I chose Cole's Spanish songs instead of the English ones. It is because ninety percent of the musicians in 1960s Hong Kong came from the Philippines. They were deeply influenced by Spanish culture, so I chose Cole's Spanish songs to accentuate that era.

I think every era has its own sounds. To be more accurate, Elvis Presley represents the voice of the early '60s; I think Nat King Cole represents the sounds of the late '50s and early '60s. It is like when people talk about the sound of the late '60s, they think of the Beatles. Their music will remind you of that era. Nat King Cole's music brings the same effect.

TL: The part of Angkor Wat appears in *In the Mood for Love* came so abruptly. Why aren't there any clues or foreshadowing?

WKW: I had originally planned some foreshadowing, but later I did not want that. I leave it to the audience [to make the connection]. Tony Leung's character became a journalist in South East Asia. He reported about the Vietnam War and then went to Cambodia with some foreign journalists. He stayed behind at Angkor Wat sightseeing. I had shot some relevant scenes [to show his trail], but I cut them out as I did not find it necessary. It was around four years after he left Hong Kong.

To me, Angkor Wat is *timeless*. This film can be understood on three levels. The first one is the fictional story: a love story between the male and female protagonists. During that period of time, we could see the events happen in history. It is like a documentary. In the film, we put the fictional drama and the real documentary together. The last level is the sense of timeless space. To Angkor Wat that has experienced ages of change, a tourist passing by is just a second, or one of many chapters. In fact, it has [written] countless chapters like this.

TL: The music and the scene at Angkor Wat seem to draw a conclusion of the film?

WKW: Yes, it is the conclusion. At any era, at any place, Angkor Wat is an *absolute* thing. I think everyone's heart has an Angkor Wat, an eternal sacred place. After living a luxurious or frustrated life, when you go back to your eternal sacred place, it is like a cleansing, a confession, or a consolation.

NOTES

1. See "All Memories Are Traces of Tears: Wong Kar-wai on Literature and Aesthetics (Part 1 & 2)" collected in this volume.
2. Wong Kar-wai used the term "Shidaiqu"(時代曲), literally translated as "song of the contemporary era" or "trendy song." In Hong Kong context, it usually refers to the Mandarin popular songs in 1950s and '60s.
3. The sleeve note can be read from: http://www.wkw-inthemoodforlove.com/livingRoom/notesGalasso.asp

2046

Mark Salisbury / 2004

From *London Net* (UK). http://www.londonnet.co.uk/ln/out/ent/cinema_wongkarwai
.html. Interview conducted in English. Reprinted by permission of the publisher.

Mixing with *In the Mood for Love*, SARS,[1] and four of Asian cinema's top female stars, Wong Kar-wai divulges why his newest film, *2046*, is an expression of Hong Kong's broken promises and regret.

Acclaimed Hong Kong writer-director Wong Kar-wai's last film was the gloriously romantic and inordinately sensual *In the Mood for Love*, which starred Tony Leung and Maggie Cheung as neighbors in 1962 Hong Kong whose other halves are having an adulterous affair and who fall in love with each other but never consummate their relationship. All achingly restrained, repressed emotions, it was exquisitely photographed and beautifully acted and confirmed Wong's lofty position in the art-house firmament. His latest film, *2046*, has been almost five years in the making. A sort-of-sequel to *In the Mood for Love*, *2046* tells of a playboy writer ([Tony] Leung Chiu-wai again) and his relationships with four women (*Crouching Tiger* [*Hidden Dragon*]'s Zhang Ziyi and Gong Li among them) several years after the end of his affair with Maggie Cheung (who appears briefly in *2046*). Presented alongside these sexual adventures, is one of Leung's character's own tales, a science fiction story in which a train heads into the future to a place called 2046 where one can capture lost memories but from where no one has ever returned. The cryptic title refers to the number of the hotel room next to Leung's, but, most pertinently, it's also the date of the fiftieth anniversary of Britain's handover of Hong Kong to the Chinese, with Wong offering up a treatise on love, memory, unfulfilled promise, and regret, as well as the impossibility of getting back one's past.

Mark Salisbury: You started making *2046* before *In the Mood for Love*. Why did it take so long to finish?

Wong Kar-wai: We had the idea for this around '97 during the handover because at that moment the Chinese government promised that for fifty years Hong Kong wouldn't change. 2046 is the last year of this promise, and I thought it would be interesting to use these numbers to make a film about promises. At the beginning we intended to make the film like an opera, with three short stories based on Western opera. By the time we got the financing and the production together it was already the end of 1999. At the same time we were working on *In the Mood for Love*, so at first it was two different projects. *In the Mood for Love* was a very simple story and we thought it would take two, maybe three months [to finish] and then we could start on 2046 again. But somehow *In the Mood for Love* took much longer than we expected, so we had to delay the production of 2046. Because the cast were very busy we had to work out the schedule again, but we also had other problems. At first we wanted to shoot in Shanghai, but we had to wait for the permits. By the time we got the permits, built the sets, and got the cast ready, we had the problem with SARS.

MS: At what point did the two films become linked?

WKW: It's because of the room numbers. One day when I was shooting *In the Mood for Love* in Bangkok in the hotel room, the room that Tony and Maggie spent their time in, I realized the room number was like 3-0-something. I said why don't we put it as 2046? At first it was like a joke, but for me, psychologically, the two films are related. Then the structure of 2046 began to change and evolve around this point. So now these two stories had something in common and the character played by Tony became the link between the two films. We didn't have this character of the writer in 2046; the original character was a postman.

MS: *In the Mood for Love* was a film about restraint and repression while 2046 is very much the opposite, much more sexual and passionate.

WKW: For me *In the Mood for Love* is a love story, and the man, Tony, the writer in the film, is a family man. He believes in commitment, in marriage. He works hard. He stays at home. Afterwards, when he goes through all the things with Maggie and his miserable days in Singapore, he goes back to Hong Kong, and he goes to another extreme. He's not married. He doesn't believe in commitment. He becomes a cynical person and prefers to stay in hotel rooms instead of finding a place to settle down. *In the Mood for Love* is a relationship about these two people. Even though we don't see any physical contact between them, we can feel the love is growing. But 2046 is more like a story about what love means to him. In this film Maggie is not a person. She's an image, an ideal woman in his memory, so he always compares this woman with all the other women he gets involved with in his life. He tries to feel that emotion again, but at the end he realizes it's not what he wants. At a certain point, these two films are a mirror of each other. And if the audience hasn't seen *In the Mood for Love*, they should watch 2046 first. If they want to know what happened between Maggie and Tony, they should watch *In the Mood for Love*—it's like the missing chapter of this novel.

MS: This time period of Hong Kong in the '60s is one you're obviously fascinated with. It's when you grew up, but its present not only in *2046* and *In the Mood for Love* but in *Days of Being Wild* too. Why are you so enamored with it?
WKW: I think the reason we wanted to make *In the Mood for Love* in the year 2000 is we realized Hong Kong was going through big changes. Hong Kong is a city that moves very fast, changes very fast, even its own history, so we wanted to capture some of the locations and places and even the manner and the way people live in those days in the film. We re-create all this, so on film, on celluloid, it will not change; we're just trying to preserve that history.

MS: In *2046* you've worked with Zhang Ziyi for the first time. Why did you cast her, and what she brings to the film?
WKW: I met Zhang Ziyi before she made *Crouching Tiger*. I still remember her in Zhang Yimou's film [*The Road Home* (1999)]. She's rather young, but she's very aggressive and very sensitive. That's why I thought she would be good in this film. In fact, the role in *2046* is extremely hard for her because she doesn't know anything about the ballroom dancers in Hong Kong during that period, so I had to give her a lot of references. I had to show her some of the Shaw Brothers' films that were made during that period about those women, at least to give her an idea about how they behave. And I asked William [Chang], my production designer, to give her all the costumes to dress up in and to rehearse in on her own because those costumes restrict the body and you have to behave in a certain way.

MS: Did Tony enjoy playing his role more this time around because his character in *In the Mood for Love* doesn't say much and is very internalized in his emotions, whereas in *2046* his character is much more expressive?
WKW: I think it's more challenging for him because he goes from one extreme to another. He's almost a very dark character at the beginning. In the chapter between Tony and Zhang Ziyi he's like a playboy, and he always asks me, "Am I the same person?" And I say, "Why not?" It's very hard for him; he has to work with the five strongest actresses in Asia. Each of them is very attractive, and they are doing a very good job. He has to have three or four very intense relationships during a few months, so it's very hard.

MS: What can you tell us about *Lady from Shanghai*, the film you're doing with Nicole Kidman?[2]

WKW: Well, we're working on the script. We have ideas. Normally I will build a story around one character, and I think it will be interesting to have Nicole Kidman play it as a woman who claims she came from Shanghai. It's very mysterious. This will be the next one and *Grand Master* [renamed as *The Grandmaster*] will be the one after because Tony needs some time to practice all these martial arts skills.

NOTES

1. In early 2003, the Severe Acute Respiratory Syndrome (SARS) epidemic broke out in Hong Kong. Within a few months, nearly three hundred deaths were reported. The epidemic has created much social and economic unrest, including a decline of international investment in the territory, resulting in a decline of jobs.

2. There has not been any news about the progress of the film since 2008. It can be assumed that the film will not be made.

All Memories Are Traces of Tears: Wong Kar-wai on Literature and Aesthetics (Part 1 & 2)

Tony Lan Tsu-wei / 2004

From *Liberty Times* (Taiwan). October 15 (Part I), October 16 (Part II). Interview conducted in Mandarin in 2004. Reprinted by permission of the writer. Translated by Micky Lee from Chinese.

PART 1

Liberty Times editor's note: An enchanting film is a result of the mix and match of different artistic aspects, a crystallization of the style and the talents of the creator. Today we publish an in-depth interview between film critic Lan Tsu-wei and Hong Kong film director Wong Kar-wai. They begin by talking about his new work *2046*. From there they extended to topics such as how Wong's films make reference to Chinese literature, how they construct a sense of visual space, and what the background of space and time are in the film, as well as the soundtrack. Through the dialogue between the creator and the viewer, the interviewer and the interviewee, Lan and Wong challenged each other's view of the aesthetics of film texts. The interview revealed the director's style: rich yet vague, retro-realism yet abstractly imaginative.

Tony Lan: Wong Kar-wai is the premier writer of romantic films. He is also an affectionate commercial seller. His films regularly use the most unique image to sell a star or a city such as Lan Kwai Fong and Tsim Sha Tsui in *Chungking Express*, the Liaoning Street night market, and Muzha Line in Taipei in *Happy Together*.[1] Wong's films emphasize mood. He uses a great deal of extremely glorious yet philosophical lover's discourse to create a *yi jing*.[2] In addition to using oldies, *qipao*,[3] old apartments, and dark alleys to re-create the beauty of 1960s Hong Kong in *In the Mood for Love* (2000), Wong also adapted from *Intersection* [*Dui Dao*] by

1960s Hong Kong writer Liu Yichang.[4] In *Intersection*, Liu wrote about a man and a woman strolling in the streets of Hong Kong, each reflecting on what they see and reacting differently. Liu shows how space and time can be experienced differently and illustrates the desire of worldly men.

A few lines in the essay seem to point out the essence of *In the Mood for Love*:

Those disappeared times,
Are obscured by a dust-covered glass,
Could be seen, couldn't be reached.
He has been reminiscing everything of the past.
If he could break through that dust-covered glass,
He would return to those disappeared times.[5]

Wong says, "Letting the public recognize and know Hong Kong as writers like Liu Yichang have is one of the happiest things to happen to me."

Wong Kar-wai told me that after *In the Mood for Love* was released four years ago, some people in Hong Kong organized a Liu Yichang symposium to revisit his literature and its historical significance. The essay *Intersection* was originally only collected in *Liu Yichang's Collection*, but it has been reprinted as a book [after the symposium]. "The most incredible thing is that after a French book publisher watched *In the Mood for Love*, he learned about the writer Liu Yichang. The publisher then translated Liu's work and published *The Work of Liu Yichang* in French. This made the old master [Liu] very happy!" exclaimed Wong Kar-wai, whose eyes brightened up behind those dark glasses.

In October 2004, after the release of *2046*, the end credits paid homage to Liu Yichang. Those in the know recognized the text on the first screen, "All memories are traces of tears,"[6] and some later quotes all come from Liu's *The Alcoholic [Jiu Tu]*. Why is Wong obsessive with Liu? What kind of charm do Liu's writings have to inspire Wong to combine words and images to give birth to new pieces of art?

Recently Wong visited Taiwan, and we began the interview by talking about Liu's work. We slowly discovered the creative process of this pioneer of romanticism.

TL: In *In the Mood for Love*, you made reference to *Intersection* by Liu Yichang and you have publicly paid homage to him. However, in *2046*, you clearly made reference to another Liu's *The Alcoholic*. You are attempting to start a dialogue with him in your films. Why?

WKW: The Chow Mo-wan character in *In the Mood for Love* and *2046* comes from Liu Yichang. He came to Hong Kong from Shanghai during the chaos. Despite his past fame, he needed to find a means to make a living. How could he live as a literati? The answer is very simple: he could only make money by writing, so he had to write all genres. He also had to write from dawn to dusk to climb across the boxes.[7] Even then, he could barely sustain his living. When I first met him, I saw him work very hard every day. He started to write once he climbed out of bed and continued until eight or nine o'clock in the evening. His greatest joy was to see a movie or take a stroll with his wife every once in a while.

Chow Mo-wan in the film is a 1960s writer. In Liu's writings one can find a lot of information about the daily lives of writers of that era. In *In the Mood for Love*, I used his lines in *Intersection* in an early scene. In *2046*, I made reference to *The Alcoholic* such as using the quote, "All memories are traces of tears," and others in three screens. The main purpose is to pay homage to intellectuals in 1960s Hong Kong. Reviewing Hong Kong literature of that time, one can tell those writers had to write a lot every day. In order to make a living, they could not write about a grand ideal. They wrote erotica and *wuxia* genres. They struggled between their conscience and reality every day. All these writings showed they had no choice in how they wanted to live; however, there were some writers who insisted on writing something that they could be proud of in addition to writing pulp fictions that sold well. Liu is one of the representative figures of the latter group.

TL: Why didn't you directly adapt from Liu's work when you like it so much? Why did you write an original screenplay?
WKW: I have always wanted to adapt *The Alcoholic*, but Liu had already sold the rights to another party. Therefore, I cherry-picked a bit of dialogue here and there, hoping to introduce young people to Liu through my films. Then they will read his work.

The writings of Liu are very referential. Reading his work makes one visualize one scene after another; his writings are very imaginative. The writers in that era had a very hard time; they were very low-profile in their daily life. They wrote without complaint. Once they sat down to write, they created millions of words [throughout the years] without realizing it. Recently Liu wanted to re-edit his past work, but I discouraged him from revising those old writings. They were composed under a specific condition of that time. He had not thought of leaving a legacy. Regardless of what the motivation [of writing in that era] was, it is better to let contemporary readers experience how the writers of that era had no choice or dignity. It is most realistic to retain the originality of the work.

TL: Your films are infatuated with the sixties. Is it because you only moved to Hong Kong then, and the new life experience gave you many unforgettable memories?
WKW: Yes, when my family first moved to Hong Kong, we could only rent a room. In *In the Mood for Love*, the tiny space accommodates people from all parts of the world. It is my own experience to live with a variety of people.

I always remember very clearly that there was a writer living next door. He was drunk every day. One could hardly imagine the boredom experienced by writers. Later I learned that he was a very famous journalist when he was in Shanghai. When he and others moved to Hong Kong, they all felt like refugees. They lived an extremely repressive life because they were caged in a tiny, worn out old room. And they had to write in every genre to make a living since they had no other means of making a living. They had to sell out to make a living. To please the market, they had to write whatever was in demand. Their lives and thoughts were full of boredom and frustration.

TL: In *In the Mood for Love*, you mastered very well the close relationships between people who live in a tiny space. However, in *2046*, you dealt with space in a very different way. The frame was wider, and it greatly enlarged the space: whether it is the sign on the rooftop, the public telephone counter, the corridor of the *2046* train compartments, or the place to exchange secrets. All the characters have been obscured by the wall in front of them and pushed to the corner. This created a much larger space for the film but the feeling of repression increased as well. What was your aesthetic choice here?

WKW: We could use a crowded space to show repressed feeling; we could also use a large space to show a liberal feeling. However, when you use a wide space to contrast with a crowd, you can strongly feel the repressive feeling brought by that space. That tactic highlights people's feeling of isolation and loneliness. In fact every time I make a film, I want to achieve one thing, which is to imagine what if the protagonists in the film are no longer characters, but space. If we can transform space into a character and to imagine the rooftop on the screen as a character, he then is a *witness*. He can see what happens on the rooftop. It is like installing a video camera on the rooftop—it can witness and record life.

In *2046*, I tried to experiment with a new visual effect. In the past I used a standard lens to achieve a 1.66 (ratio aspect). Space in Hong Kong is very tiny, so the dimension is vertical. The standard aspect ratio is the most suitable to show this feeling. This time I hoped to use *CinemaScope* on the big screen so the dimension is horizontal.[8] All the space on the screen was suddenly enlarged; however, the actual space is as tiny as before. This technique highlights the visual expression, but it poses a challenge to cinematography and sound recording. We [the crew] did not have anywhere to hide, and it was easy to catch us on the camera. Therefore, this time we used a lot of stationary camera shots; we did not move too much.

TL: Your previous stories about love and desire take place in a small room, [but this time] you took everyone to the rooftop in *2046*. Going from a closed space to an open one, from the location and the expression of the rooftop, you have shown a new visual world to the audience. What was your conception?

WKW: I have not thought about that carefully; it was a natural reaction. The location was originally a prison where they jailed the political dissidents during the riots in 1960s Hong Kong.[9] The location has been preserved until now. When I shot the film, I transformed the prison into an inn.

To me, the rooftop is a very nostalgic place. When I was young, we always went to the rooftop to play. We chatted about this and that there, or we went there for an escapade. But now the space and the concept of the rooftop seem to have all but disappeared.

In *In the Mood for Love*, Tony Leung (who plays Chow Mo-wan) has a home. All the activities take place inside the home. In *2046*, his activities take place in an inn. An inn is a public place. It is hard to find a private space; Therefore, the rooftop is the best arrangement. the rooftop has become their private *space*.

TL: Speaking of the use of the rooftop space, it reminds me that in every scene on the rooftop, you use *Casta Diva* of *Norma* written by the famous Italian opera composer Vincenzo Bellini. From the music in the prelude to the voice of the female soprano, [the image and the music] form an intriguing combination. Film scholars noticed that in this edited segment, you used music to show the characters' emotions. You have accurately corresponded a make-believe world to the emotions in the drama; this also enriches the imaginative quality of the film. Did you start from the music? Or was the music something you thought of during postproduction?

WKW: The original story of *2046* was not as complicated as the final cut of the film. I wanted to use the number 2046 to tell three stories—each with an opera music theme. They are *Norma*, *Tosca*, and *Madama Butterfly*.

Western opera has to have a recurring theme. At the end of the day, Bellini's *Norma* talks about vows and betrayal. This is very close to what we thought of vows at the beginning [of the production]. (TL's note: Norma is a priestess of Druids, she should represent her people and defend them against Roman invasion, but she falls in love with the Roman Proconsul and bears him a son. She has broken the vow she made with the Druids people. However, the Roman Proconsul falls in love with her assistant, the deputy priestess, and Norma experiences her lover's betrayal.) During the film development, only *Norma* remains [out of the three operas]. The reason is that the story of this opera is quite similar to the plot involving Faye Wang. In fact, the music came first, then there was the rooftop. Because we had the rooftop, then we had Faye Wong in it.

I used *Casta Diva* in Norma because of two simple reasons: the rooftop is like a stage. First, the story of every character in *2046* is like a play on the stage;

second, at the beginning of *Norma,* the priestess is on the balcony confessing to the moon. She is praying for her people and lover. Because I believe the rooftop is the private space of the protagonist, the rooftop eventually becomes the portrayal of every female character. The three female characters all go to the rooftop: Faye Wong is expressive; Zhang Ziyi feels hopeless; Dong Jie [who plays the younger sister of Faye Wong] is hopeful. Dong goes out to stroll around and is full of anticipation.

TL: There are several number codes in the film. Some feel that *2046* is a political film because 2046, while not meaningful to most people, is a vow made by the Chinese communist party to the people of Hong Kong. The party promised that from 1997 to 2046, the governing system of Hong Kong will remain unchanged. From this perspective, does it mean that [2046] is a political code that you hide in the film? Other than the lover's discourse, can *2046* be read as a politically conscious film?

WKW: I don't deny that the inspiration of *2046* comes from a political language, but I put the language into another context: not politics, but love.

Why did I go far away to Argentina to make *Happy Together* in 1996? I don't deny that in that era, I had my own thoughts about Hong Kong being returned to China and about its future. But I think political influence casts a long shadow on one's life. The real effect is not realized today. We cannot feel the influence in one moment or two. The influence will become clear after a considerable length of time. Of course, everyone is concerned about Hong Kong being returned to China, so we all become very politically sensitive. We want to emphasize Hong Kong will remain unchanged, but this is impossible because the world is changing. If you don't change, you will be left behind, so you have to follow the change.

At the beginning, why did I pick the number 2046? It is because we all say it is very important for Hong Kong to remain unchanged before 2046. It is a very serious political topic. Here are the problems: first, whether there is change or not cannot be determined by us [Hong Kong people]; second, we don't know what will be changed. Therefore, I use this number to tell a love story. To everyone, what does "unchanged" mean? If we love something, of course we hope it will not change; or if we lost something already, we'd say it'd be great if that thing would stay the same forever.

Therefore I invented a place called 2046. In that place, nothing will change. Because in a love story, the most sensitive and important question is whether the lover will change or not. We make promises to our lovers, but we cannot guarantee we will not change at the end. Is it true that you will remain the same? Wouldn't it be interesting if the film starts from the question: will the lovers change or not?

PART 2

TL: You apply a great amount of lover's discourse in every film. That creates a very philosophical "Wong school" style. Why?

WKW: The love story is the most surface layer in the films. Everyone can easily receive the relevant message and understand the film. But a love story is not only about love between a man and a woman, it can also be about the emotions between one person and another.

When an audience watches one of my films, people usually won't compare me with other directors. Instead they compare the film with my previous films. Sometimes they think the previous one is better; sometimes they think the present one is better. This sentiment is like the situation of Chow Mo-wan. In his impression and memory, the previous love relationships have brought many sweet memories. However, when the present love relationship becomes the past, he adds many subjective opinions and regret about the past. Directors cannot forget about their past films, so how should they encounter their current situations?

TL: You seem to be unable to forget your previous films and the soundtrack. In 2046, the soundtrack obviously repeats itself a lot. Whenever a short segment of music begins, it is like a diffusion of beauty or like temptation. The short segment teases the audience but immediately stops. When the same segment is played again and again, the audience starts to get familiarized with the music. Then the people start to naturally appreciate and get brainwashed by your musical aesthetics. Is this what you intended to do?

WKW: I am actually like a DJ. Other people are music DJs, I am a film DJ. But the purpose is the same. If I like the music, I will find every way to use it in the film. Other people may think it is repetitive, but I don't think repetition is a problem. Of course I am self-conscious that sometimes I will use music to a point of saturation. This is a very dangerous inclination. I try hard to avoid it.

For the Cannes cut of 2046, as we start editing the film from the middle, it was hard to accurately estimate the length of the soundtrack. Some of the melodies and rhythms became too saturated. I was very dissatisfied with that; therefore, when we edited the film again we remixed the soundtrack. I insisted the musical arrangement had to start from the beginning. Among my previous eight films, the sounds and music of 2046 were the most difficult. I spent a lot of effort on them.

I had a few basic principles for musical arrangement in the past. For example, there was little music in *Days of Being Wild*. The music would only appear at very important moments; there was no music at other times. However, in *Chungking Express*, seventy percent of the film had music. Contrary to that, there was no music in the most important moments. In *In the Mood for Love*, I used the theme music of Shigeru Umebayashi and Nat King Cole (and Michael Galasso) as accompaniments. In *2046*, I wanted to abandon all these principles. On the surface, some of the music is specifically for certain characters, but the music can also reflect other characters. For example, to accompany the entrance of Carina Lau, I used *Perfidia* because I used it in *Days of Being Wild*. [Editor's note: Carina Lau plays the same character in the two films.] But I kept on using this music until Faye Wong's entrance. Why? Because the two characters basically belong to the same category—they have a very insistent attitude towards love. They don't give up easily, so I use music to link them together.

TL: When you made *In the Mood for Love*, you not only required the viewers to see that era, but you also wanted them to hear that era. You had to show the *time reference* of the particular era, and you had to use a suitable *rhythm* for the film. This concept seems to have further applied in *2046*. For example, Nat King Cole's "The Christmas Song" and Connie Francis's "Siboney" both express a mood of the 1960s and reflect the characters' emotions. However, in *In the Mood for Love*, you adapted from music that Japanese composer Shigeru Umebayashi created for Seijun Suzuki's *Yumeji*. In *2046*, you further used Umebayashi's soundtrack along with [the soundtrack of] Truffaut, Fassbinder, and Kieślowski. Why?
WKW: I love watching films, and I am interested in film soundtrack. Truffaut, Fassbinder, and Kieślowski have deeply touched me. In *2046* I used their music because I feel their music is very suitable for my own films, I wanted to pay homage to those masters this way. But the most important thing is they are experts at romance; each of them used a new angle to interpret love. Would adapting their music create a new chemical effect for my films? I am hoping for that result.

TL: In *In the Mood for Love*, you use Umebayashi's waltz and tango to symbolize the interaction and power struggle between lovers. This time when Umebayashi created the theme music for *2046*, what requirements did you give him so that there is an obvious difference between *2046* and *In the Mood for Love*?
WKW: I asked Umebayashi to compose for me again mainly because the male protagonist [in *2046*] Chow Mo-wan comes from *In the Mood for Love*, so there is a relation. Therefore, I asked Umebayashi to compose the *main theme*. I simply told him if the music in *In the Mood for Love* is like *chamber music*, then the music structure would be grander.

Basically the music talks about a journey, but it changes according to the plot. For example, I gave him three female characters (Gong Li, Zhang Ziyi, and Faye Wong) and asked him to compose different kinds of music. To me, these three women represent the past, the present, and the future, respectively. But I asked

Umebayashi to write music with a *dance* feeling, something with a strong *rhythm*. He made many versions. I did not use the tango and cha-cha because those are too similar to *In the Mood for Love*, repeating the rhythm that I have already used. [In 2046], I used the rhythms of rumba and polonaise dance.

But the final composition of Umebayashi is not only restrained for one particular character, I feel he has linked the entire theme while making changes throughout the film. At the beginning, the mood was very severe, very *over the top*, the feeling is very *operatic*. Then it became the feeling of rumba—very seductive, like the feeling of getting drunk. At the end it is the dance rhythm of polonaise: at its beginning it appears to be very light, but as it goes on the feeling becomes very *sentimental*, very *sad*.

TL: You don't want others to say *2046* is the sequel to *In the Mood for Love*, but the characters and plot in *2046* clearly make reference to *In the Mood for Love* and *Days of Being Wild*. How should the audience understand this?

WKW: The ending of *In the Mood for Love* shows Tony Leung telling a secret to a tree hole in Angkor Wat. *2046* begins from this hole. The two films are certainly linked. But I suggest the audience reverse the viewing order— start with *2046*. They may discover from there Tony Leung was once in love with a married woman. You may then want to know who Maggie Cheung is in the taxi. Then when you see *In the Mood for Love,* you can see the story of Maggie Cheung. Similarly, if you are interested in the character of Carina Lau, you may find a connection with *Days of Being Wild*. To me, *2046* is a final summary. Every character can be seen as a chapter. I made the three films as a 1960s trilogy, and it is now done. Perhaps I will wait for many, many years to use another new *perspective* to discuss this topic.

TL: You have used a lot of close-up angles to show the relation between women and clothing, making every actress have her own style and narration. How do you categorize their qualities?

WKW: All these come from the quality of each of the actresses. The strength of Faye Wang is her body language, which is extremely good. You can give her the simplest action to express how she feels, which is much better than twenty lines of dialogue. She acts best when she moves. That's why when I introduce her in the film, the first scene starts with her feet. When she wears shoes, not only do you feel the beauty of the feet, but the shoes become alive. When I shot the legs of Zhang Ziyi, I asked her to be *naked*. That gives others a sensual feeling.

I have this arrangement because I am very sensitive towards female beauty. I have a lot of prejudice. I believe that the sexiest part of a woman is her legs, so they have to look good on the screen. In addition, because I know each of the actresses' quality and I understand their strengths, I amplify each of their strong points and make her attention-grabbing when she enters the scene.

TL: A good romance film relies on the mastery of the lonely feeling. In 2046, you use 1224 and 1225 as time codes to show how during Christmas holidays, lonely hearts hope for love, yearn for warmth, want to experience some intense emotions through a lover's embrace, but in this scene you use the sober song "The Christmas Song" to create those lonely feelings during the holidays. Is it because at a time when you feel lonely and sad, you have a desire to be in a crowd and let the strange and bigger desolation comfort your loneliness?
WKW: Correct. The more sadness there is, the less one should isolate oneself. To be in a crowd, one will experience a sense of loss and loneliness more strongly, but that is the best cure. It is like after one cries heavily, the wound will get healed.

NOTES

1. In *Chungking Express*, the fast food shop where Faye Wong works is located close to Lan Kwai Fong. The blond played by Brigitte Lin lingers in Chungking Mansion located in Tsim Sha Tsui. In *Happy Together*, Tony Leung's character Lai visited the Taipei night market en route from Argentina to Hong Kong. The Muzha Line (now part of the Wenhu Line) is the first line of the Taipei Metro, which opened in 1996. Trains run across Taipei from east to south above ground. The Liaoning Street night market is located near one of its metro stations.

2. *Yi jing* 意境 is a Chinese concept of how artists create an artistic world, though not necessarily a make-believe one, through both objective observation and subjective emotions.

3. The tightly fitted dresses that Maggie Cheung wears in *In the Mood for Love* were first popular in Shanghai in the 1920s. In Wong's anthology film, *The Hand*, the young tailor played by Chang Chen made *qipaos* for Gong Li.

4. *Intersection* is a novel written by Liu Yi-chang. The title comes from the term in philately, *tête-bêche*, which means a joined pair of stamps in which one is upside-down in relation to the other. The English translation of *Intersection* was published in *Renditions* (Nos. 29 & 30, 1988), a journal published by the Chinese University of Hong Kong. It is available at: http://www.cuhk.edu.hk/rct/toc/toc_b2930.html.

5. We use a more word-by-word translation. The North American version has the following subtitles: "He remembers those vanished years. As though looking through a dusty window pane, the past is something he could see, but not touch. And everything he sees is blurred and indistinct."

6. The literal translation is "All the memories are humid."

7. An expression of "filling up the page"—Chinese writers used to write on manuscript papers preprinted with grids. One character fills in one box.

8. CinemaScope is used to shoot widescreen movies with a ratio aspect of 2.66.

9. The 1960s riot started with the Star Ferry protest in 1966. The public took to the streets to protest the fare increase. The British colonial government suspected communists were behind the protests, so dissidents were arrested and charged. Curfew was imposed for the city. Wong refers to the White House in Mount Davis on west Hong Kong Island. It is known for jailing pro-Beijing protestors during the 1967 Riot as they wanted to launch a cultural revolution in Hong Kong and caused casualties. It was the most serious threat to the British colonial government in Hong Kong history.

Because of Norah Jones: *My Blueberry Nights*: Exclusive Interview with Wong Kar-wai

Hong Kong Film / 2007

From *Hong Kong Film* (Hong Kong). December. Interview conducted in Cantonese in 2007. Translated by Micky Lee from Chinese.

After Wong Kar-wai wore the dark glasses, he became a symbol of a particular style: cigarettes, tango, and Iguazu Falls [of *Happy Together*]; *qipao*, music, afternoon tea at Gold Finch restaurant [of *In the Mood for Love*][1] . . . narcissists usually like to be alone. Narcissists can hardly avoid being obsessed with objects. Smoking the same brand of cigarettes for years, insisting on something that can hardly be understood by bystanders, extensively quoting lines from Wong Kar-wai's films, [these] have become the lifestyle practiced by certain people.

When Wong Kar-wai was a minor scriptwriter, he understood that the audience want to watch movie stars when they watch films. His films have never been short of a heavy-weight star-studded cast. The charm of the stars will always be amplified under his camera lens. He really knows how to show the sexiness of East Asians—examples include the *cha cha* [dance of Leslie Cheung] and the one-minute friend in *Days of Being Wild*; the high contrast light and shadow of Peach Flower (played by Carina Lau) and the horse in the lake in *Ashes of Time*. At the time of shooting *Chungking Express*, the way Cop 663 talks was very popular [in Hong Kong]—boredom and grievance are one kind of disease suffered from city dwellers, but once muttering is demonstrated by Tony Leung Chiu-wai, all of a sudden the mutters become very beautiful. One should not miss the alluring body underneath the *qipao* and the provocative gaze in *In the Mood for Love* and *2046*. This kind of sexiness does not require nudity; it is entirely diffused from the deepest part of the soul. All this sexiness comes from Wong Kar-wai's precise mastery of people—not only of the characters but also of the actors. Then *My Blueberry Nights* was released, [despite it being a film in English] we discover that the stars only use English to express Wong-Kar wai's dialogue. [The actors] are like the kiss between Yuddy (played by Leslie Cheung) and Su Li-zhen (played by Maggie Chueng) [in *Days of Being Wild*]; the careful probing between Cop 663 (played by Tony Leung) and Faye Wong [in *Chungking Express*]; and the way that Ho Po-wing (played by Leslie Cheung) and Lai Yiu-fai (played by Leung) smoke and stand by the bar windows [in *Happy Together*]. . . . Wong Kar-wai is born to be romantic; he is also nostalgic. He has a thorough understanding of romance, including what happens before and after a relationship. At the same time, he allows himself to drown in a romantic ambience. His mood is not affected by the characters' loneliness or sorrow. His metaphors are too obvious; his narrative is too much of a stream of consciousness. Certainly Wong is not an excellent realist director, but no one can deny that he is an expert at creating a mood.

Gradually, people have started to only remember Wong Kar-wai when he wears dark glasses. But perhaps this is what he wants.

Hong Kong Film: Can you tell us the creation process of *My Blueberry Nights*?
WKW: Every film has a starting point. This time the starting point is like a juggling act. I did not have this film in my plan. When I was in New York City, I had an opportunity to meet Norah Jones. I quickly felt this woman is quite fun, so I thought perhaps we should make a film together. She was in New York for two months to make a record, so I started to consider making a road movie that is about a woman wandering around. She goes everywhere as she wishes. To use the road movie genre, the story can follow the path of Norah Jones. Then I started to think: what is the reason that makes her leave a place? If we say love or something like that, it is very superficial. I feel the first image that I have about this film is the legs of a woman who stands by the road side. She ought to go ahead or something. I used another route to walk this path. Maybe it is because I want to give myself a bit more time. Drawn from this way to think [about the story], one segment after another, every segment has a story inside. Every beginning scene has a tentative structure, like a juggling act or like an orchestra. *My Blueberry Nights* is built upon many previous films, some from *Days of Being Wild*, some from *In the Mood for Love*. I see this film as a light suitcase that I pack for a new journey. It is like the last line in *2046*, "You have to start anew." You should carry a light suitcase rather than a big trunk to start the journey.

HKF: The narrative follows a chronological order; all the events follow a straight timeline. This gives the audience a very straightforward concept. It is like there is no special design to create suspense.
WKW: There is nothing much about memory in this film. There isn't too much design [about time]. I think this is related to the impression that Norah Jones

gave me. She is very straightforward. She does not have much unspoken intention. She likes what she likes, doesn't like what she doesn't like. When I asked her if she wanted to make a film, her question was not "Am I capable?" but "When? Do you think I am capable? If I can, then I will." She does not have too many complications inside. It is like when I am dubbing the Chinese dialogues, I asked Dong Jie to be the voice of Norah Jones. In this dubbing process, Dong Jie was inspired by Norah Jones. Dong explained, "Well, normally a young woman like Norah Jones would wrap herself up in a cocoon." To her surprise, she found Jones completely at ease. Norah Jones is very straightforward; perhaps at that point she had not thought too clearly [about the film]. But she will do what she feels comfortable with; she does not plot.

HKF: Based on what you said, *My Blueberry Nights* is actually a tailor-made film that you designed for Norah Jones.
WKW: Actually every film of mine is based on a person. The most difficult parts of making a film are the beginning and the ending. There are many ideas at the beginning. Where do you start? Everything can be a beginning; a story can be told from any point. But what is the reason for wanting to make a film? The starting point of *My Blueberry Nights* is my meeting Norah Jones. She made me wonder [if she would act]; then I began to pair her up with others. It is like *2046* comes from Tony Leung. I begin with this person; then I pair him up with others. Another example is *Chungking Express*, I saw Faye Wong [sings], and I started to pair her up with others.

HKF: Do you create all other work in this way?
WKW: Not entirely. Because there is the country Argentina, I wanted to go there to make a film. The result was *Happy Together*. [The reason why I wanted to make] *Chungking Express* was because I often went to that fast food restaurant and noticed what was going on there, so I suddenly wanted to shoot a story about that fast food place. *Ashes of Time* is because of Louis Cha [Jin Yong]. I feel Eastern Heretic and Western Venom are two of his best characters. Everyone says Eastern Heretic is a very carefree character, but to me, he is the most conservative and the most restrictive. Then I thought about how the two characters might have been when they were young, what kinds of encounters they may have faced that made them who they are.

HKF: In this film you chose two stories to illustrate Norah Jones's experience: one is related to family, the other is a father-daughter relationship. Why does her encounter relate to family relationship?
WKW: Actually it is because I have decided the protagonist is Norah Jones. The

first story takes place in New York City. I chose to re-use a site that I used for Tony Leung in *In the Mood for Love*. The site is a fast food restaurant. This woman has run away. Where should she go to? I was driving [in the US] when I chose the location. I thought: first, if I choose to make this film, at least I should understand what it feels like to be on the road. That's why I asked the producer and the cinematographer to go on a road trip with me—from New York to Los Angeles on the West Coast, from the Atlantic Ocean to the Pacific Ocean. Actually I originally wanted her to go farther away, tentatively Beijing. I had scouted locations in Beijing, but I heard others said this site will be demolished because of 2008 Beijing Olympics. That's why Norah decided not to go. At the end we stopped at Los Angeles. We return to where we begin to hang around. Afterwards when we chose locations on the road, there were many choices from the East Coast to the West Coast. Eventually we chose Memphis because when we drove to Memphis at dawn we stopped by the road and saw street cars honking, I felt this reflects the world of Tennessee. I told myself, "Why not have a segment here? I do not know if I will have another opportunity to make a film here, do I?" Because there was an opportunity to have some fun, I wrote a story about Tennessee about an alcoholic meeting a wandering woman. Then I thought he could be a police officer. From there I developed their relationship which is partly like friends, partly like father and daughter. Then I thought more [about it]; the next story has to take place on the West Coast. One has to pass through Nevada when passing the large desert. That place should also be included because it gives the feeling of a Western genre. That's why I developed the gambler character. She and Norah Jones are like sisters, but in fact they are the two sides of one person, two possibilities [of a person]. And the element of the father, it may come from [the father-daughter relationship between Faye Wong and her father in] the previous film [2046]. In fact all the stories are chronological.

HKF: What consideration did you have when you picked the actors, such as the character of Jude Law?

WKW: Because you have the main female character, Norah Jones, you have to find a counterpart male character. At that time we auditioned a few, and at the end I picked Jude Law. When I met him in Los Angeles, I felt he has . . . first he is British. Many British live in New York City. He has an inherent quality of being [emotionally] distant. Second, he has an excellent sense of acting pace. Third, he is not a very complicated person; he is a very easy going person.

HKF: Did you know him before this film?

WKW: No. I only know him because of this film. First, I thought Norah Jones and he might create some chemistry. Also, he is a veteran actor; he has a lot of acting experience. It is like the effect of Tony Leung. He can control the rhythm very well because [this skill] comes from a theatrical training. Norah Jones had to have a counterpart like him so that she would feel safe and confident when acting. So I told Jude Law, "To me, if you have to act with a professional actor, you probably understand how each other acts so that would be boring, but if you act with someone who is new to acting, she may have many unconventional ideas that may inspire you." After choosing Jude Law, the second actor I chose was Natalie Portman because I felt when she is in the car, the dark hair of Norah Jones matches with Natalie Portman's very much. Coincidently, Natalie Portman had time in her schedule, so we picked her. We contacted Rachel Weisz beforehand because I think she is suitable for the role. Basically Rachel Weisz is like Gong Li. Rachel Weisz just got married and had a baby. She told me if I gave her two months, she would immediately lose weight. When we were shooting in New York, the restaurant was close to her home, so she visited the crew every day. Every day she would tell me how much weight she lost, how much weight she lost together (chuckle) . . . she is a very hard-working actress. And David Strathairn was decided on last because I decided that Rachel Weisz is the wife. I decided that David Strathairn should be the husband.

HKF: With so many stars, is the production cost high?
WKW: Many people thought, "God, the production cost of this film could be high." But I discovered that there are two tendencies among American actors: one is if there is a commercial blockbuster, they will ask for a high compensation that is proportional to the estimated budget. But if there is a film like our independent production that has a fresh idea, they all showed interest when we chatted. They felt, "I want to act in this film, [it is] very meaningful." Their attitude is to have fun, so they were not too calculating with the compensation.

HKF: Can we say that the actors' compensation is very low for this film?
WKW: When compared to their previous films, the compensation is indeed very low. Actually what they made was very similar to our Chinese actors. To them, this is a film that they were willing to make, so they did not mind the compensation too much.

HKF: Do you think *My Blueberry Nights* is a road movie?
WKW: Actually it is not a road movie. Although a road movie is about a journey, basically this film does not have a clear journey in the story. It is just a journey of a woman's state of mind. Her heart is still in New York City wherever she goes. We focus on expressing her many emotional thoughts. It is a road movie about the soul.

HKF: About the time limit that she set for herself—three hundred days—why wasn't the time limit longer?

WKW: Actually it could be three hundred days or a year, two years, or even five years, but my feeling is that this experience is not a big deal. This may just be an episode in her entire life. Also, the three hundred days in the screenplay is the duration that I spent working on this film—about a year. From preproduction, production, and postproduction to Cannes, it had been a year. That's why the set-up of a year in the story can be said to be my own journey.

HKF: What is the origin of the film title? Last time at Cannes you said you don't like blueberries.

WKW: I don't like [blueberries]. I absolutely detest them. But to the woman in the film, she eats blueberry pie not because she has always liked it, but because others don't like eating blueberry pie. She wants to understand why others dislike it, and she eventually ends up liking it. In fact I am a very lazy person, as long as [the title] is simple and catchy, that's okay with me. In the film, she eats blueberry pie all day. Wouldn't it be fun to called it *My Blueberry Nights*? In addition, in the restaurant where we shot the film, they have a large selection of desserts. We asked the boss which one is the least popular, and he said blueberry pie is the least popular. That's why we decided on blueberry pie. It was as simple as that. In fact [the blueberry pie] represents one type of things, a representation of the abandoned. This blueberry pie is not sweet; it is bitter.

HKF: Other than blueberry pie, there are many symbolic objects, such as keys and chips.

WKW: Oh, strictly speaking, the chip was not my idea. During the preproduction process, we were driving on the road, but I was not the driver. We were on the road for sixteen hours a day. What should the passengers do? I was reading and listening to music. I was reading a book about quitting drinking; it is the case study of giving up drinking. The book is written for people who want to quit drinking. That inspired me to use quitting drinking as an analogy to love. Both are about giving up an addiction. That is to say, when you want to forget your lover of five years, [but] he has become part of you, part of your addiction. When you don't feel right, you wonder what you should do in order to get rid of that addiction. That's why in the first segment, we could see it from the police officer. Americans like to use reward to encourage quitting drinking. Americans like having rewards! You will be given a reward. If you don't drink for a day, you get a chip, you get a chip numbered 90 if you don't drink for ninety days. As you hang out with other alcoholics, you have a sense of achievement [when you have the chips]. When one has an addiction problem, confidence alone is not enough. You need others' recognition.

In addition, this chip symbolizes more than encouragement. When you focus on minor things [such as a chip], you won't think about drinking or something like that all day long. That's why I thought this method is not bad. To this woman, she needs this kind of chip so that she will forget her boyfriend. She has two part-time jobs in Memphis [because] she does not want to stop [and think]. This shows that she is still thinking of him. But she slowly changed, and that is a gradual process of getting rid of the addiction.

HKF: How about the door and the key?
WKW: The door and the key don't have much symbolic meaning. The man who left Norah Jones did not appear in the film. It is not important whose boyfriend he is and how he looks. Everyone can imagine how he is; everyone can fit her boyfriend in it. The door key, basically, is the relationship [between Norah Jones and her ex]. I have to give you a chain of keys [in order to] confirm our relationship. You are welcome to my space. But if I return the key to you, this shows I am not willing to enter your world.

HKF: The key may interest women. There is this pub with many keys—every key represents a feeling. To women, every key contains a mystery.
WKW: Actually [there is] nothing special about the key. At a summer job in college, I worked in a pub. Many things like this happened in a pub. Many people forgot to take along their little things with them, such as lighters, cigarettes, spare change, and even keys. I have seen someone saying [in the pub], "Let's split up here." Then one gave the other the key. I have witnessed that.

HKF: Why did you use a restaurant in New York City?
WKW: Because the woman spends most of her time in New York. She is living and working in New York. That's why, to us, New York is the starting and ending points. This sounds reasonable. She can arrange her own work schedule.

HKF: After watching this film, I had a feeling from what I have read and watched about this genre, especially among American films, this film is very sexually innocent.
WKW: Yes, innocence is not popular nowadays. That's why I retain some innocence on screen. Actually Americans are very conservative, [but not in cities] like New York, Los Angeles, or others. But if you go to other places you will see a different attitude. You will understand it after seeing this film. Why did Americans elect [George W.] Bush as the president? In addition there are [social] problems such as alcoholism. In fact, the US is a very conservative place; their people are very simple and honest. Also they are very religious, especially in the south.

HKF: So from the beginning of conceptualizing this film, you did not think there would be any sex scene?

WKW: There is no such need. This is not part of the story because sex itself should be a topic, not a strategy. If this is only a strategy, then there is no point. If it is a topic, you can touch upon it, but you have to find a way to talk about it.

HKF: What do you think of how Ang Lee used sex in *Lust, Caution* (2007)?

WKW: To him, this may be the topic of film. I think he used it very well, very cleverly because I think he has applied the image of Tony Leung both inside and outside the cinema very well. Let's just say Tony had a transformation and exerted a big impact [on the audience].

HKF: We have talked about your films before. You are not like a lot of directors who like to give love and women a miserable condition in the story. Sometimes you allow the women and men to end up together, like those in this film. There is a happy ending, but some films don't have a happy ending.

WKW: Nowadays many people ask, "Why do you shoot so many love stories?" I told them I do not; these are not conventional love stories. Maybe this is a story about love, but this is not a love story. Like this film, one should say this is not a love story. The love story only begins at the end of the film. The ending is the starting point of the love story. We can imagine what happens next is a love story. But what has happened [in the film] is a story about a process of finding love, finding a feeling of love. It is like saying 2046 is an aftermath of love. [2046] is not about love, but the aftermath of love.

HKF: You have made many love stories. How do you see the effect of love in daily life?

WKW: We say nowadays love is a part of our daily lives. This is something that cannot be denied. I need to find something with which everyone can identify. I believe love is a commonly identifiable topic. Some other things may not be too popular, but in a film you can include many, many types of emotions—you can talk about husband and wife, father and daughter, many kinds of relationships.

HKF: Do you feel love is a reliable emotion?

WKW: Actually in the film, love has already given you a feeling, which is to say you need to believe in it to enjoy [love]. But we need to ask what would you do if you failed? We have provided all the answers for you. If you are like Natalie Portman who does not trust others like how she is at the beginning, if you have to be always careful, you can be like this, but you have not enjoyed the process. It is like I know I have eaten some spicy things [which is uncomfortable], but I enjoy them. What

I can tell you is that [after eating spicy things], you can have a cup of hot tea, and then the spicy sensation will be gone.

HKF: I found that for some films, you could work very fast. But on the whole, your production is slow. Why?

WKW: I have high expectations! Just like this time when we have a version with Chinese dubbing, they said, "You'd better not come [to the production]." Usually when people work on dubbing, the director should not be here. The dubbing usually only takes two days, but it had already taken ten days and was not done yet. This kind of dubbing is like the dubbed foreign films of the old days, such as those films from the USSR or Yugoslavia. The original dialogues have constrained how the speech and expression could be translated. That's why I said we should do a domestic version: if the story took place in China, what it would be like. Actually people's emotions are the same. We have transformed the film into one that would be comprehensible for the Chinese audience. They would feel, "Oh, it is like the people around me."

HKF: So is this your starting point of choosing people for the dubbing, such as picking Chang Chen for Jude Law's voice because he came from Taipei? How about others?

WKW: He has some [Taiwanese] accent (chuckle). For Jiang Wen and Gong Li, I told them that people in Memphis speak with a southern accent. It is like Chinese who speak with a Beijing accent. Cheng Chen has a bit of a local Taiwanese accent, so in the film he represents a foreigner! Isn't it great to allow him to have a bit of an accent?

HKF: We can understand why you chose Jiang Wen as the voice of the police officer and Gong Li as the wife, but why is Dong Jie the voice of Norah Jones? I feel Norah Jones's voice in this film is very mature and deep, but the voice of Dong Jie gives us an impression of being a young girl.

WKW: Yes, when you see this film when it is done, the pitch of the voice may be adjusted, but you cannot adjust the emotion of the voice. Dong Jie gives me a similar impression like that of Norah Jones. She is very innocent, very raw. She is a very authentic person. Because when we hear the voice, at least when Dong Jie is doing the voice and when the audience sees this character, they imagine, "Would Dong Jie react like this when she encounters such a problem?" Does she have to have a voice that is close to Norah Jones? I don't think it is necessary as long as she gives the same feeling. Aren't there some people who like to say dubbing a film is a kind of remake? I say it is not; it is original.

HKF: Is this the same reason why Zhao Wei is the voice of Natalie Portman? I feel Natalie Portman's character is quite cunning.

WKW: You should go and see; it is very good. You can think whether Zhao Wei can play a character like Natalie Portman. She comes from Anhui Province. You know it is right for her to perform the role of a gambler when you hear her tone. We even got Xu Jinglei to dub the voice of Cat Power (the Russian girlfriend of Jeremy [played by Jude Law]); you would not believe it. That was great!

HKF: It is a special way of thinking. Did you consider them initially because they are all movie stars?

WKW: Not all voices are movie stars. I asked my driver to do dubbing because I think he has a great voice. I also asked Hung Huang to do the voice of a black woman; that *waitress* [performed by Hung Huang] is very fun.

HKF: After you make a film, do you hope to be like some directors who only make films for those who understand their films?

WKW: I don't have this kind of sentiment. I am the most scared of [comments that say] this film is a piece of art, [that piece is] commercial, or whether the film is made for a specific group of people or for everyone. I feel all these questions are meaningless. Making a film is like how you engineer a watch or you work as a cook, the most important thing is you have tried your best and have some fun during the process. You have to feel that this is a very good thing. You present [your work] to others hoping everyone can enjoy it. It is this feeling [that I want].

HKF: Have you ever thought of using a completely different way to express yourself, to make a film that is completely different?

WKW: If there is an opportunity, if there is such a topic or reason, of course, I could do it. This is not a question about money or actors. Many people say, "You are making films; you should not worry about money." But this is not true. Actually at the beginning of every film, there is a condition; there exists some problem, big or small. When I say opportunity, I mean the most important thing is my time is not wasted when I have this concept. It is because I feel it is getting more and more complicated to make movies. You are not only making a film, but you also have to spend a lot of time on preproduction. Afterwards you also have to spend a lot of time promoting the film. Like *My Blueberry Nights*, you thought it is a very simple film, but we have spent two years on this. What I ought to think is "Do I want to spend almost two years to make this film?" If I want to do it, let's do it. But if I feel exhausted, then there is no such need. It is better to think of doing something more meaningful.

HKF: Let's make a supposition. Let's say *Harry Potter VII* is inviting you to be the director. Will you accept this offer?

WKW: I will. Why? A simple reason is that my son asked me why he could not see the films that I make (chuckle). Therefore, if one day someone asks me to make a film for children, I am willing to do so. That's why if there is such an opportunity, I will accept it regardless of the outcome. I chatted with my son [and told him] if he has a story concept, I will make a film. This will solve the problem [of his not seeing my films]. He has begun to think [about a story] (chuckle), but I have not seen him for almost a month.

HKF: Isn't it a part of the life of filmmaking? You are always away from your family.

WKW: Yes, it is like this. That's why now I gradually feel I need to think very carefully about making a film. Because when you spend time on one very important thing, you know you lose time on other very important things, such as spending time with the family.

HKF: Last time you said the reason why you wear dark glasses is because you want to mark a distinction between working and living.

WKW: Actually lately I have a better explanation, a clearer explanation. One day last month I was doing an interview in France; the interviewers are all old friends. One of the new journalists asked, "Director Wong, why do you wear dark glasses?" One old friend said my dark glasses are like the moustache of Charlie Chaplin. He said Charlie Chaplin had a son or daughter; he/she had the impression that there are two fathers. When he smelled glue, it is the man with a moustache; he was Charlie Chaplin. When he did not have a moustache, when there was no smell of glue, that man was the father.

HKF: Do you have other habits?

WKW: No bad habit. Is smoking a bad habit? (chuckle) You can see that I never finish one cigarette. That is to say it is a habit that I need to light up a cigarette and inhale. I smoke one pack or two in a day. I smoke less at home because my family does not like it that much; they would complain. (chuckle)

HKF: Do you like to smoke the more expensive cigarettes?

WKW: No, I have been smoking this brand for a few decades, Benson and Hedges from Britain. One day I smoked one, it felt right, and I continued getting this brand. Smokers always follow a brand, just like drinkers. But it's too bad that it does not sell well! So now you can't buy it in Hong Kong. This brand is not very popular. It does not plan to have any advertisement, but it is a very good cigarette.

HKF: You are working with Nicole Kidman on *Lady from Shanghai*. What is the progress?

WKW: We are working on preproduction. We are still collecting some information in New York. There is also a problem with scheduling; we need to look into when production can begin.

HKF: You have worked with William Chang for so many years. Is the stylistics in your films your or his ideas?

WKW: Basically, he and I have the same ideas about most things. He knows how I see things well, and I know his ideas well too; therefore, many things don't need to be explicated. Mainly you need to see how we can collaborate for a film. Simply speaking, there is no Christopher Doyle [as the cinematographer] in *My Blueberry Nights*. He was making other people's film at that time; therefore, you would feel the cinematography of *My Blueberry Nights* was very different from my previous work.

HKF: You seem to have largely used red and blue hues [in your films].

WKW: Not necessarily. I did not have any "taboo" in *My Blueberry Nights*. When we saw a place and felt that the location was right, we added some simple things to the set and then we shot. There wasn't any special arrangement. Also, there was only red or green inside a pub. (chuckle) *Chungking Express* is in blue hues though. The lighting in the fast food shop has a blue hue, and the home [of Tony Leung] is also blue. There is also a yellow hue, such as the mackintosh jacket of Brigitte Lin and Chungking Mansion.

HKF: Because of your film *Chungking Express*, Chungking Mansion has become a landmark in Hong Kong, but everyone says actually it is very seedy and chaotic inside.

WKW: It is because the audience's understanding of it is not the same as mine. I grew up in the district [Tsim Sha Tsui]. Chungking Mansion used to be a very up-scale residence in the 1950s; many Shaw Brothers Studio movie stars lived there.[2] In the 1960s, the lowest floors were occupied by the largest, most luxurious night club in Hong Kong. Because of the night club, there were many foreigners, in particular Indians living there. Later it gradually became more chaotic; it was rumored to be a hotbed for drug dealing and such. Because of this reason, I have always been very curious about this place. My father would never let me go inside. *Chungking Express* gave me a reason to go inside to make a film, to investigate why [my father did not allow me to go inside]. (chuckle) *Happy Together* also gave me a reason to go to Argentina to make a film. It is like this to make a film! The only advantage of being a director is it gives you a reason to do something that you want to do. It is like how Ang Lee uses films as an experiment. (chuckle)

HKF: There is criticism that your films are all alike; some even say Wong Kar-wai spends his entire life making one film. Do you agree with this thought?
WKW: It is like taking pictures. Today I took three pictures of you. Ten days from now I take another picture. Your face probably has changed a bit, but they are still [like those] three pictures. They belong to you! Some directors could make a horror film today, a comedy tomorrow, but you can still see that something does not change.

HKF: To many women, the image that they have of Wong Kar-wai's films is the night. Why is that so?
WKW: I think there are two reasons: first, it is a very objective thing. Many of my films were shot at night. Also I like to film at night because it is very complicated to film during the day—you have to lease a place and to clear the location. At night, as long as it is slightly quiet, it is fine. Second, I believe that in a city we make our living during the day. We only own the time at night, don't we? We can sing karaoke with friends; we can have dinner or drinks with them. If we don't have friends, it is rather hard to live in a city. That kind of feeling can inspire many writings.

HKF: Your films have many dialogues that reflect a modern lifestyle. There is always some foretelling, or there are some deep philosophical thoughts [such as] using objects as metaphors . . . a key or a tree hole.
WKW: In fact many dialogues are full of self-mocking. One theory is most people say much the same thing. Sometimes, when they are too blatant, they will be too corny, won't they? In my daily life I never talk in this way. Because at that time, people talked like the characters in *Chungking Express*, so I made this way of talking into a phenomenon. I don't talk like this; that's why I put dialogues that I would not say in daily life in my films. I use my films to express all those ways of talking. But it is very hard to evaluate one thing in one single way, which is when the audience is watching your films they may not be in the same train of thought as you. For example, like the voice dubbing of Jude Law to me, things he says are half true, half false. He self-mocks what he says. But the audience may believe that he is always serious with what he says. Therefore I always say we have to see more clearly. Some people may appear to be very serious when they talk when, in fact, they are just joking.

HKF: About the concept of time, your films seem to use the concept of time to create tension in the films.
WKW: Not true. In *My Blueberry Nights*, our focus is on distance, not on time. But 2046 is about time because my feeling was . . . when we were scouting for locations [for *My Blueberry Nights*], we did not check how much time we spent [on

the road], but we counted how many days since we left New York. We only looked at the distance on the dashboard; that's why I did mention the concept of time.

HKF: In other people's mind, Wong Kar-wai is someone who has to find actors to accommodate his stories. He has already decided how to film [before interacting with the actors]. Is it true?

WKW: Never. I have never thought like this. I don't have this habit. The other evening I had dinner with Gong Li, and we talked about this. She said she only discovered very recently that I don't have a script. She used to believe that I already had a script, but I did not allow actors to read it. She discovered that it is not true. Because I don't have any bad intention, I only think of what the actors should do when I work with them. My habit and feeling are not like: I have thoroughly thought out every role and try to find an actor to play that role. It is not like I need to find a model to wear a piece of already-made clothing; that is not true [for me]. Usually I see a person, then I think of what clothing this person should wear.

HKF: But many people say Wong Kar-wai intentionally refuses to let the actors read the script. He lets them improvise during the filming so they give a fresh performance.

WKW: Never. This has never happened. Of course I can't say I take a piece of blank paper to the filming location, impossible. As I started as a scriptwriter, I will have a very rough script. I mostly know what the story is about. When we film, there may be changes of dialogue here and there. That change is possible. But because *My Blueberry Nights* was a script in English, I found a novelist, Lawrence Block [to write the script]. The story is constrained by the script, but I also told the actors that the dialogue could be changed—this dialogue could be cut, that could be included. It is like we have a scene in which Jude Law has a ten-minute monologue. At the beginning that monologue was very long, but at the end we felt it did not need to be that long. We changed it when we filmed. Lawrence wrote some, and I wrote some. The change gave people a feeling that the monologue comes from the heart [of the character], not from the pen of the scriptwriter.

NOTES

1. Goldfinch Restaurant is the location where Maggie Cheung and Tony Leung have coffee and dinner in *In the Mood for Love*.
2. Shaw Brothers Studio was a major film production company in Hong Kong from the 1950s to the 1980s. Its films cover various genres such as *wuxia*, romance, and musicals.

The American Way

Tony Rayns / 2008

From *Sight and Sound* (UK). No. 18 no. 3 (pp. 32–34). Interview conducted in English in 2008.
Reprinted by permission of the publisher.

Wong Kar-wai's *My Blueberry Nights* may be the director's first English-language film, but his trademark focus on characters and relationships remains. As the recut road movie goes on release, Wong talks to Tony Rayns about being an outsider looking in.

Wong Kar-wai spent last year working on two main projects. One was *Ashes of Time Redux*, a freshened-up version of his legendary 1994 martial arts movie. The original won a prize in Venice but was distributed almost nowhere because of a rights dispute that has only recently been resolved. Its belated international release promises a lot, partly because Wong and some of his stars (Tony Leung Chiu-wai, Maggie Cheung, the late Leslie Cheung) are much more widely recognized these days than they were fourteen years ago and partly because the genre itself is now much more familiar to non-Chinese audiences. Wong has faced the choice of either polishing the old cut by remixing the sound or revising the cut by adding some of the many deleted scenes he has warehoused in Hong Kong. Either way, *Ashes of Time* will resurface in 2008.

The other project was *My Blueberry Nights*, his first English-language movie, which stars singer Norah Jones in her first acting role. This had its premiere on the opening night of the 2007 Cannes Film Festival, where it didn't go down all that well. Wong had a characteristic rethink last summer, and the film now being released around the world is a recut version. It's some fifteen minutes shorter, its rhythms are changed, and it has fewer voiceovers, though the basic structure remains the same. The tweeness of the title gives fair notice that this is never going to be thought of as major Wong Kar-wai, but it's now a tighter and in some ways more persuasive film.

Many earlier Wong Kar-wai movies have been through a similar process of revision, including his last feature *2046*, which changed quite a bit in the six months between its Cannes premiere and its release. That was very much a film about a writer's relationship with the fictional world he creates (symbolized by 2046 itself, both a far-off time and a space in which lost memories are recaptured and fixed) and was anchored in the writer's voiceovers, some spoken by himself and some by the Japanese character [played by Takuya Kimura] he invents. The voiceovers were the element most extensively rethought in the revision process, and the final version of the film finesses a rather moving coup by reassigning one of them from the fictional character (who spoke it in Japanese) to the writer himself ([Tony Leung] who speaks it in Cantonese). The effect, sadly, was lost on most western audiences, who couldn't tell the two languages apart.

One recurrent voiceover heard in the Cannes version of 2046 had disappeared by the time the film reached release. That version opened and closed with the writer's reflections on his own relationship with 2046, and the same words also popped up in the middle of the film. They went something like this: "Those who go to 2046 never come back. But I'm the exception. I went to 2046, and I have come back. Because I want to change . . ."

I once asked Wong Kar-wai why he had rewritten that voiceover, and he told me he did so because he thought the original was too obvious. What he meant, I think, was that his own relationship with his writer character too closely mirrored the writer's relationship with his Japanese surrogate. He feared that audiences would take the voiceover as an autobiographical mission statement. 2046 felt like some kind of summation of Wong's themes and motifs. This voiceover gave the whole thing an air of valediction; it suggested a director who was feeling an urgent need to move into entirely new areas. I was reminded of an earlier conversation with Wong in which he wryly commented, "Too many people are 'doing' Wong Kar-wai these days, so I have to do something else."

So, is *My Blueberry Nights* something entirely different? Yes and no. Yes, in that it's in English and offers episodic, linear storytelling of a kind not seen in Wong's earlier films. No, in that the focus is still on characters who are working their way through relationship problems—and in that the story itself is one that Wong dug out from his files. Still, as the film's opening voiceover observes, "The stories have all been told . . ."

Tony Rayns: What was the primary impulse behind the film?
Wong Kar-wai: I was in New York, doing some research for *Lady from Shanghai*, a project I have with Nicole Kidman,[1] and I somehow got the chance to meet Norah Jones. We sat and talked in a café in SoHo. I found her character very straightforward and confident, so I asked her if she'd ever thought about acting. She didn't ask why I was asking; she just said, "You think I can act?" So I said, "Why not?" I

suggested that we should work together and told her I had a story I'd come up with a few years ago that might be the idea we could start from.

The story was one I used in a short film called *In the Mood for Love 2001*, which was screened in Cannes that year but hasn't really been seen since. It's about a chance encounter in a convenience store in Hong Kong between two people, played by Tony Leung and Maggie Cheung, who may or may not have a relationship. I showed Norah Jones the short film, and we started thinking about moving it to the United States and expanding it. So the main reason to make the film in English was that Norah obviously couldn't do it in Chinese. And I guess some of her attitude rubbed off on me—that "Why shouldn't I give it a try?"

TR: Was it very intimidating to work in the US?

WKW: I know I'm not the first foreign director to make a film that looks at America. I think the way I work is quite well known: I don't build stories; I build characters. I always have to know all about the people in the film, so even if we see this woman only in a café, I have to know where she came from, what she was doing yesterday. I need all that background. If I shoot with Tony and Maggie in Hong Kong, I can easily imagine what's around them and what's behind their characters. But I needed to be able to do that with my American characters too. When I look at an Edward Hopper painting, I can feel the existence of the people he shows. The question I need to ask is always, "What impression do I get from this face, this gesture?"

TR: How did you settle on the novelist Lawrence Block as your script collaborator?

WKW: Since the film was going to be in English, I knew I'd need help to write the script. I can't be the one telling the story myself. I have to be behind someone else, outside looking in. I knew Larry's novels and short stories from long ago, but I hadn't met him. I especially liked his character Matt Scudder, a private eye in New York who has a drink[ing] problem. He used to be a cop but he accidentally killed someone, so he had to quit the force and become a private detective. Knowing those stories made me think I should try to get Larry to help me.

Actually my first thought was to get a different writer for each chapter of the film: one for the first and last chapters in New York; one for the chapter in Memphis, Tennessee; and one for the chapter set in a small town in Nevada. But Larry is very fast and understood immediately what I was trying to do, so I asked him if he could write it all. It was only about two months from the time we had the idea to the start of shooting.

TR: How did you decide where the chapters would be set?

WKW: Once we'd decided on the first and last chapters in New York, we had to figure out what would happen in between. So I got into a car with my cinematographer Darius Khondji and my production manager and started driving. We made several trips, each ten to twelve days, driving for fourteen to sixteen hours each day. Mostly we started in the evening, drove through the night, and reached a place in the early morning. Sometimes it was the other way around. The basic idea was that Elizabeth, Norah's character, should move across the country from east to west.

I felt from the start that one chapter should be set in the south. A lot of the Americana I like originates there, including much of the music. Norah herself is from Texas, so I asked her if she could recommend any place for us to check out. She told us there was a town called Love, which sounded interesting, but it turned out to be very ordinary. We finally settled on Memphis.

We also headed for Las Vegas, which is in every way the opposite of the south. But somehow we got lost in the Nevada desert and ended up in a small town outside Vegas. Basically it's just one main street, but it has a very old hotel with a casino in the basement. We reached this place one morning after driving through the night. It was totally empty, hardly anyone in the casino, but we realized it had once been an important town. The hotel had Nevada's first elevator. It had been a staging post for Hollywood stars on their way to Vegas, and so the rooms were named after them. I thought this would be a good place for Elizabeth to get lost.

TR: And Elizabeth's emotional trajectory? How did you determine that?
WKW: I always have books with me when I travel, and I had three on these trips, all of which influenced my thinking. One was Sophie Calle's *Exquisite Pain*, which is a kind of photo album with texts that chronicles the most unhappy days of her life from a vantage point of fifteen years later. She has been stood up by a man. She keeps repeating her story to different people, and each time she tells it, it becomes less detailed until by the end it's very vague. The book is full of things I like. At one point she wanders around an unfamiliar city, goes into a diner, and orders sausage—a dish she hates!—and she doesn't know why.

Another book (I've forgotten the title) was a guide to quitting addictions—smoking, drinking, bad relationships, everything. It's very schematic: the writer says that when you reach this stage, you can expect to have this symptom and so on. I found myself using this book like a menu, with the chapters in the film becoming like the stages in the writer's analysis of withdrawal from addiction,

And the third book was a collection of Lawrence Block's stories. All his recurrent characters appear in it, and I came to see that many of them are variations on Larry himself. That got me thinking that one of our characters should be a cop. Since we were going to shoot in Memphis, I found myself also thinking about Tennessee Williams and that we should maybe do a tribute to him. So I proposed that to Larry: "I want to have a story about a cop and his problems with his wife." Larry didn't travel with us, but I drew a lot of inspiration from him. For instance, he's an active marathon runner and that ended up becoming part of the background of Jeremy, the Jude Law character.

TR: I know the actual shoot was fairly tight, so I wonder if you found any time for the "trying out ideas" approach you bring to your Chinese films?

WKW: In some ways there was even more of that than in the Chinese films. I had to involve all the cast and crew. At the start of the shoot I told everybody, "We've seen so many films about Chinese people—made by foreigners—that look very weird to us, and I don't want to repeat that mistake! Even if I spent three years here working on this film, I'd never see things as an American does. So I need all of you to be involved in commenting and giving advice." They were a bit shocked at first because of course they're used to having directors tell them exactly what they want. But they got into it, and we ended up having a lot of fun together. They were surprised when I gave them a script; they thought I didn't work with one at all. We did make changes as we went along, often in response to their suggestions, though all of the changes were to bring us closer to the characters.

NOTE

1. There has not been any news about the progress of the film *Lady from Shanghai* since 2008.

Exclusive Interview: Wong Kar-wai (*Ashes of Time Redux*)

Damon Houx / 2008

From CHUD.com (US). http://www.chud.com/16553/exclusive-interview-wong-Kar-wai -ashes-of-time-redux. Interview conducted in English.

On the subject of a recut and remastered re-release, you would expect George Lucas to become something of a talking point, either for or against. That he made his way into my conversation with Wong Kar-wai at the start was not surprising, but that Wong Kar-wai talked favorably about one of his films at the end of the interview was nothing less than a bombshell. Yet the recut *Star Wars* was never a point of reference for our discussion of his *Ashes of Time Redux*. This, though, has more to do with my respect for [Wong Kar-wai] as an artist.

Instead, I approached this interview balancing my film lover side with my— what in polite society would be called—fanboyishness. For, you see, one of my favorite working directors is Wong Kar-wai, and when I told Jeremy Smith [a fellow critic and writer at the publication] about the interview he was nervous for the master's health in my presence. I kept myself mostly in check, but what surprised me more than anything was that he was happy to have a conversation. He wanted some back and forth, and you'll see at several points I can't help but digress with him.

We were together to speak about the release of *Ashes of Time Redux*, his recut of the 1994 martial arts epic. The film was famous in Hong Kong for Wong having spent a year in postproduction, so lost in it that in the middle he went and shot *Chungking Express* to re-energize himself. As I described it to Devin [Faraci; a fellow critic and writer of the publication] as we walked out of the screening, it's as if Woody Allen in 1982 made a science-fiction film with the help of ILM [Industrial Light and Magic, founded by George Lucas] that was at once both a sci-fi film and a Woody Allen movie. It's a strange marriage and deserves to be seen on the big screen, and this version is now the only version as the *Redux* happened partly to save the film, which did not have its elements properly preserved. It opens on October 10 in New York and Los Angeles and will likely play around after that.

Damon Houx: I was trying to find out who said it first. I want to say it was Francis Ford Coppola, but I've also seen George Lucas credited, though I was thinking it might be Jean-Luc Godard. Anyway, someone said, "Films aren't released; they escape." And with this film that seems to be the very definition of it. You edited for a year on this film which led to the 1994 version, and now you've got to go back with a butterfly net and spend more time with its skills.

Wong Kar-wai: But in a way this film was never released in this part of the world. It just, it took a long birth. I should put it this way.

DH: Most of the versions that came stateside—I have the Mei Ah DVD—were those approved and shipped over here from Hong Kong.

WKW: They always say, "Director Approved" (laughs). They never have approval.

DH: You did go back and tinker with it? It seems some of the transitions are different.

WKW: It's more than that, I think. In a way it's very savage because we took quite a lot of things out of the film and replaced them with something else. It used to be five courses, but now it's only four. It's less dressing, but it's the same thing. The process is not as easy as you would think. The original version we cut in '94 is in a delicate balance. The story, the structure of the story, is so complicated that you need a certain way to tell it. Everything is in a certain balance, but if there was a missing piece, the story collapses. So, it's not just that we take out the parts that have problems; we had to take out more, because it didn't make sense. We had to do a lot of work. It's not only a few trims.

DH: You're known for spending a lot of time in the editing room, going back to this one. How was it? Could you get this one a little faster?

WKW: I couldn't do too much on this film because—actually the restoration took two years. They had to scan all the footage and all the extra takes and fix scratches, watermarks, and sounds.[1] So, I did what I could based on the material. There's not a lot of options to do that. I don't want to change it completely because, otherwise, what's the point? You'd better to just do another film.

DH: In the production notes it mentioned that you were basically rescuing it.

WKW: We call this film *Saving Ashes of Time*.

DH: Was there a longer cut at some point? Were there things that went missing? Do you feel that you got it all?

WKW: No. We were not able to retrieve 100 percent of the material, and, in a way, it's so strange the reason why we had to look for extra material from Chinatown copies is that we noticed the film has been released here and in different territories in different versions longer than the original. I think at that point distributors wanted to have more action than the rest of the world because the Chinatown audience just look for action. So we looked to see if we could get some extra material from there, but it's not very rewarding.

DH: Where *Fallen Angels* has some gangster/action elements and *2046* has some science fiction, here you were working fully in genre. I mean, you've played with genre since, *My Blueberry Nights* was something of a road picture, but do you like having that form to fall back on? Do you ever want to do something like that again?

WKW: Of course, I think I'm quite good at action. The last few years we've been developing a project called *The Grand Master* [renamed *The Grandmaster*]. It's a story about the teacher of Bruce Lee. It's a film about the fight club in Hong Kong in the '50s. So this is something we all feel excited to do, and maybe this time we might do the film next.

DH: (at that moment, I think my eyes dilated a little) That's very exciting. One of the great things about your movies is how you're able to wed a piece of music, be it Cat Power or Astor Piazzolla, to images. When you're working with a period piece like *Ashes of Time*, was there ever a moment where you wanted to apply something you had in mind to this movie?

WKW: Do you know what the reference I gave to Frankie Chan [the music composer of *Ashes of Time*] in '94? Do you know?

DH: No.

WKW: I said, well, the music should be like Mark Knopfler, so in a way it's a very wild soundtrack at that point. It's not a normal martial arts film. We had, like, Tangerine Dream versus Dire Straits. There was "Private Investigations." Do you know the song "Private Investigations"?

DH: Not off the top of my head.

WKW: Ah!

DH: If you're recommending it, I'm going to go find it tonight.

WKW: I'm telling you; you can match the pictures, the scenes when there's a big fight in the desert. The second one, the ambush, you can score it to "Private Investigations." The introductions, the guitar lick. You should do that, the best, original.

DH: Going back . . . it seems Criterion is about to put out *Chungking Express*. Were you supervising that?
WKW: No. I just try and stay away from that as much as possible because once a film is done it's done. It's like if you take a picture when you're fourteen, and then you want to go back and photoshop it.

DH: So then how involved were you with this *Redux*?
WKW: That's different because of what's happening. The film was becoming incomplete, so I think it's very rare and very lucky to have a chance to work on a film twice. It's like you had a car—you built the car and it's broken, so you have to dismantle the car to fix it. By the time you put it back together you experience the same things twice. Then you realize why you had to build this car in this way years ago. It's fascinating.

DH: An interesting form of nostalgia.
WKW: Exactly. How can we do something digitally for this Internet medium?

DH: In terms of cinema?
WKW: Yeah.

DH: I don't know; we'll get there. Everything right now seems to be bite-sized pieces. I don't know. With this as an act of restoration and preservation, what about your other films, *As Tears Go By* and *Days of Being Wild*? Are they safe?
WKW: I wouldn't say I'm saving it. My feeling after all this, this job, is that finally this film is in a fixed form. When you used to have to do the developing of film, you had to put it in certain chemicals, and you could see the image coming out. But you had to fix it; otherwise, it would become overexposed or too dark. I think *Ashes of Time* as a film needed the time to be in this fixed form. Now, this is the film, finally. In Chinese we call this the ultimate version because maybe this is the best version to be seen by audiences.

DH: But with your older films, are the negatives safe?
WKW: No, no, because there won't be regional versions anymore, I won't be able to restore them. They will only exist as the DVD or VHS that still exists today. But I'm sure that will be gone very soon. So what we have to do right now is the final look of this film. That will be the only existing format.

DH: So you see your films as existing on DVD now more than ever screening theatrically? How do you feel about people watching stuff at home instead of theater?
WKW: It's not the best condition. One of the reasons we wanted to do this *Redux* was so the audience would be able to watch this film on the big screen. But, you know, it's not the habit of people today to spend a couple hours getting to the cinema to watch a film and go back home. It's too time consuming. People now are more lazy. They have so much stuff to do, so there's nothing you can do. I don't understand. There's the computer and at home on DVD or TV.

DH: There's a revival house here in Los Angeles, the New Beverly; I spend quite a bit of time there.
WKW: Really?

DH: Obviously, as you well know, there's something about the communal experience. That's always . . .
WKW: Yes, it's very different.

DH: I don't know. I think people will always want to go to the cinema. They'll always want to go out. A lot of people are attracted to convenience, but there's something to going to the theater that I don't think will ever be replaced, that group thing. Or, if it goes away, I will be very, very sad.
WKW: Right, but the thing is there are so many things you can watch today on the Internet. It's not only film. There's YouTube that occupies a lot of time.

DH: Yeah, it's very distracting, but—and I'm something of a cinéaste as well—there are films I have been waiting years and years to see—Sam Fuller's *White Dog*—films that were never released in America. . . . Let me put it this way, there're people who go see two foreign films a year and say, "Okay, I'm good," and there're other people who say, "I've just seen *Ashes of Time*, so now I've got to see *Fallen Angels* and *Chungking Express*." It's just a small percentage of people who get excited.
WKW: Also, the thing is they don't know what they are missing. With the big screen at home, they feel like "I've seen the movie," but that's not the case. When you look at it in that format, it's something else. The best way is to go to the cinema to watch it. It's what it's supposed to be.

DH: Yes. Exactly. A friend of mine was telling me about being at Cannes for *2046*, and there was a huge drama if the print was going to show up on time. There was, like, a race from the airport. It seems Cannes has been a deadline for you on a couple of occasions. Do you like working against that timeline, or would you rather have another couple of extra months?

WKW: No, every time I say, "I don't want to repeat that." But somehow it's like your nature to work against it. So last time, after 2046, we decided to be the first film to be shown at the festival, and still we rushed for that.

DH: Is editing your favorite part of the process?
WKW: No, it's about letting go. It's like you just want to make sure that this is the best you can do before you let go because once you let go you never look back. The film, once it's in the theaters, it's not yours anymore. There's nothing you can do about it, so you just want to see your daughters get married, that she looks as good as possible as she walks down that aisle.

DH: Do you like to go back? Have you ever gone back?
WKW: I haven't watched 2046 again because I know the film very well, and I've watched it hundreds of times to the point that I should stay away from it for a long time.

DH: So then what is your favorite part of the filmmaking process?
WKW: I don't think there's a job like a director. We can travel in time. We can make a film about now; we can make a film about five hundred years ago. In normal life you can't play around with time. You can make one minute forever, or you can make ten years just like (snaps), right? That's the best part of being in this business because you enjoy this. I can say, "Well, I'm in control of certain things which is beyond control in normal life."

DH: Creating fiction is as close as we come to being God.
WKW: Yes. You won't actually see these things, but when you are in this business you have to make things to believable.

DH: So, what artists do you draw from? Who would you say are your biggest influences?
WKW: I can't single out one person, but if I have to say I would say my mom because she was the one who introduced me to this world of cinema.

DH: Is there a film you go back to?
WKW: From time to time, yes, but now I enjoy watching films when I least expect it. I believe I've seen a lot of films, but somehow . . . you watch certain films because of recommendations, so you have certain expectations. But I enjoy watching films by accident. It's great when you say, "I wasn't going to watch this film," but now somehow, it works for you. It's the most satisfying experience. It's like, two

days ago, I watched this black and white film on TCM (Turner Classics Movies). It was amazing. I had never heard of it.

DH: Do you remember the name of it?
WKW: It's a film with Ginger Rogers but not a very well-known one.

DH: Do you feel like you need to make time to watch movies, to spend time with movies?
WKW: Yes.

DH: I think it's nourishing. Every once in a while you get overwhelmed with mediocrity, but something will be in there that's just . . .
WKW: Yes, that's why I watch movies. But I still remember . . . A few years ago, I was in Los Angeles, and it was the opening of *Star Wars*. The first *Star Wars* from the new series. I went to the cinema with my friend who was a big fan. And I had never seen anything like this in the Chinese cinema. It's like a bunch of people, the parents, you know are big fans of the first series, and then the kids. When the music started, and the Lucasfilm logo appeared, it was like a party. They screamed and clapped, and you couldn't hear the film for the first ten minutes. They just had to lose it, and it was a party.

With that we were told to wrap it up, and I asked him to sign my poster of *Happy Together*. He obliged, and I told him that I had a French girlfriend who told me about this movie and that I fell in love with her and the movie. He asked, "Are you still together?" I said, "Of course not." And we both chuckled.

NOTE

1. The warehouse where the film reels were stored was closing, so they asked Wong Kar-wai to retrieve the reels. The condition of the film reels was not good, so Wong had to improve the quality. In addition, Leslie Cheung passed away, so they tried to save the original reels for redubbing.

The Grandmaster or the Grand Barber? Multiple Choice Questions for Wong Kar-wai

Li Hongyu / 2013

From *Southern Weekend* (China). January 10, 2013. Interview conducted in Mandarin.
Translated by Micky Lee from Chinese

In the film, *The Grandmaster*, there is a line that says some people will become the *mianzi*—the public face, the winner, the main character—and some others will become the *lizi*—the loser, the supporting character.[1] [Who becomes *mianzi* or *lizi*] is a consequence of circumstances, not because of one's talent and potential. But what is more touching is that many people work hard in silence. They don't have a halo above their heads. Still, they carry on with a low profile the legacy of the older generation.

Wong Kar-wai had a head full of people and stories from the Republic of China when filming *The Grandmaster*. In the film Zhang Ziyi plays Gong Ruomei (Gong Er), the daughter of Master Gong. To avenge her father, she vows that she will not wed and have children. Gong's character may be based on many outstanding women during the Republican era of China, one of those was Shi Jianqiao. Her father Shi Congbin, a Commander of the Fengtian Clique, was a prisoner of war under the control of warlord Sun Chuanfang [of the Zhili Clique]. Shi was killed and his corpse was publicly displayed for three days. Shi Jianqiao vowed to avenge her father. At the beginning she hoped her brothers would do it, but they failed her. Later a man who was pursuing her promised he would avenge her father if Jianqiao agreed to marry him, so she did. However, the husband was climbing up the political ladder, and he kept on saying, "The time is not yet ripe [for the revenge]." Jianqiao left with their sons without bidding farewell to the husband. She found out the whereabouts of the warlord. When the warlord paid a visit to a Buddhist temple in Tianjin, Jianqiao shot him three times with a Browning pistol. This incident became a major event in the Republican China. By the time she carried out her revenge, Jianqiao's father had already been murdered a decade ago.

"The determination of the people during the Republican era reached this ultimate level," Wong Kar-wai told *Southern Weekend*.

In the film, Ip Man of Foshan began practicing kung fu at the age of seven. He became an apprentice of Wing Chun master Chan Wah-shun. Later Ip Man was named Ip of the Peide Lane because the family owned the entire lane. Before Ip Man turned forty, he did not have to work for a living. He could indulge in his kung fu practice. The real story of *The Grandmaster* began in 1936 when Ip Man was chosen by kung fu schools in Guangdong and Guangxi to have a match with Master Gong Bao-sen. He went to the south to hold his retirement ceremony—he had retired from the chairmanship of the Northern Martial Arts Union. Ip won the match. The daughter of Master Gong challenged Ip by inviting him for a match. This time Ip Man lost. Then the war between Japan and China broke out, and kung fu masters of that era such as Ip Man, Gong Er, and Razor (Yixiantian) left Guangdong and became exiles.

In fact *The Grandmaster* should have belonged to the wave of kung fu genre Chinese films. Ang Lee made *Hidden Tiger, Crouching Dragon* in 1999. Zhang Yimou made *Hero* in 2001. The script of *The Grandmaster* was registered [with the authority] in 2001, but production began only at the end of 2009. Some popular faces [in the wave of kung fu genre] such as Tony Leung Chiu-wai, Zhang Ziyi, and Chang Chen showed up again. But this time, Tony Leung really started to practice kung fu. Tony Leung told *Southern Weekend*, "I have always liked kung fu and have starred in many television shows [of this genre], such as *The Heaven Sword and Dragon Saber* and *The Deer and the Cauldron*,[2] but I have never learned kung fu. When I started to practice Wing Chun a year before *The Grandmaster* went into production, I was forty-seven." *The Grandmaster* was supposed to be released in 2012, but it did not happen. Luckily *The Grandmaster* has not become "a disappearing master." The self-mocked "Wong the procrastinator" Wong Kar-wai really handed in his work. He wanted to release it in 2012 to mark the centennial of the establishment of the Republic of China. Wong Kar-wai hoped that the Republican era would be revisited [in *The Grandmaster*] in which the beauty of Chinese would be shown.

Wong Kar-wai: When we look back today, there are many fine things during the Republican era. But fifty years from now when we look back to 2013, it will have its own fine things as well. It is the same every time we look back. We always say that a lot of fine things are no longer here when, in fact, they may just be temporarily obscured.

Many films talk about the ugliness and darkness of human kind. The story [of those films] is well developed and the script is also well written. But then you meet some people and feel the beauty in them. There is something beautiful about the Chinese.

From the time of preproduction, *The Grandmaster* has taken ten years [to finish]; the shooting took three years. Until early November 2012, the crew was still working in Kaiping city in Guangdong. Even on the last day of filming, they spent nine hours working. Wong Kar-wai had a hard time calling it a day because that might be the only time in his professional life that there was such a star-studded cast and crew and such a huge effort put into the production. He even said this might be his last time to shoot a feature on film stock. The Fuji film reel used to shoot *The Grandmaster* was the last batch manufactured for this camera model. Wong Kar-wai deliberately kept one for himself: "Very sad, you look at those movie cameras and wonder what will happen to them."

The last scene of the film takes place in the Buddhist temple where Gong Er decides to avenge her father. That is the Grand Hall (Daxiong Baodian) of Fengguo Monastery located in Yi County, Liaoning Province (in Northeast China). It was built in 1020, and it represents the highest achievement of Buddhist architecture in the Liao Dynasty (915–1125). In 1948, Liaoning was a war zone. One cannon shot through the roof of the Grand Hall and landed on the palms of the Buddha, but it did not explode. It only burned the right hand of the stature. The camera panned across brightly-lit candles on the dust-covered altar. The candle echoes the preaching of the older kung fu generation to the younger one, "Be determined to light a lamp."[3] Wong Kar-wai said, "Fine things would be preserved one day."

Southern Weekend: What do you miss the most about the Republican era?
WKW: It is not that I am particularly interested in the Republican era. I am only interested because this is a film with Ip Man as the main character. Ip Man's life is a vivid story about the history of the Republic. The Republic was a golden age of Chinese kung fu. At that time everyone believed China needed to be strong. The Republic was a very special era [that can be reflected from] the nationalist sentiments of kung fu masters. Many films showed the realistic face of Chinese. I hope this film shows the beauty of Chinese.

For example, between Master Gong and his senior classmate Ding Lianshan, one of them [Master Gong] was willing to become the public figure. The other was willing to live in the shadow because each of them has a different responsibility. They were separated for thirty years. To Master Gong, kung fu masters ought to weigh life and death lightly but separation heavily. This belief is not shared by other cultures.

SW: How can the viewer understand the concepts of *mianzi* and *lizi*?
WKW: In the scene where Ding was stewing snake soup, you may notice that

he said he left the Northeast in 1905. In that year, there was a major event in Chinese history, the assassination of five Qing officials by Wu Yue of the Northern Assassination Corps. Heroes like Wu Yue and Zhang Rong wanted to revolt against the Manchurian Qing rulers, and their means was assassination.

Liang Qichao [a writer and an intellectual of the late Qing Dynasty and Republican era] said that era was marked by assassinations. To revolt against Manchurian China, some chose republican revolution. Others chose the most extreme means such as assassination. The former choice was on the bright side, the latter one on the dark side. When Ding Lianshan and Master Gong separated, Ding asked Gong whether it is easier to be the head of a sect [of martial arts] or to wander in wilderness. Master Gong said, of course, it is easier to be the head of the sect. Then Ding said he is going to do the less easy thing, [that is, to assassinate.]

There was a real story: there was a Japanese wanderer called Bo Wugui. He used a samurai sword to mark a circle in the main street of Fengtian city [Shenyang City of today] in Northeast China. That circle symbolized the Japanese territory, and any Chinese who stepped inside would die. That was the plot. Many hot-blooded citizens walked into the circle and died. The circle then grew bigger and bigger. Ding killed Bo Wugui. Afterwards he left the Northeast and lived a life in shadow. That's why he gained the nickname the "Rascal of Guandong."[4]

Master Gong was the *mianzi*. He took over after his senior to become the chairman of Chinese martial arts association. The association had a stated purpose of saving the nation, but it was actually the Northern Martial Arts Union. It is like the Yagyu clan in Japan that had the "Bright Yagyu" and the "Dark Yagyu." The legal branch was the training place for the samurai class, while the illegal branch was the ninjas who specialized in assassination.

The story was very touching. But Zhao Benshan [who played Ding] had some health problems, so there was no way to fine-tune that story.

SW: In the film you arranged many characters who made completely opposite choices when facing the same problem.

WKW: From the late Qing Dynasty to the Republican era, resistance against Japan, and arrival in Hong Kong, that was a trying time [for Ip Man and others]. Many things happened during those years. Everyone had to choose—some chose to go forward, some chose to stay in the same place, and some made wrong choices.

In such a trying time, the most challenging thing in life was to live. Regardless of how good your kung fu skill was, living was the most challenging obstacle. It can frustrate you and ruin your profession. At the end of the film, many people could have become a grandmaster: Zhang Ziyi [who plays Gong Er] could have, Razor [played by Chang Chen] could have, and Ma Shan [played by Zhang Jin] also had the potential. But at the end, only Ip Man became the grandmaster who continued what the older generation passed on.

SW: That's why you feel Ip Man overcame the largest obstacle.

WKW: Correct. At that time, many people believed that the secrets of each kung fu school should only be passed on to fewer than sixteen people. Apprentices could not be someone who came from another background. When Ip Man arrived in Hong Kong, he made Wing Chun flourish. Some said he destroyed the essential spirit of Wing Chun, and that's why Wing Chun was started and ended by him. But to Ip Man, he did not believe in tribalism. He felt kung fu should be universal.

SW: Other than making important choices, the film also has two key phrases, which are "moving on" and "looking back."

WKW: The reason I contrast Ip Man with Zhang Ziyi is because one is on the bright side, one is on the dark one. This contrast is the same as their schools of kung fu: basically Wing Chun is about a straight line; you can only go forward. The main strategy is to face each other. Ip Man believes that the shortest distance between two points is a straight line. But the practitioners of *Bagua* Palm of Gong School believe that although the line between two points is the shortest, it may not be the fastest route. She can circle [her counterpart] and go behind his back. This also represents the life attitude of both: some only look forward, but Zhang Ziyi always looks back. At the end she chose to stay at the same point because she chose to look back all her life.

That's why Tony Leung told Zhang she does not move on. She does not look forward. The Gong School has a pair of moves: "the old monkey hangs up his badge" followed by "turning back and looking at the moon." [That was the move that Master Gong taught Ma San.] The key of that move is to "turn back." That is to say, many times looking back is about introspection, about reflection, but sometimes it is also about nostalgia.

SW: Chang Chen plays Razor, but he does not have a scene with Tony Leung. What is their relationship?

WKW: He and Tony Leung have parallel lives: both of them are kung fu masters, and both of them have suffered much. When they arrived in Hong Kong, they had to do less than ideal things in order to make a living. At the end they build their own business, but one has a halo and became a grandmaster, the one became a barber. Like what the film said, in one's life, some become the public figures;

some become the supporters. [What one becomes] has less to do with talent and potential, but more to do with circumstance. The most touching thing is many people work hard in silence and don't complain [even though] they are not given a halo. They silently pass on what the older generation teaches them and they move forward.

SW: That's why the touching thing is those grand barbers?
WKW: When I was small, there was a barbershop beneath my home. I heard rumors that many skilled kung fu masters mingled there. When they came to Hong Kong, they became local bullies.

Chang Chen plays Razor. The character comes from two historical figures: one was a *Baji* Fist master called Li Shuwen. He always killed when he fought, but he was very lazy. He said he only needed one move. Another historical figure is a master from Taiwan. His name was Liu Yunqiao. He was a spy during the Republican era. He had done much killing during the resistance to Japan. When he arrived in Taiwan, he made *Baji* flourish.

Many people were skilled, but some were given a halo because of fate. But for those who didn't have that fate, it does not mean they didn't need to do what they ought to do. Some people didn't have a halo, but they continued doing what the older generation passed on to them. I feel this is a very important thing.

SW: The kung fu masters liked to gather in the brothel. One dialogue says it well, "among all the worldly people, there would be those who act from the heart."[5] Is that what you discovered in historical research, or is it your own conclusion?
WKW: That is my conclusion. Notice that the Gold Pavilion (that brothel) is [also] called "The Republic House." Before Master Gong said in the scene, "I have done three things in my life," there was actually another scene, but it was too long [so it was cut]. Master Gong said that year when he led his clan to escape from the Northeast, they kept on taking off the warm clothing until they reached southern China. When they arrived in Foshan, only when they visited the brothel did they realize they are country bumpkins. The brothel was adorned with gold and was extremely well-kept . . . However, they went to the brothel, not because of the women but to deliver a bomb. The bomb was made by [revolutionist] Cai Yuanpei. Three days later, the bomb killed Feng Shan, a Guangzhou military leader of the Qing government, and thus began the Republican era. That's why the brothel was renamed the Republic House. That is a place with worldly people, but inside it had many heroes.

That scene was cut, so many people asked why the kung fu masters were all in a brothel. You have to know that the concession announcement of [the last Emperor of Qing dynasty] Puyi was drafted there. It was written by a few people who hid inside the brothel. Their existence had to be kept secret.

SW: There is also a line that says, "If you have faith in what you believe in, one day it will be answered." What is the belief?
WKW: The belief is one's dream. Heroes are those who don't change their intention [because of the circumstance]. You can't be a great master if you don't insist on your own thoughts. You have to bear in mind your intention, you have to concentrate on [making it happen]. After you water your plant enough, there will be a tree sprouting there.

Those from the first generation of Northern Martial Arts Union said strong country, strong race; martial arts can save the country. The snake stew made by Ding is their intention and belief. They hope this belief will continue. Master Gong was a very great elder, he saw that hope from Ip Man. So he conceded to Ip Man and said he would pass his reputation to Ip Man. He had a hope that Ip Man would relay the torch to the next generation.

SW: Gong Er defeated Ma San. The key move was to place her palms on his chin and press up [to break his neck]. Master Gong hit Ma San in the same way. Was this your decision because of aesthetic reasons, or was it a decision based on literature about *bagua*?
WKW: I hope the kung fu moves in the film correspond to the plot. There is a move in *xingyi* (part of Gong School) called "the old monkey hangs up his badge [*Laoyuan Guayin*]," which is very simple. When one lifts the knee to the opponent's sternum, that is "hanging up the badge."[6] That move is lethal. Ma San at that time worked for the Japanese militants. She hoped to take an official post. But Master Gong told her that the key of that move is "turning back." I feel that corresponds to the plot: Old Master hoped Ma San would realize his mistake [for working for the Japanese], but he did not turn back. The move of Zhang Ziyi is called "a hidden flower below the leaf" (*yedi canghua*). It breaks the "the old monkey hangs up his badge" move. [This arrangement] emphasizes both brain and brawn.

SW: During the shooting, the actors' kung fu teachers and action choreographer Master Eighth (Yuen Woo-ping) were on location. They must have a different view of the action sequence. Who had the final say?
WKW: That is the most intriguing thing about this film. To an action choreographer like Master Eighth, there is a saying: children, dogs, and headmasters are the most difficult to deal with. Children are difficult to teach to play kung fu; animals, needless to say, are more difficult. Then there are the headmasters. They all have

their perspectives—"This is not acceptable because this is not something from our school." But this time the collaboration was quite good because everyone had a clear objective, which is every move of every kind from every school had to be precise. When making a decision, sometimes a move is not precise enough—but it looks great—and that is acceptable. There is a balance in the film.

These teachers always tell me, "We can kill a person in one move (of our school)." But you can't just have one move. That would kill the film. It will not make a good film. Like Akira Kurosawa, you could have one move with a knife and sword, but one move won't do for fists and legs.

SW: During your interview process with kung fu masters in China, some masters would say they are willing to demonstrate their kung fu in the film only under the condition that they cannot lose to Wing Chun. What do you think about that?

WKW: That's why at the end I am very thankful for Master Wang Shiquan and a few *bagua* masters. They did not mind that much. Generally, when they found out this film is about Ip Man, they wanted to know whether their school would lose or win. They did not want to be the one who loses because they would be blamed [by people in the school]. I explained to them that there is more than one grandmaster in this film, so the question is not about who wins and who loses. At the end those elderly masters put their trust in me. I was very lucky.

Actually out of all the martial arts in the film, some of them are very interesting. For example, in the scene when Ip Man and Master Gong were fighting for a piece of cake, most people don't know why one time Tony Leung has the palm up, another time the palm down. But if you are in this world [of martial arts], you'd know when the palm faces up, it is the *yang* hand. Generally it is a mercy hand—your gravity comes from the ground. You will injure but not kill your opponent. *Yin* hand is "beyond the boundary" [meaning expiating the sins of the dead in Buddhism and Taoism]. Ip Man had tried the *yang* hand and the *yin* hand, but neither could make him win. At the end he used *ting qiao* [literally: listening to the bridge]. It is like the *nian* hand [literally: sticky hand] of Wing Chun. This is similar to the *tui* hand [literally: push hand] in tai chi, which is you feel the power of your opponent and follow his move. That is actually very fun. But some of these things only make sense to the practitioners who later think, "Hey, Director Wong, you know a bit [of kung fu]!"

SW: At the beginning of the film, Ip Man says, "Kung fu has two characters, one horizontal, one vertical. The loser lays flat; the winner stands proud and is qualified to talk." Isn't this a tactic for the winner?

WKW: No, this is not a tactic for the winner. At the end martial arts is like a kind of art. There are more than one hundred and twenty kinds of Chinese kung fu.

Each school has its own methods. At the end it is a tactic. At the end it is about the purpose, either you lay flat or you stand proud. Only those who stand proud are correct. Others say your fist is not very powerful. My fist is more powerful than yours. But this does not need any discussion because you only need to have a match and you can tell [who the winner is and who the loser is].

For the masters, they only need a light touch (with their opponent), and they will know how skillful the opponent is. In the old days, the masters could save face for others and spare the opponents the embarrassment [of losing the match]. I think this is quite interesting. It is a big deal to destroy someone's reputation because he does not represent himself, but his school. Different schools would avenge for themselves, and the revenge never stops.

SW: You spent three years visiting kung fu masters. What is your opinion about Chinese kung fu nowadays?

WKW: Now there are two kinds of Chinese kung fu: one is institutional martial arts [for competition]. It sees martial arts as a sport. There is nothing called a school; all are tactics. But if there is no school, there will be no tradition to pass on; there will be no masters and apprentices. Actually Chinese used to say, "Learning by hands-on teaching." This is very important because some things are taught by an oral tradition from the heart. The apprentices have to practice until they reach a certain level. When they are ready, the master would test and inspire them. Then the apprentices' horizons of kung fu would be broadened. Kung fu development outside the state is worrying. Nowadays, parents won't allow children to practice kung fu. They learn taekwondo, art, music . . . but kung fu is not acceptable. I have interviewed many students who are in their fifties, and they said they could only concentrate on practicing kung fu after retirement. The youngest apprentices are in their fifties. You could say this is indeed worrying. "The poor study [to make money] while the wealthy [have the money to] practice kung fu."[7] To make a living, you can't spend time practicing kung fu.

NOTES

1.   The pair *mianzi* 面子 and *lizi* 裡子 can be seen as a *yinqyang* concept. "*Mianzi*" can be translated as appearance, face, reputation, and the outer side, while "*lizi*" can be translated as actuality, soul, and the hidden or inner side. The meanings of both words change in different contexts. In the rest of the interview, the meanings are translated without citing the original Chinese words used in the interview.

2.   *The Heaven Sword and Dragon Saber* (1961–1963) and *The Deer and the Cauldron* (1969–1972) were novels penned by Jin Yong (Louis Cha). Tony Leung starred in the

television adaptations of *The Heaven Sword and Dragon Saber* in 1986 and *The Deer and the Cauldron* in 1984. Both shows were produced by Television Broadcast Ltd. in Hong Kong.

3. This is the line that Master Gong says to Ip Man after their match. Master Gong hopes Ip Man can pass on the torch and never give up his faith.

4. Guandong (or Kwantung) was a Japanese-occupied territory in Northeast China during the late Qing and Republican era. Chang Ta-chun, a well-known Taiwanese writer as well as the script consultant of *The Grandmaster*, has written an article on the story of Ding Lianshan. It can be found at: http://blog.sina.com.cn/s/blog_6b736b5b0102e272 .html

5. In DVD, this dialogue is translated as "Good men can be found among rogues."

6. In ancient Chinese, hanging up the badge (official stamp) means becoming an official.

7. This saying means those who don't have money need to study hard to sit for examination so that they can get a good job. Those who come from a wealthy background don't need to have a job to make a living, so they can indulge in their hobbies, such as kung fu. This was true in Ip Man's days, and Wong implied that it is still true: Chinese parents want their children to learn something useful so that they will be admitted to good universities.

The Grandmaster, Director Wong Kar Wai

David Poland / 2013

From *DP/30* (US). https://www.youtube.com/watch?v=VeCfktjSlyc. Interview conducted in English in 2013.

David Poland: Have you been to Comic Con?[1]
Wong Kar-wai: Yes, two nights ago.

DP: Did you just go down for fun?
WKW: No, we have a screening over there.

DP: So, how is it?
WKW: It's very, very strange.

DP: (laughs) Is there a geek universe in Japan, not in China, that you're a part of?
WKW: No, the thing is I expect it's all kids. It's mainly for comic fans and kids, so we went there. Actually you find most people are not kids. They are very mature, but all in costume. It's fun.

DP: Is there any culture like that in China?
WKW: No, none. I think in Japan, yes.

DP: All the manga stuff.
WKW: The manga is something very important in Japan. They have a big following.

DP: Is it fun to watch [your own film *The Grandmaster*] with this crowd? I'm sure they went crazy.
WKW: No, it's not true. At first I did a mix for this Comic Con version, a bit stronger than it's supposed to be, because I thought the crowd is a different crowd. They might need something more exciting, but in fact they are very quiet, in a way they

are not quiet for bad reasons. They're very patient and very into the film, and the reception is very, very warm.

DP: So does this film feel like the rest of your body of work to you? Does it feel like a different thing and that it's the first WKW chopsocky movie?[2]
WKW: No, I'm not doing a chopsocky kung fu film. It's been a long time since there was a kung fu film, like what we saw in the '70s Shaw Brothers, very hardcore, very authentic. There's no flying. There's no fancy move. Everything is very precise, and it's hardcore.

DP: It is hardcore. So how do you see it? I mean you were talking [about it] before the screening.
WKW: Right, I did say something.

DP: I would say you said a lot of good things. You were talking about how when you wrote the script there was room for improvising the words because you already knew very clearly what the visuals were in your head. Do you start conceptualizing doing something like this from the very beginning?
WKW: No, because after all, we are filmmakers. We are not writers, but we need writings to make a movie. You have to think in terms of a visual; that's why we spent so much time on doing interviews with different masters from different schools. It's not just talking. I had to get them to do demonstrations, and when they showed you the demonstration, you just looked at the move. You understood the move: What is the mechanisms of the body? How to make this kick? And how to do this fight? And then it's in your mind already because you already have the shot, have the set up. You know how to [film it]. I don't practice martial arts, even though I've watched thousands of martial arts films, but it's a different thing. You have to actually feel it. And every time I did an interview with a master, I would say, "I want [you] to show how hard that punch goes." In some of these Chinese schools they are not talking about force, they are talking about the power. So it doesn't seem very strong, but somehow it hurts a lot. So you have to feel that.

DP: How did you get to the point where you decide to tour and to meet everybody, to meet the kung fu universe?
WKW: When I wanted to make this film, I already decided that this is a once in a lifetime chance for me to actually understand what Chinese kung fu is. We've seen so many kung fu films, and at a point people just think Chinese kung fu is a show. It is like a trick. It's not that efficient (Wong may mean *effective*) or practical. So I wanted to find out how good it is because it has a long history, and there must be

a reason why this arts stays for so long. When you have the chance to meet with these people, [it is not] just listening to stories, reading books, or watching films. You have to go exactly where they live, see how they practice, and know what exactly the skill is. I think that's very fascinating to me.

DP: So the journey was your journey first?
WKW: Yes, I spent three years on the road.

DP: Have you done this kind of research for any other films?
WKW: Yeah.

DP: All of them or some of them?
WKW: Some of them because if I'm going to make *Chunking Express* or *Happy Together*, I don't have to do much research because the stories are contemporary. But if you make a film like *The Grandmaster*, you have to understand the world. You can never understand the story of Ip Man without knowing the time he went through, the background of his family, and the martial arts movement at that time.

DP: So did you approach *2046* in this way as well?
WKW: No, *2046* is more like a fantasy. It's about a writer in the '60s, I know many of them. These are people that I know from my childhood, and the futuristic part is basically a very low-tech futuristic vision from the '60s. I intended to make it like that because it's the imagination of a writer in the '60s, not [how a writer imagines the future] today.

DP: When I think of you, I think of you as a twenty-five-year-old still. Somehow, you're not quite twenty-five anymore. When you started out did you think, "I wanna make a certain kind of film," or are you just trying to be in the moment and find your voice as you are working?
WKW: You never know what it's like when you start on a project; you somehow have a hunch. I always say the first people who visit a place are called adventurers, like Christopher Columbus. After that they are all tourists because they know exactly what they will get. I don't want to be a tourist. I want to be someone who discovers something.

DP: So that was your philosophy from the beginning?
WKW: Yes. Otherwise, what's the point?

DP: So why film?
WKW: It's the only thing that I know, which I think I'm good at.

DP: Did you figure out you were good at it from the beginning?

WKW: First of all, writing is too hard and too boring. Acting is not something that I want to do, so I think I will make films. Remember we are from a time when film really was a very exciting medium. When I was a kid we would spend almost every day watching films.

DP: But when you started, not a lot of work that was done in the Chinese film industry was like your work. It was very melodramatic, very kind of old fashioned in a way.

WKW: No, not true. When you look at some of the old classics in the '30s they were very expressionistic, and when you look at the films from the Shaw Brothers in the '70s, they were also in a way full of energy. So it's not true [that no work was like mine when I started]. I must say when we started it was the beginning of the so-called Hong Kong New Wave.[3] It was a time that was very exciting. You had a lot of chances to make films and to express your ideas.

DP: So you felt an absolute freedom to do your work from the beginning?

WKW: Right, but of course you have to because we are independent. We have to manage a lot of things. When we first started, we were not mainstream filmmakers, and we did not produce mainstream products. So you have to really make your voice heard, to make extra efforts to convince people that it's something that they should pay attention to.

DP: So did the Western world's embrace of your work change the game for you? Did it make it easier? Did it make it harder? Was it something that everyone's excited about in Hong Kong?

WKW: I think it helps because that makes our audience bigger, and that means more resources to make the films that we want.[4]

DP: So did you ever have the urge to do something more commercial?

WKW: I think all my films are very commercial.

DP: But I don't imagine you doing a *Star Wars* episode any time soon.

WKW: If I have this passion like George Lucas, why not? I think he has this passion to make a world of his own, like in *Star Wars.* Somehow I have a passion to make a film about the world of martial arts. I think it's the same thing. It's really what drives a filmmaker to do his best. He must have this kind of passion that is almost like an addiction. He wants to makes sure everything's right. He's so curious about this world, and I think that's the driving force.

DP: So you don't have a judgement about filmmakers' choices in terms of their subject. Whatever their passion is, hopefully they make it interesting and do a good job.

WKW: There're so many filmmakers today. Everybody can be a filmmaker with your iPhone, with your camera. So all of us are actually providing a vision and sharing our angles. Some people get picked up because they get appreciated by a lot of people. Others have less following, but that doesn't mean that their work is [of a] more or less [quality]. It's our job to do something to convince ourselves, then we have to convince others.

DP: At Cannes this year, and almost every year, there's this kind of huge [star] that most film critics are talking about all the time.

WKW: That's their job.

DP: Yes, but there's an extreme response sometimes. Obviously all of the films have been qualified by the festival, but there's this kind of rage about some films. The critics hate them, and then there are films they absolutely love, almost all generous too.

WKW: I think film critics are more generous than before. Today, I always feel like when you go to a film festival, you have a kind of mission. You have to deliver some message. You have to have social conscience [editors' note: Wong may mean social consciousness]. I'm not saying that's wrong, but that doesn't mean films have to be made in this way. Not all the films have to address [social consciousness] because there are so many more things we need to address. We can address some urgent issues [of the present], or something else, that is more about life.

DP: So are you into all genres, or are there things that you would pass? Do you like animation? Are you interested in science fiction? Well, I mean you've done science fiction.

WKW: Genre is basically like a uniform. You are the same person, but you can put on different uniforms. That's why you need this uniform. We call this a form. So what you are going to say has to go with the form, and you pick the right uniform for this occasion or this message. That's it.

DP: So what was the very first inkling on *The Grandmaster*? Was there a moment when you first thought that someday you'd like to make a movie like this?

WKW: I always wanted to make a kung fu film.

DP: Since you were a kid.

WKW: Yes, I am a big fan, but I have to find my angle because most of the kung fu films are about who's the better fighter—whether I'm the best in the world—or revenge. What's my angle? I don't think I'm going to make many kung fu films. If this is the only chance, I want to make it right. I want to make a very different kung fu film. It's not only about the skills; it's also about the wisdom, the philosophy. Why has the tradition of martial arts been like this for so many years? There is a certain wisdom in it. I think it's a time for not only the action audience, but we would like to have more people look at this film to understand this world.

DP: Did you go into the journey to meet people to explore the world after you had an idea of what your hook was that made it uniquely yours, or did you go looking to find it as part of that journey?
WKW: I wanted to make a film like this, but I don't have all the keys. I need to find those keys. I need to walk through that door and find all the answers myself.

DP: At what point did you feel you'd figure it out, or have you?
WKW: I can't say. I think this is the beginning. There're just so many interesting aspects of Chinese martial arts tradition. I hope we have taken the lead, and some filmmakers in the future can continue doing it because I think it's very worthwhile.

DP: Well it's interesting because you took a long time to make the film, and people knew you were working on a film and roughly knew about the story. So a bunch of people made movies [about Ip Man] before your movie even came out. There were even sequels that came out before you started. Are you conscious of that when it's happening? Are you thinking about the commercial world around while you're working?
WKW: People work at a different pace. Like what I said last night, if you want to do something original, of course it will take time. You are not just copying something. In fact after we announced the film *The Grandmaster* there are so many films about Ip Man that were made even at a greater speed. [Those filmmakers are] more efficient than I. But I don't mind. I don't feel pissed because I think it's good to have films talking about this character, to bring an awareness of Ip Man and his ideas and to bring the awareness that we have to revisit the traditions of martial arts because it's not in very good shape now.

In China today two forms of martial arts exist: the form that is encouraged by the government—the competitive martial arts. There is no school, just a combination of skills from different schools. There is no history; it's a sport. It's a sport for the Olympics. There is no teacher; there is no student. You only have a coach and the athletes.

The second form is the traditional martial arts that exists only among individuals. They are not supported by government. Most of the masters I interviewed are in their '70s. The youngest student is fifty-five because [these students] are retired, and they can focus on this practice. So you can see that traditional martial arts is dying. I hope this film can bring out the awareness of that.

DP: So the younger ones are doing a copy of a copy?
WKW: Yeah, come on, let's be honest. Today people say they practice Tai Chi because Tai Chi is like Chinese yoga. That's not true because when you look at the first two generations of the Tai Chi masters, they died very young. Tai Chi is a very, very lethal weapon. It can kill.

DP: So taking a Tai Chi class in the mall in the suburb, it is probably not the core of it.
WKW: Well I'm sure it helps, and it's good exercise. But the thing is you cannot label Tai Chi as yoga. It's not the essence of Tai Chi. Tai Chi is about the balance. It is, in a way, a weapon.

DP: So you're not talking about the philosophy and the spirituality of the forms; you're just doing exercise.
WKW: Yes.

DP: In terms of how you work, people see you as a mysterious figure in some ways because your films are so beautiful and intimate.
WKW: Why? [Because my films are] hard to understand?

DP: Well, sometimes hard to understand, but sometimes not as accessible to a general audience as they are to people who are really focused on the work. There is a degree of passion among the people who are very interested [in your films] as you saw last night at the academy. People went crazy when you walked in the room. At the same time in terms of the Average Joe who goes to the multiplex, he can't even figure out where to start. I guess you are conscious of this because you are saying that. Are you aware of how it presents. Do you want a broader audience? Do you want to make it more accessible, or does it even matter because the work is just what you're doing? Your focus is on your work.
WKW: Well, just look at a film like *The Grandmaster*—we released a film in China in January, and the film has been showing all around the world. So we have a huge audience from different backgrounds, from different cultures, and this film speaks to this audience.

DP: Do you like that? Do you see it as an entryway to a *2046* or *Chungking Express*? Or do you hope it is?

WKW: Just imagine, I'm not a painter and to make films you need an audience. You need to speak to an audience. Otherwise, what's the point of making a film? Of course we are very happy to communicate with the audience, but that doesn't mean you have to do something to find an easy way out. I think we want to have our own language but will appreciate having more people understand this film.

DP: So in terms of this film, last night you talked particularly about the sequence of the train track at the train station, with Zhang Ziyi and the other actor's name whose name I don't know offhand.
WKW: You have to find it out. Don't be lazy.

DP: I will look it up in a second, but it's a remarkable sequence. You did mention that it took two months to shoot it. So the sequence is five minutes, six minutes, seven minutes long?
WKW: Eleven.

DP: Eleven minutes long. But two months is a long time to shoot, and it's very intimate. I mean, it's beautiful. It's not like any other kung fu you'd see anywhere else because it's so much about the moment: the facial expressions, the movement of the hands, and all the different little pieces. Did you know what that sequence would look like, or roughly, what it might look like when you started?
WKW: Are you kidding?

DP: Or were you finding the pieces to put them together?
WKW: Of course.

DP: You had it all in your head?
WKW: You can make that scene in three hours or three days. With all these doubles and flying wire, you can do it in three days. The thing is, once you have seen the actual demonstrations, you want to give to the audience exactly the same feeling—to understand the skill, the movement. I think you need to spend that much time.

DP: So how do you do it technically? Did you use multi camera, or was it single camera?
WKW: Single camera. How can you do these shots with multi camera? It doesn't work that way.

DP: Maybe you have a trick to do it.
WKW: No, I don't have that trick.

DP: So when you wanted to get the arms moving in a certain direction, are they going through the whole sequence of the fight to get that moment?
WKW: First of all we have sessions called choreographing, so we do all the choreography beforehand. Then we have to set up. We have a setup for this part of the movement; we want to capture this movement. But before the setup we have to choreograph the whole movement on scene. As you can imagine, shooting on a train station like that is extremely difficult because it was sometimes, like, minus thirty degrees Celsius at night. You can only do a few set ups.

DP: So that seemed like the only way to do it? Is it the only way it can be done?
WKW: No, no. Only for me, it is the only way to do it this way—to be true and to be authentic.

DP: Are you looking to capture a specific beat or a moment or an image, and then you shoot until you get that and move on to the next image?
WKW: No, when you're shooting action, it's highly technical because it's not like just one take will get you the shot. Because there is a lot of coordinating, you have to have the action, timing, and angle, and the camera movement. Everything has to be coordinated, and it takes time.

DP: You're also well known for your postproduction. You know what is in your head when you're shooting. So what is post-production like for you in a situation like that? Is it refinement? Is it changing your mind about what you wanted? Or are you just trying to create the thing you had in your head?
WKW: They're options. Postproduction means there are so many options in front of you. There are so many ways to tell the stories, so you're trying to find the best way. When you are shooting a film you want to see more, but when you are doing postproduction you are aware that there is a running time. Some people say, "Well, I don't care. I want to make this film three hours long, and it should be three hours long." But sometimes you have some restrictions about running time, so you have to find the most efficient way to tell the story within a certain running time. For instance, in China the film is two hours and ten minutes, and in Europe it's two hours and five minutes. Here it is one hour and fifty minutes. You have different requirements or different restrictions for different markets. You can't simply just make it shorter. You have to tell the story in a certain way. It's the same film, but in a way it's a bit different.

DP: So it's not really tweaking the scenes as much as finding the energy of the whole thing, coming together at the right amount of time to fit?

WKW: You have to tell the story in the most efficient way and at the same time in a way that you feel is the most satisfying.

DP: Is there a preference for you between the 2:10 and the 2:58 and whatever the American length is?
WKW: It's the same film for me.

DP: It's the same film?
WKW: Right.

DP: So we shouldn't go running out to try to find the longer version?
WKW: First, you have to watch this version.

DP: What is your relationship [with this film] after the movie is done? Obviously you are doing press and having conversations about the movie, but are you emotionally ready to move on to the next thing? Are you still lingering in the experience that you had and thinking about how it's going to affect you?
WKW: I think I'm still in 1936, and it will take a while to leave. Then you can move on to something else.

DP: Do you look back at your work much?
WKW: No.

DP: Once you're done, you're done?
WKW: Just imagine. I've seen this film so many times.

DP: But if you see a film from ten years ago show up on television or something . . .
WKW: I'd enjoy it.

DP: You'll watch it?
WKW: Yeah, yeah, but the thing is accidental. You are not intentionally trying to get a DVD, to get the film. It's like you just came across an old friend you haven't seen for a long time. When you look at the film you are not actually looking at the film. You have all these memories of how this scene got made, and it's a different experience.

DP: Do you see a younger you when you watch your old work? Do you see a younger man who worked on those films? Do you see your own evolution?
WKW: No, I don't see myself. I see the people working with me, and the moment when we made that scene.

DP: Can you imagine ever not making films?
WKW: Sure.

DP: Just one day you might decide to go off and paint, or do something else?
WKW: Yes, of course. I always have a dream like that. When I don't have to work, I will just be reading, eating, and having a different life.

DP: So in some ways it's still work. You are clearly an artist, but there is still an element of it that is work for you.
WKW: No, it's the passion. It's the curiosity.

DP: As long as you have that passion, you'll keep shooting?
WKW: Yes, we all do, I think.

DP: For some people, I mean, it's career, and it sounds like you aren't interested in a career as such.
WKW: I think of a different definition, right.

NOTES

1. Comic Con is a comic convention that takes place in multiple US cities. It aims to bring fans to the creators through sale booths, talks, and screenings. The convention is known for passionate fans dressing up in their favorite characters. The event attracts a lot of media attention because of the colorful crowds.

2. Chopsocky kung fu film is a derogatory term used to describe cheaply-made Chinese films that have loose storylines, compromised acting, and lots of action. It is drawn from the term chop suey—an Americanized Chinese dish that mixes different ingredients together. Many Western audiences first learn of Hong Kong cinema from chopsocky films.

3. Hong Kong New Wave started in the late 1970s when film directors started seeing themselves as auteurs and their films have their signature styles. Wong Kar-wai is one of the latecomers to the scene. Some of them are working in the mainstream (such as Tsui Hark and John Woo), and others remain in art house cinema (such as Ann Hui and Stanley Kwan). See introduction for a detailed explanation.

4. Since *In the Mood for Love*, Wong Kar-wai's films have been financed by Hong Kong, Chinese, and French production houses.

Interview: Wong Kar-wai

Jake Mulligan / 2013

From *Slant Magazine* (US). http://www.slantmagazine.com/features/article/interview
-wong-kar-wai. Interview conducted in English. Reprinted by permission of the publisher.
The interview collected in this volume is the entire conversation. The magazine version is
abbreviated.

Jake Mulligan: In *The Grandmaster*, as in your other films, much is made of reflecting on the past. How much of what you film is dictated by your own memories
and personal experiences? And how does that affect something like *The Grandmaster*, set in a time before you were born?
Wong Kar-Wai: It's actually not really about memories; it's about curiosities. I
think for *The Grandmaster*, it's about a time I only ever heard of and never actually went through. Most of my films are about Hong Kong in the '60s—the im-
migrants, the Second Generation [of immigrants]. And this film is a bit more . . . I
wanted to know where they came from. We went to the early days of the Republic
of China,[1] and for me, it's like a new territory. It's not going back. It's a discovery.
When you look at the film, you see that a lot of people end up in Hong Kong for
different reasons. That is how Hong Kong has become [what it is] today.

JM: Much as the time period has shifted. I personally feel there has been a shift
in your past four pictures away from the type of photography you were composing
in your earlier works. Do you feel that your aesthetic preferences have changed at
all? Do you consider your previous pictures while making a film?
WKW: I never want to make beautiful pictures. I just want to make sure it's right.
Every set up, every shot represents a choice: what you want to see and what you
don't want to see. If you want to see precisely this button [referencing the button
that Ip Man gave to Gong Er as a love token in *Grandmaster*],[2] then you have to
look at this button. It's not just a button, it's a history, right? If you are going to
show a punch, how can you show a punch is very powerful? I remember when we
shot the scene in the train station, they said that the first punch was too strong

[since] it breaks the nails coming out of the pillars. They asked, "If we want to be authentic, is it too over the top?" I said, "We'll see." I think it's good enough to tell you that his [Ma San played by Zhang Jin] punch is very, very strong.

JM: So you're telling me you've never once composed a shot with the conscious intention of creating something beautiful?
WKW: No. (Thinks) No. I'm not going to frame a beautiful shot [for the sake of beauty].

JM: Yuen Woo-ping is credited as the fight choreographer of the film. He's created a distinctive signature for himself through his work. How do you two work together, and does his work influence the rest of the film, like the dialogue scenes, at all?
WKW: The way I work with Yuen Woo-ping is very straightforward. At the beginning of our meeting, I told him that I wanted this to be a hardcore kung fu film. It has to be authentic. I don't want wires. I don't want tricks, and I want my actors to perform their kung fu, like in the early days—like in the Shaw Brothers films. So he was quite shocked, actually. I brought him to the training rooms with Tony [Leung], and he realized that I was serious about it. Because [Yuen's] from that background, he knows this world very well. Together we created action scenes that were choreographed with the trainers. If Tony is [playing] a Wing Chun master,[3] then all his moves should be Wing Chun moves.

JM: So I assume you mean you dislike the wires and overuse of CGI effects.
WKW: In the last ten years, a lot of kung fu films have become over the top. And at a point, audiences start to think, "Kung fu films are just a show, or a gimmick . . . the Chinese martial arts—does it [actually] work?" But you look at the popularity of MMA (Mixed Martial Arts) today, [you see that they do work.] The Chinese martial arts, especially Wing Chun, they are the beginning of MMA.

JM: Then is this film intended as a corrective to the genre as it stands now?
WKW: No, I think [the film] opens a window. It's more like a question than an answer, "Do you really know what Chinese martial arts is? Are you interested? Do you want to learn more?"

JM: There's a lot in the film about different styles, about mastering different techniques, about fostering a command of many different styles. Hong Kong cinema has always been defined by a collection of different genres and styles. Is that something that attracted you? Did you think about that parallel while making the film?
WKW: Because of the Chinese market, most of the Hong Kong filmmakers work

in China, through co-productions. So at a point, people said, "Well, where is Hong Kong cinema?" But in fact, the Hong Kong cinema has gone through a different stage. It [now] has a bigger playground. But in a way you also have to keep the essence, the spirit, of Hong Kong cinema.

When we were shooting this film, we were conscious to do a homage because kung fu film is a big genre. So in a way, you can see in the first thirty minutes, when Tony is doing the three challenges in the brothel, it's basically an homage to Lau Kar-leung films,[4] the Shaw Brothers, and the Tsui Hark period. We are trying to get everything in. It's not just one kung fu film. It's like, *Once Upon a Time . . .*

JM: So the music cue you borrow from *Once Upon a Time in America*,[5] that's not just because you liked the music, then? There's a thematic connection between that film and *The Grandmaster*?

WKW: Oh, it's an homage. We had these discussions, like two days ago, with a very good writer who wrote many big films. The interesting thing he said was, "It used to be that film was about stories. Today, film is about short stories." And I think the reason I wanted to pay homage to *Once Upon a Time in America*, to Sergio Leone, to Morricone, is because people don't make films like that anymore—people don't have the patience for epics. Epics are really about time. It's a journey and not just action.

JM: There's a lot of footage out there for this film. I've seen two different cuts of the picture, and there was plenty of footage exclusive to each. If it weren't for that lack of patience among audiences, would you like to release a version that comprises most of the footage—a version of *The Grandmaster* that would be as long as most Leone movies? Or are the running times dictated by other things?

WKW: Yeah, sadly, today, the distribution of films is very competitive, so in China we can [only] afford to release this film in two hours and ten minutes, [and] we have an obligation to release this film under two hours in the United States. But I don't want to just do a shorter version—do some trimming, take out some scenes—because I think the structure of the Chinese version is very delicate and very precise. Instead I want to do a new version. I want to tell this story in a different way.

And, in fact, American cinema, besides Chinese cinema, has the longest history of kung fu films. So I think [in the American edition of *The Grandmaster*] we can focus and go directly to the story. In the Chinese version, it's really about time. And here it's really about the characters. We follow the story of Ip Man and go through this world of martial arts.

JM: You've been quoted in the past saying that your editing process is so arduous because you love your movies too much and don't want to let them go. So the multiple edits, the way you've gone through and re-edited different cuts of your movies from the ground up—for you, is that as much about finding a way to release as much footage as possible as it is about creating the perfect final product for separate markets?

WKW: You have to imagine, when you're shooting a scene and you really love that scene, it's a lot of work. It's not only the work of the director, it's the actors, writers, the whole crew. And sometimes that footage that doesn't go into the final edit, it will wake you up. [Those scenes] will call you. So you want to think, "Is there any way I can put this back, and tell the audience [the story] in a different way?" Just imagine if they said to you, "Well, you only have five minutes for this interview." Then you have to make choices, right?

NOTES

1. The Republic of China (1912–1949) is the period after the Qing Dynasty collapsed and before Mao established Communist China.

2. The button is a token of love between Ip Man and Gong Er. Ip Man keeps the button from the winter jacket to show her that he had intended to visit Gong in the Northeast but the Japanese invaded southern China, so the trip was not made. When Gong Er passed away, she returned the button to Ip Man.

3. The school of kung fu that Ip Man practiced.

4. Lau Kar-leung (1934–2013) was a choreographer and film director of many kung fu and *wuxia* films such as *36th Chamber of Shaolin* (1978) and *Drunken Master II* (1994).

5. *Once Upon a Time in America* (1984) is a drama film directed by Sergio Leone and scored by Ennio Morricone.

Wong Kar-wai: *The Grandmaster* Should Have Been a Trilogy

An Ying / 2015

From *The Beijing News* (China). January 9, 2015. Interview conducted in Mandarin. Translated by Micky Lee from Chinese.

The Grandmaster in 2D that was released earlier has the best box office figure among all Wong Kar-wai's films. In addition, its unique artistic achievement helped Wong's career reach a new peak. This time the re-edited, re-released 3D version[1] undeniably created a suspicion of recycling old materials or grabbing money. But the re-edited and renewed contents and format gave fans something to look forward to. Wong says: "To me, I hope more people will see this film. This film is about an era that has been forgotten by us. If more people revisit that era, I believe it will be very beneficial."

An Ying: There has been a rumor that there is a four-hour version of *The Grandmaster*. Later you said there is no such thing. So among all the versions,[2] is the 3D one the version that you are the happiest with?
Wong Kar-wai: I have always said those of us who make films have an idea, but it cannot be expressed in one single film. Sometimes you have enough materials, but you cannot simply divide one film into two. [*The Grandmaster*] should not be like this. Everyone says there is a four-hour version, but in fact there is not. To me, the 3D version is the ultimate version of *The Grandmaster*. I think many things in this version are very good, but they are not included in the 2D version. This time I let [the 3D version] greet everyone, and this is also the last time [that a version of *The Grandmaster* will be released].

AY: In addition to the tighter narration in the 3D version, the most important additions are the two extra segments of footage at the end. Can we say these two clips are the biggest surprises that you bring to the audience?[3]

WKW: Actually, no. After you watch the 3D version, you will have a clearer idea [of the story] when you re-watch the 2D version. The 2D version talks about a certain era, the Republican China. We can see the martial arts novels of Pingjiang Buxiaosheng or Gong Baiyu[4] because the narratives of the novels were linear. But in the 3D version we follow the path of one person, the path of the grandmaster. There are three stages of his path: facing himself, facing the world of kung fu masters, and facing the era by keeping the legacy of kung fu.[5] In this story only one person has completed all the stages; that person is Ip Man. Therefore, we follow the path of Ip Man's life: people he met, things he encountered, and eventually how he achieved the path of being a grandmaster.

About the footage, we all want to know something that many people don't. The narration of the 3D version has no space to accommodate the two clips. The unknown is very attractive for the audience and I would like to share the footage with them.

AY: Can we say the two clips are best not to be included in the narration because they contradict the story?

WKW: You can say that's the case.

AY: At the end of the 3D version, there was a clip that re-enacts the "64 Hands" kung fu move [of the Gong School].[6] This implies a slight change in the relationship between Ip Man and Gong Er. Some audience members feel their relationship has moved forward; others feel it is not as despairing as before, [and therefore less good]. What do you think?

WKW: This is like what Zhao Benshan [who plays the Ding Lianshan character, a senior classmate of Master Gong] said in the 2D version [in the snake stew scene], "It is hard to please everyone. It is very difficult to anticipate what everyone thinks." In the clip where the "64 Hands" move was enacted, it is to fullfil Ip Man's wish. He said he wishes that one day he could see the "64 Hands" of the Gong School. Earlier he also said he dreamed of walking in the snow a few times. You understand that in reality he has never been to Northeast China [where Gong Er came from]. but in his heart he has visited the place many, many times.

AY: In the footage Zhao Benshan has a dialogue that says, "Life and death, success and failure, right and wrong, glory and humiliation." Are these four pairs of opposites something that you most want to express in this 3D version in order to talk about life value and philosophy?

WKW: In fact that dialogue is very important to me. Because in the film, Master Gong and Ding Lianshan represent the older generation of masters. In this duo, one is the *mianzi*—the public face, the winner, the main character. The other is the *lizi*—the loser, the supporting character. A lot of times, whether in the kung fu world or in reality, many people start at the same point. At the end, some become the winners; many, though, become the losers. The vicissitude in life is clearly reflected in this dialogue. Also, the most important thing for those who are losers is that they have to finally find out who they are and reconcile themselves.

AY: After the release of the 2D version, Chang Ta-chun[7] wrote a blog entry entitled, "The life, death, and exile of Ding Lianshan."[8] He talked about Ding's assassination of a Japanese militant [Bo Wugui] in occupied northern China as well as the unknown stories between China and Japan, the (Northern) *Beiyang* government and the (Southern) Nationalist government.[9] Have you read that essay?
WKW: Of course, we two edited it together.

AY: Part of a Chang's story adapted some historical facts about Ding Lianshan. Is this a clue of the whole story?
WKW: Why did Chang Ta-chun include this fable [of Ding killing a Japanese militant] in his book? All history is actually contemporary history. Very often when we read about history, we feel the facts are true. In truth, they are probably something that we made up and interpreted. Chang put this fable in the unofficial story about Ding Lianshan. Many people believe Ding Lianshan and some loser characters existed in history, but that is only a tale we made up for the film. First we had the concepts of *mianzi* and *lizi*; afterwards we designed the characters to fit those concepts.

AY: Like, that was only a background—you shot many scenes of those materials, but they did not deal with the face and the inner self?
WKW: But it would make a good film. It is a great idea to make a film about the story of the face and the inner self.

AY: This sounds like a grand historical epic.
WKW: I think if *The Grandmaster* was really talking about the world of kung fu during the Republican era, it would not be one film. It ought to be three. The first one is about Gong Er and Ip Man; the second one is about the face and the true self; and the last one is about how Razor (played by Chang Chen) was exiled to Taiwan.[10]

AY: Is the story about Razor's exile to Taiwan just an idea?
WKW: I have a concrete story. Why did I choose *Baji Quan*?[11] *Baji Quan* has a legendary background. All the bodyguards of Chinese leaders in the past century were trained in *Baji Quan*: [the last Emperor of Qing Dynasty] Pu Yi's bodyguard,

Chiang Kai-shek's, and Chairman Mao's was said to be. The prototype of Razor is based on Liu Yunqiao, the master of Taiwanese *Baji Quan*.

AY: Will you make a film about this?
WKW: If the opportunity arises.

AY: After the release of *The Grandmaster*, many fans online talked about their close readings of it. You have once said in the scene that took place in the tea house,[12] Tony Leung Chiu-wai's character [Ip Man] is like Chow Mo-wan [in *In the Mood for Love* and *2046*]. You wish Ip Man and Chow Mo-wan could have met. There are even some fans online who suggested because you used "Deborah's Song" from *Once Upon a Time in America*, *The Grandmaster* is like "Once Upon a Time in the Republican China." Do you read the online fans' close readings and find joy from their discussion every time after your film is released?
WKW: I believe that no matter what one does, someone will try to find clues throughout the entire process: from the time you conceptualize the film to the final product. This is actually a very happy thing. This is interaction in another dimension; you can say this is a friend in the know. I have always said *The Grandmaster* is not called *The Story of Ip Man* or *The Story of Gong Er* because it is about a past event in the Republican China. It is about a past event in the world of kung fu. That's why I used "Deborah's Song."

Many people's impression of Tony Leung comes from Chow Mo-wan in *In the Mood for Love*. The audience is very familiar with his character. I suddenly realized Chow Mo-wan is a character who lived in the '60s of the last century. The grandmaster Ip Man also lived in the '60s. If the two characters met at a tea house, it would be quite intriguing. Certainly, I did not do this in the film, but I did have a scene in which Tony Leung [as Ip Man] wore a western-style suit. Historically, that was true. Ip Man only wore a western-style suit once, and that was when he took his passport photo. His apprentices told him, "When in Rome, do what the Romans do; do wear a western-style suit to apply for an identity card." He wore that once, and he never wore it again. He felt that is not something he likes.

AY: During the film promotion in Guangzhou, Li Yuchun was invited to re-interpret a song of Tony Leung. The audience wonder how Wong Kar-wai and Li Yuchun are connected.
WKW: Just because of *The Grandmaster*. The biggest motivation of editing the 3D version is I could not forget about the film. I kept on thinking about it. I tried to express this motivation so I thought of Tony Leung's song "It Is so Hard to Forget You." At that time I wondered who would sing it well. When I was contemplating it, I saw the serious attitude of Li Yuchun when she makes music. Her aura, her

pursuit for the ideal is very much like Tony Leung, or perhaps like a grandmaster. Another point is that I never thought she would say yes when we talked to her about this arrangement. She was willing to do it, she said, "I like *The Grandmaster* very much." I never thought Li Yuchun would like *The Grandmaster*, but she told me she really likes *The Grandmaster* very much. That's why she was willing to do it, hoping to promote *The Grandmaster* for us. Here I thank her a lot.

NOTES

1. The 3D version was only officially released in mainland China and Taiwan in 2015. It was in the theater two years after the 2D version. In 2016, the 3D version was shown at the 40th Hong Kong International Film Festival as part of "In the Mood for Films—25th Anniversary of Jet Tone films."

2. The four versions are the North American (108 min.), the Cannes/European (123 min.), the domestic (130 min.), and the 3D (111 min.). The differences among them are described in http://ent.ifeng.com/movie/dayinmuhou/special/dymh012/.3. The footage contains Gong Er showing Ip Man the "64 Hands" of the Gong School, and Ding Lianshan talking about "life and death, success and failure, right and wrong, glory and humiliation."

3. Pingjiang Bixiao Sheng (1889–1957) and Gong Baiyu (1899–1966) were martial arts writers.

4. This is one of Gong Er's lines of Gong Er; she quoted from her father, Master Gong. The English subtitle in *The Grandmaster* states that the three stages of mastery are being, knowing, and doing. Gong Er says to Ip Man, "I know myself. I've seen the world. Sadly, I can't pass on what I know. This is a road I won't see to the end. I hope you will."

5. The move "64 Hands" is the signature move of the Gong School. In the 2D version, Gong Er vowed to the Buddha that she would not have an apprentice, would not marry, and would not have children if she was allowed to avenge her father.

6. Chang Ta-chun (1957–) is a well-known Taiwanese writer and critic. He is also the script consultant for *The Grandmaster*.

7. Chang's blog can be found at: http://blog.sina.com.cn/s/blog_6b736b5b0102e272.html.

8. The Republican China was a politically chaotic time in modern Chinese history. It started in 1912 and ended in 1949 when the People's Republic of China was established. During the Republican era, the country was ruled by different local warlords and governments as well as foreign powers. The Japanese military government was resisted by the Nationalists (Chinese National Party, as known as Kuomintang).

9. The Razor character is fictional but is based on two *Baji Quan* masters. Many *Baji Quan* masters were assassins or military leaders who rebelled against the Japanese occupation. In *The Grandmaster*, an injured Razor was shown in a train after an

operation. Gong Er asked him to lean on her shoulder to disguise them as lovers. This fooled the Japanese army who overlooked Razor being the assassin.

11. *Baji Quan* can be literally translated as Eight Extremities Fist.

12. It is the scene where Ip Man last meets Gong Er in a tea house in Hong Kong. Gong Er returns the button to Ip Man and says, "I once cared about you."

Additional Resources

BOOKS

Alovisio, Slivio. *Wong Kar-wai*. Milano: Il Castoro, 2010.

Bettinson, Gary. *The Sensuous Cinema of Wong Kar-wai: Film Poetics and the Aesthetic of Disturbance*. Hong Kong: Hong Kong University Press, 2015.

Binh, N. T. *Wong Kar-wai*. Paris: Scope, 2008.

Botz-Bornstein, Thorsten. *Films and Dreams: Tarkovsky, Bergman, Sokurov, Kubrick, and Wong Kar-wai*. Lanham, MD: Lexington Books, 2008.

Brown, Andrew M. J. *Directing Hong Kong: The Political Cinema of John Woo and Wong Kar-wai*. London: Routledge, 2003.

Brunette, Peter. *Wong Kar-wai*. Urbana: University of Illinois Press, 2005.

Chow, Rey. *Sentimental Returns: On the Uses of the Everyday in the Recent Films of Zhang Yimou and Wong Kar-wai*. Hong Kong: Hong Kong University Press, 2006.

The Conference of Wong Kar-wai: Repetition, Differentiation, and Variations. [*2008 Wang Jiawei Dian Ying Yan Tao Hui Lun Wen Ji*]. Taipei: Department of Radio, Television and Film, Shih Hsin University.

Dissanayake, Wimal, and Dorothy Wong. *Wong Kar-wai's "Ashes of Time."* Hong Kong: Hong Kong University Press, 2003.

Doyle, Christopher. *Happy Together: Christopher Doyle Photographic Journal* [*Du Kefun Chung Guang Zha Xie She Ying Shou Ji*]. Hong Kong: City Entertainment, 1997.

Ferrari, Jean-Christophe, Adrien Gombeaud, Franck Kausch, and Frédérique Toudoire-Surlapierre. *In the Mood for Love*. Paris: Éditions de la Transparence, 2005.

Gliatta, Leonardo. *Wong Kar-wai*. Rome: D. Audino, 2004.

Jiang, Xin. *All the Films by Wong Kar Wai*. [*Chun Guang Ying Hua Wang Jiawei*]. Beijing: CCTV, 2004.

Jousse, Thierry. *Wong Kar-wai*. Paris: Cahiers du cinéma, 2006.

Khoo, Olivia. *Love in Ruins: Spectral Bodies in Wong Kar-wai's "In the Mood for Love."* Honolulu: University of Hawaii Press, 2007.

Lalanne, Jean-Marc, David Martinez, Ackbar Abbas, and Jimmy Ngai. eds. *Wong Kar-wai*. Paris: Dis Voir, 1997.

Liu, Yonghao. *Wong Kar-wai: The Imbalance Filmic Texts*. [*Shi Heng De Dian Ying Wen Ben: Wang Jiawei Dian Ying Fen Xi*]. Taipei: Garden City, 2015.

Ma, Jean. *Melancholy Drift: Marking Time in Chinese Cinema.* Hong Kong: Hong Kong University Press, 2010.

Mauer, Roman, Thomas Koebner, and Fabienne Liptay. *Wong Kar-wai: Film Poet in Hong Kong Cinema.* [*Filmpoet im Hongkong-kino*]. München: Edition Text + Kritik, 2008.

Nai, Kang. *The Ambiguous Taste: The Cinematic World of Wong Kar-wai.* [*Ai Mei De Pin Wei: Wang Jiawei De Dian Ting Shi Jie*]. Beijing: Gold Wall Press, 2008.

Ngai, Jimmy. *Four Films of Wong Kar-wai, Los Angeles.* [*Si Chu Wang Jiawei, Luoshanji*]. Hong Kong: Chen Mi Ji Cultural Affairs, 1995.

Nochimson, Martha, P. *A Companion to Wong Kar-wai.* New York: Wiley-Blackwell, 2016.

Poon, Lawrence, and Zhaoxing Li. *The Cinematic World of Wong Kar-wai.* [*Wang Jiawei De Ying Hua Shi Jie*]. Hong Kong: Joint Publishing, 2004.

Redmond, Sean. *Studying "Chungking Express."* Leighton Buzzard, UK: Auteur, 2008.

Robinson, Luke. *Wong Kar-wai's Sensuous Histories.* London: Routledge, 2006.

Schnelle, Josef. *Signs and Wonder: The Cinema of Zhang Yimou and Wong Kar-wai.* [*Zeichen und Wunder: Das Kino von Zhang Yimou and Wong Kar-wai.*] Marbug, Germany: Schüren, 2008.

Su, Mi. *The Blooming Era's Wong Kar-wai* [*Hua Yang Nian Hua Wang Jiawei*]. Beijing: Chinese Literature Publishing, 2001.

Tambling, Jeremy. *Wong Kar-wai's "Happy Together."* Hong Kong: Hong Kong University Press, 2003.

Teo, Stephen. *Wong Kar-wai.* London: BFI, 2005.

Tête-bêche: A Wong Kar-wai Project. Hong Kong: Block 2 Pictures, 2000.

Wong, Ain-ling, Lawrence Poon, and Zhaoxing Li. *The Cinema of Wong Kar-wai* (2nd ed.). [*Wang Jiawei De Ying Hua Shi Jie*]. Hong Kong: Joint Publishing, 2015.

Wong, Kar-wai, and Jet Tone. *"The Grandmaster": A Wong Kar-wai Film.* Taipei: Thinkingdom, 2013.

Wong, Kar Wai, and John Powers. *WKW: The Cinema of Wong Kar Wai.* New York: Rizzoli, 2016.

Wu Xuanhong. *Love Runs Amok: The Cinematic Map of Wong Kar-wai* [*Ai Qing Pa Pa Zou : Wang Jiawei De Dian Ying Di Tu*]. Taipei: National Taiwan University Press, 2006.

You, Qingyuan. *Two Chinas: The Republican China of Wong Kar-wai and Strong Country of Peter Chan.* [*Liang Ge Zhongguo : Wang Jiawei De Min Guo Yu Chen Kexin De Qiang Guo*]. Hong Kong: Shang Shu Ju, 2013.

Zhang, Lixian. ed. *Kar-wai's Jungle* [*Jiawei Sen Lin*]. Beijing: Modern Publishing, 2001.

JOURNAL ARTICLES, BOOK CHAPTERS, AND INTERVIEWS

Aoun, Steven. "2046." *Metro Magazine* 147 (2006): 205.

Arther, Paul. "Philosophy in the Bedroom: Wong Kar-wai's *2046.*" *Cinéaste* 30, no 4 (Fall 2005): 6–8.

Ashbrook, John. "Wong Kar-wai and Christopher Doyle: Available Light." In *Heroic Bloodshed,* edited by Martin Fitzgerald, 58–73. Harpenden, UK: Pocket Essentials, 2000.

Bear, Liza. "Wong Kar-wai." *BOMB* 75 (Spring 2001): 48–52.

Biancorosso, Giorgio. "Global Music/Local Cinema: Two Wong Kar-wai Pop Compilations." In *Hong Kong Culture: Word and Image*, edited by Kam Louie, 229–45. Hong Kong: Hong Kong University Press, 2010.

Blake, Nancy. "We Won't Be Like Them": Repetition Compulsion in Wong Kar-Wai's *In The Mood For Love. Communication Review* 6 no. 4 (2003): 341–56.

Boltin, Kylle. "In The Mood for Love." *Metro* 129/130 (2001): 152.

Botz-Bornstein, Thorsten. "Wong Kar-wai's Films and the Culture of the 'Kawaii.'" *SubStance*, 37, no. 2 (2008): 94–109.

Bruno, Giuliana. "Surface, Fabric, Weave: The Fashioned World of Wong Kar-wai." In *Fashion in Film*, edited by Adrienne Munich, 83–105. Bloomington: Indiana University Press, 2011.

Cameron, Allan. "Trajectories of Identification: Travel and Global Culture in the Films of Wong Kar-wai." *Jump Cut*, 47 (2007). Accessed at: http://www.ejumpcut.org/archive/jc49.2007/wongKarWai/.

Cheng, Sinkwan. "Comparative Philosophies of Tragedy: Buddhism, Lacan, and *Ashes of Time*." *Mln* 123, no. 5 (2008): 1163–87.

Choi, Heawon. "Oblivion beyond Forgetting: A Buddhist Reflection on Suffering in *Ashes of Time*." *Journal of Religion and Film* 14, no. 2 (October 2010). Accessed at: http://www.unomaha.edu/jrf/vol14.no2/ChoiAshes_Time.html.

Chow, Rey. "Nostalgia of the New Wave: Structure in Wong Kar-Wai's *Happy Together*." *Camera Obscura: A Journal of Feminism, Culture, and Media Studies* 42 (1999): 31–48.

———. "Sentimental Returns: On the Uses of the Everyday in the Recent Films of Zhang Yimou and Wong Kar-Wai." *New Literary History* 33 no. 4 (2002): 639–54. (Also in *Reading Chinese Transnationalisms: Society, Literature, Film*, edited by Maria Ng and Phillip Holden, 173–87. Hong Kong: Hong Kong University Press, 2006.)

Ciment, Michel. *Film World: Interviews with Cinema's Leading Directors*, trans. Julie Rose. (Chapter 13 "Wong Kar-wai") Oxford: Berg, 2009.

Crompton, Nils. "Towards a Postmodern Avant-Garde: The Temporality of the Refrain in Three Films of Wong Kar-Wai." *Metro Magazine: Media & Education Magazine* 142 (2005): 52.

Deppman, Hsiu-Chuang. *Adapted for the Screen: The Cultural Politics of Modern Chinese Fiction and Film*. Honolulu: University of Hawaii Press, 2010. (Chapter 4 "Liu Yichang and Wong Kar-wai: The Class Trap in *In the Mood for Love*").

Dumas, Raechel. "A Look at Hong Kong's New Wave Sentimentality: Rey Chow's Reconceptualization of Nostalgia and the Allegorical Implications of the Image in Wong Kar-Wai's *In The Mood For Love. International Journal of the Humanities* 5, no. 4 (2007): 135–39.

Geuens, Jean-Pierre. "The Space of Production." *Quarterly Review of Film and Video* 24, no. 5 (2007): 411–20.

Greenhalgh, Cathy. "How Cinematography Creates Meaning in *Happy Together*." In *Style and Meaning: Studies in the Detailed Analysis of Film*, edited by John Gibbs and Douglas Pye, 195–213. Manchester, UK: Manchester University Press, 2005.

Huang, Tsung-yi Michelle. "Hong Kong Blue: Flâneurie with the Camera's Eye in a Phantasmagoric Global City." *Journal of Narrative Theory* 30, no. 3 (2000): 385–402.

Hughes-d'Aeth, Tony. "Psychoanalysis and the Scene of Love: *Lars and the Real Girl, In the Mood for Love*, and *Mulholland Drive*." *Film & History: An Interdisciplinary Journal of Film and Television Studies* 43, no. 2 (Fall 2013): 17–33.

Kraicer, Shelly. "Tracking the Elusive Wong Kar-wai." *Cinéaste* 30, no. 4 (Fall 2005): 14–15.

Law, Jo. "Wong Kar-Wai's Cinema." *Metro* 126 (2001): 92.

———. "Years in Bloom." *Metro* 133 (2002): 198.

Lee, Vivian P. Y. *Hong Kong Cinema since 1997: The Post-nostalgic Imagination.* New York: Palgrave Macmillan, 2009. (Chapter 1 "Post-nostalgia: *In the Mood for Love* and *2046*").

Leung, Helen Hok-sze. "Queerscapes in Contemporary Hong Kong Cinema." *Positions* 9, no. 2 (2001): 423–47.

Lim, Dennis. "Wong Kar-wai, Kung Fu Auteur." *New York Times* (February 16, 2014). Accessed at http://artsbeat.blogs.nytimes.com/2013/02/16/berlin-film-festival-wong-kar-wai-kung -fu-auteur/?module=Search&mabReward=relbias%3Ar.

Mazierska, Ewa, and Laura Rascaroli. "Trapped in the Present: Time in the Films of Wong Kar-Wai." *Film Criticism* 25, no. 2 (2000): 2–20.

Morrison, Susan. "John Woo, Wong Kar-wai, and Me: An Ethnographic Meditation." *Cineaction* 36 (1996).

Ng, Konrad, Gar-Yeu. "Hong Kong Cinema and Chineseness: The Palimpsestic Male Bodies of Wong Kar-wai." In *Mysterious Skin: Male Bodies in Contemporary Cinema*, edited by Santiago Fouz-Hernández, 43–58. London: I.B. Tauris, 2009.

Nochimson, Martha. "Beautiful Resistance: The Early Films of Wong Kar-wai." *Cinéaste* 30, no. 4 (2005): 9–13.

———. *World on Film: An Introduction.* Malden, MA: Wiley-Blackwell, 2010. (Chapter 9 "Hong Kong: Wong Kar-wai, Now You See It")

Ong, Han. "Wong Kar-wai." *BOMB* 62 (Winter 1998): 48–54.

Pang, Yi-ping. "*Happy Together*: Let's Be Happy Together." *City Entertainment* 473 (May 29, 1997): 41–44.

Perks, Sarah. "My Noir: Ambiguity, Ambivalence, and Alienation in 1990s International Noir." *Film International* 11, no. 5 (2013): 47–51.

Phathanavirangoon, Raymond. "Interview at *Ashes of Time Redux*." Toronto International Film Festival, Ryerson Theatre (September 8, 2008).

Rayns, Tony. "Poet of Time." *Sight and Sound*, 5, no. 9 (September 1995): 12–16.

———. "In the Mood for Love." *Sight and Sound*, 10, no. 8 (August, 2000): 14–17.

Reynaud, Berenice. "Entretien avec Wong Kar-wai." *Cahiers du cinéma* 490 (April 1995): 37–39.

Rohter, Larry. "Wong Kar-wai on *The Grandmaster*." *New York Times* (July 10, 2014). Accessed at http://carpetbagger.blogs.nytimes.com/2014/01/10/wong-kar-wai-on-the-grandmaster/?_ php=true&_type=blogs&module=Search&mabReward=relbias%3Ar&_r=0.

Tsui, Clarence. "Berlin 2013: Wong Kar-wai on *The Grandmaster*." *Hollywood Reporter* (February 6, 2013). Accessed at http://www.hollywoodreporter.com/news/berlin-2013-wong-kar -wai-418839.

Tsui, Curtis K. "Subjective Culture and History: The Ethnographic Cinema of Wong Kar-wai." *Asian Cinema* 7, no.2 (1995): 93–124.

Udden, James. "The Stubborn Persistence of the Local in Wong Kar-Wai." *Post Script: Essays in Film and the Humanities* 25, no. 2 (2006): 67–88.

Wilson, Flannery. "Viewing Sinophone Cinema through a French Theoretical Lens: Wong Kar-wai's *In the Mood for Love* and *2046* and Deleuze's *Cinema*." *Modern Chinese Literature and Culture* 21, no. 1 (Spring 2009): 141–73.

Yeh, Emilie Yueh-yu, and Lake Wang Hu. "Transcultural Sounds: Music, Identity, and the Cinema of Wong Kar-wai." *Asian Cinema* 19, no.1 (2008): 32–46.

VIDEOS

Kwan, Pun-leung, and Amos Lee. *From Buenos Aires Zero Degree*, Hong Kong: Jet Tone and Block 2, 1999.

The Road to the Grandmaster. [*Zong Shi Zhi Lu*]. Hong Kong: Jet Tone, 2012. Accessed at https://www.youtube.com/watch?v=Tl17_Ku7CUM.

Wong Kar-wai vs. Kevin Tsai. Eros DVD, Taipei: Jet Tone, 2005.

Index

Abe, Kobo, xvi; *The Woman in the Dunes*, 49

Acting, xv, 12–14, 38, 65, 118–19, 129–30, 154; improvisations, xi, 6, 56, 76, 81

Action scenes, xiii, 5, 40, 65, 131, 159, 163. *See also* Fight scenes

Allen, Woody, 134

Always Good Film, 3, 8, 94

Ambiguity, xv, 23, 65, 89

Antonioni, Michelangelo, xv–xvi, xixn3, 38, 92; *The Eclipse*, xvi

Architecture: Angkor Wat, xiv, 88, 98; Buddhist, 143; Chinese, 44, 52; Greek, 52; Roman, 52

Argentina, xi, 76–80, 82–83, 90, 109, 113n1, 117

Art direction, viii, ix, 71, 94. *See also* Chang, William Suk-ping

Art film (art house film), ix, xv, 12, 33, 74, 100, 124, 161n3. *See also* Commercial movies; Independent film productions

As Tears Go By, vii, x, xiii, xvi–xvii, xixn1, 3–7, 9, 12–13, 19–20, 32–33, 39–40, 42, 46n4, 47, 53, 57–58, 60n1, 67, 137

Ashes of Time, x–xiii, xvi–xvii, xixn1, 21–26, 30, 32–34, 38–45, 47, 50, 52–57, 59, 64, 94, 115, 117, 129, 135–38

Ashes of Time Redux, xiii, 129, 134–35, 137, 140n1

Audience response, vii, xiii, 4, 6, 7n2,

29–30, 69, 71, 122; international, vii, xviii, xixn1, 31, 68, 129–30, 136, 161n2; local, vii, ix, 31, 35n11, 87, 123, 126

Auteurs, viii–ix, xii, 161n3

Avid (editing), xvi, 80

Balzac, Honoré de, *La Comédie Humaine*, xvi, 49

Bangkok, Thailand, 88–91, 93, 101

Beatles, The, 98

Beijing Olympics, 118

Bellini, Vincenzo, *Norma*, 108

Bertolucci, Bernardo, xv, 37

Betrayal, 43, 108

Block, Lawrence, xi, 128–30

Blue Kite, The, 30, 35n7

Body language, 13–14, 82, 90–91, 112

Book of Jin, 50

Borges, Jorge Luis, 50

Box office, 9, 54, 67, 166; domestic, vii; overseas, 40

Bresson, Robert, xv, 25, 37, 41, 45, 91–92

Buenos Aires. *See* Argentina

Buraiha (Decadent School), 49. *See also* Dazai, Osamu

Bush, George W., 121

California Dreaming, 59, 95–96

Cambodia. *See* Architecture: Angkor Wat

Camus, Albert, 27; *The Stranger*, 48

Canton: ethnic groups in, 40, 85, 92;

films from, 46n3, 47, 57, 60n4, 64; as
language, x, xiv, xviii, 14n1, 40, 45,
130
Carax, Leos, xvi, 29
Censorship, 29
Cha, Louis. *See* Jin Yong
Chan, Frankie, xvii, 94–95, 136
Chang, Cheh, 53, 55n7
Chang, Chen, 82, 123, 142
Chang, Ta-chun, 150n4, 168, 170n7
Chang, William Suk-ping, ix, xvii, 52, 64,
73, 82–83, 102, 126; as art director, ix,
xvii, 13, 43, 52, 71, 79, 83; as editor,
xiii, xvii, 5, 26, 77, 83
Chaplin, Charlie, 125
Characters: emotions of, 12, 25, 56, 65,
111; expressions of, 23, 41–42, 66,
102, 127; names of, 45, 52; one-
dimensional, 82; personalities, 4, 13,
18, 23–25; thoughts of, xii, 13
Cheung, Alex Kwok-ming, viii
Cheung, Jacky, 13, 43, 58
Cheung, Leslie, xi, 12–13, 23–24, 79, 81,
140–41
Cheung, Mabel, ix
Cheung, Maggie, ix, xviii, 13, 87, 89–90,
93, 129
Chinatown, xiii, 90, 136
Chinese history: Jin dynasty, 50; Liao
dynasty, 143; Qing dynasty, 144, 147,
168; Republican era, vii, xiii, 142–43,
162, 165n1; Song dynasty, 44; Tang
dynasty, 50
Choreography, 6, 42, 79, 147–48, 159, 163,
165n4. *See also* Fight scenes
Chow, Valerie, 58
Chungking Express, vii–viii, x–xi, xiii,
xivn1, 21, 23–28, 32–34, 39–40, 43–44,
47–52, 54, 56–59, 65, 69n4, 76, 94–95,
97, 104, 110, 113n1, 115, 117, 126–27,
134, 137–38

Chungking Mansion, 44, 57, 60n2, 69n4,
113n1, 126
Cinema City (production company), 8,
38, 46n2
Cinematography, 7, 40, 94, 107, 126;
close-ups, xv, 41, 79, 112; handheld
cameras, 39–40; lighting, xvii, 7, 24,
39–40, 73, 79, 89, 115, 126; single cam-
eras, 158; ultra-wide angle lens, 61–62
City dwellers, 56–59, 64–65, 115
Cole, Nat King, 90, 98, 111
Comic Con, 151, 161n1
Comics, 52, 82
Commercial movies, vii, ix, xv, 63–64, 68,
119, 124, 154, 156, 159
Communication, 32, 39, 67, 69, 70–73
Compensation, 43, 119
Coppola, Francis Ford, 135
Copyright, 5, 21
Countrysides, 47, 65
Crew members, xi, xviii, 6, 11, 19, 23, 82,
107, 119, 132, 143, 165
Criterion Collection, xiv, 137
Critics, viii, xvi, 21, 26–27, 33, 61–62, 66;
comments from, xi, xiv, 20, 155; Hong
Kong, vii, 30; international, vii–viii.
See also Film reviews
Cultural Revolution, xvi, 36, 54n1, 88,
114n9

Dancehall girls, xii, xixn3, 3, 14
Dark glasses, 28, 105, 115–16, 125
Days of Being Wild, vii, ix, x, xiii, xiv, xvii,
xixn1, 11–15, 16–20, 21, 23–24, 26, 28,
32–33, 35n11, 38–40, 43, 47–48, 52, 53,
56, 57–58, 64, 71, 80, 85–86, 96–97,
102, 110–11, 112, 115–16, 137; unproduced sequel to, xiii, 14, 15n4
Dazai, Osamu, xvi, 49–50; *No Longer
Human*, 49
De Gaulle, Charles, 88

De Niro, Robert, 39

De Sica, Vittorio, 64

Deconstructionism, 27

Delon, Alain, 37

Dire Straits, "Private Investigations," 136

Disappearances, xv, 57–58, 105, 108

Distance, 4, 62, 127; between characters, 27, 56, 61; between the director and the audience, 67; psychological, 57

Distribution, x, xiii, 18, 33–34, 62, 129, 136, 164

Dong Jie, 109, 117, 123

Doyle, Christopher, 24, 39–40, 62, 77, 81–82, 89, 126; working relationship with Wong, xvii–xviii, 73, 79, 83–84, 89

Dubbing, 5, 96, 117, 123–24, 127, 140n1

Editing. See Film editing

Eros. See Hand, The

Existentialism, 54

Fallen Angels, xiii, 56–60, 61–65, 76, 82, 136, 138

Fassbinder, Rainer Werner, 111

Father, Wong Kar-wai's, xvi–xvii, 36–37, 48–49, 59, 126

Fifth Generation (Chinese filmmakers), 45, 47, 54n1. See also specific filmmakers

Fight scenes, 6, 22, 28, 42, 53, 148, 158–59, 162–63

Film festivals, vii–viii, 30; Berlin, viii, xixn1, 82; Cannes, viii, xii–xiii, xixn1, 80–81, 92, 94, 97, 110, 129–31, 138–39, 155; Toronto, viii; Venice, xixn1, 30

Film versions, varying, xiii–xiv; 3D, xiii, xiv, 159–60, 166–67, 169, 170nn1–2; Chinatown, xiii, 136; Europe, xiii, 159, 170n2; Hong Kong, 170n2; Mainland China, xiii, 123–24, 159, 164; North

America, xiii, 91, 113n5, 159–60, 164, 169, 170n2; premiere, xiii, 25, 110, 129–30; Taiwanese, 7n3; VHS, 16–17

Films: budgets, vii, x, 9, 18, 34, 43, 58–59, 68–69, 70, 75, 119; business of, 9, 18–19, 47, 64, 67, 70, 139; editing, xii–xiv, 5, 26, 32–33, 38, 41, 53, 73, 80, 92–93, 110, 135, 139, 165, 169; education and training, ix, 12, 37, 64, 66, 68; independent productions, ix, xi, 62, 119, 154; markets, ix, xiii, 17, 30, 33, 47, 67, 159, 163, 165; political, viii, 29–30, 109; reviews, 21, 27–28, 33, 61, 67; titles, xv, 3, 7n1, 7n3, 11, 14n1, 15n3, 18, 55n3, 60n1, 76–77, 89, 100, 120, 129, 137, 169

Fin de siècle, 64

Flynn, Errol, 37

Fong, Allen Yuk-ping, viii

Footage, xii, xiv, 135, 164–65, 166–67, 170n2

Ford, John, The Searchers, 23, 51

Forrest Gump, 68

Frame rates, 6, 82

Frears, Stephen, 77

French New Wave, 64, 91

Fuji film, 143

Gable, Clark, 37

Galasso, Michael, 97, 111

Genres: action, 38; animation, 155; comedy, ix, 38, 41, 127; experimental, 31; film noir, 42, 53; gangster, ix, 4, 7, 136; kung fu and wuxia, vii, ix, 33, 35n2, 38, 54, 55n7, 65, 178n2, 142, 147, 152, 155–56, 161n2, 163–64, 165n4; melodrama, 67, 91, 92, 154; period, vii, 22–23, 41–42, 44, 53, 136; pornography, 38; road movie, 22–23, 40, 45, 53, 78, 116, 119, 129; sci-fi, 72, 100, 134, 136, 155

Godard, Jean-Luc, 25, 29, 37–38, 45, 135; *Little Soldier*, 83
Gold Finch restaurant, 115
Golden Harvest, 38, 46n2
Gong, Li, xixn3, 111, 113n3, 123, 128
Grandmaster, The, vii, x, xii–xv, xviii, 103, 136, 141–42, 143–48, 151–53, 155–60, 162–64, 165n2, 166–70
Graphic design, ix, 36, 66
Greene, Graham, 52
Gu, Long, 53, 55n6
Guangdong, 142–43. *See also* Canton
Guangxi, 142
Guangzhou, 59, 146, 169

Hai Pai. *See* Shanghai: style
Half a Lifetime Romance, 23, 35n3
Hand, The, xvi, xixn3
Hanrahan, Kip, 80
Happy endings, 43, 91, 122
Happy Together, viii, xi–xii, 76–79, 80–84, 86, 90, 104, 109, 113n1, 115–17, 126, 140
Hemingway, Ernest, xvi, 49
Hero for a Day (unproduced), 39
Hitchcock, Alfred, x, 32
Hollywood films, ix, xv, 31, 64, 68; 1950s, 53
Homosexuality, xi, 76–77, 86
Hong Kong, 89–90; 1930s, 17; 1960s, xiv, 11, 13, 14n1, 17, 40–41, 96, 98, 104–8, 112, 114n9; 1970s, 13, 14n1, 87; culture, xviii, 27, 29, 57; return to China, 29–30, 35n4, 76, 100–101, 109; studio system, viii, ix, 12, 38, 46n2, 68, 126, 128n2
Hong Kong Film Awards, xii, 46n7
Hong Kong Film Critics Society Awards, xii
Hong Kong New Wave, viii, xvi, xixn3, 46n3, 161n3
Hong Kong Polytechnic, 46n1

Hong Kong Stadium, 57
Hou, Hsiao-hsien, xvi, 30, 35nn7–8, 39, 46, 48, 89; *A City of Sadness*, xvi, 30, 35n7, 46; *Daughter of the Nile*, 30; *The Puppetmaster*, 30, 35n8
Hu, King, 42, 44
Hui, Ann, viii, ix, 46n3, 161n3
Hung, Sammo Kam-po, 42
Hung Huang, 124

Iguazu Falls, 79–80, 115
Immigration, 48, 88, 92, 162
In the Mood for Love, x, xii, xiv, xvi–xvii, 85–88, 93–94, 96–98, 100–102, 104–8, 111–12, 113n3, 115–16, 118, 128n1, 131, 161, 169
In the Mood for Love 2001, 131
Intellectuals, 105–6, 144. *See also specific writers*
Ip Man, xiii–xv, 142–45, 147–48, 150n3, 150n7, 153, 156, 162, 164, 165n2, 167–69, 170n2, 170n5, 171n12
Isolation, 54, 107, 113
Itami, Juzo, xvii, 7

Jiang Wen, 123
Jin Yong, xvi, 21–22, 44, 53, 117; *The Deer and the Cauldron*, 142, 149n2, 150n2; *The Heaven Sword and Dragon Saber*, 142, 149n2; *The Legend of Eagle-shooting Heroes* (*The Legend of Condor Heroes*), xvi, 21, 35n1, 41
Jones, Norah, xi, 116–19, 121–23, 129–31
Judge Dredd, 68

Kafka, Franz, 45
Kam Kwok-leung, 8
Kaneshiro, Takeshi, 58, 63
Kawabata, Yasunari, xvi, 49–50; *The House of the Sleeping Beauties*, 49; *Snow Country*, 49

Khondji, Darius, 132
Kidman, Nicole, 102, 126
Kieślowski, Krzysztof, xvi, 63, 111; *The Double Life of Veronique*, 28; *Three Colors: Blue, White, Red*, 28
Kimura, Takuya, 130
Kowloon, 17, 44, 60nn1–2, 69n4, 77
Kung fu. *See* Genres: kung fu and *wuxia*; Martial arts
Kurosawa, Akira, xv, 37, 89, 148
Kwan, Stanley, ix, 5, 161n3

Lady from Shanghai (unproduced), 102, 103n2, 130, 133n1
Lai, Leon, 58, 63
Lan Kwai Fong, 57, 60n2, 104, 113n1
Language barriers, xiv, 40, 48, 73–74, 130
Lao She, 51
Lau, Andy, 12–14, 28
Lau, Carina, 12–13, 14, 93, 111
Lau, Jeff Chun-wai, ix, 52
Lau, Kar-leung, 164, 165n4
Lau, Andrew Wai-keung, 39, 46nn4–5
Law, Clara, 9
Law, Jude, 118–19, 123, 127
Lee, Ang, 126, 142; *Crouching Tiger, Hidden Dragon*, 100, 102; *Lust, Caution*, 122
Lee, Bruce, xiii, 136
Lee, Mark Ping-bing, 89
Leone, Sergio, *Once Upon a Time in America*, 164, 165n5
Leung, Tony Chiu-wai, xi, xviii, 14, 45, 81, 90, 100, 115, 119, 122, 131, 142, 149n2, 163, 169–70
Leung, Tony Kar-fai, xviii, 43–44
Li Yuchun, 169–70
Liaoning Street night market, 104, 113n1
Lin, Brigitte, ix, 23, 28
Literature, xiv; classical Chinese, xvi, 41, 49–50; English, xvi, 36; French, xvi, 36, 49; Hong Kong, xvi, 53, 105–6;

Japanese, xvi, 27–28, 49–50, 52; Latin American, xvi, 50, 76–77; Modern Chinese, xvi, 36, 51–52; North American, xvi, 49, 131; Russian, 36, 45, 49. *See also* specific writers and titles
Liu Na'ou, 51
Liu Yichang, xvi, 91, 105; *The Alcoholic*, xvi, 105–6, 113n5; *Intersection (tête-bêche)*, xvi, 104–6, 113n4
Lizi. *See Mianzi* and *lizi*
Los Angeles, California, 118, 121, 135, 138, 140
Love relationships, 3, 5, 11–12, 17, 23, 25, 56–59, 63–65, 76–78, 81, 86–87, 97, 98, 100–102, 109–10, 116, 121–22, 167
Lu, Xun, xvi; *Dawn Blossoms Plucked at Dusk*, 51
Lucas, George, 134–35; *Star Wars*, 134, 140, 154
Lynch, David, 27; *Twin Peaks*, 52

Madama Butterfly (opera), 108
Man, Alex, 5
Mandarin films, 45, 48, 86
Márquez, Gabriel García, xvi, 52; *Chronicle of a Death Foretold*, xvi, 42, 50; *One Hundred Years of Solitude*, 50
Martial arts, xv, 142–49, 156, 163; *Bagua Palm*, 145–48; *Baji Quan* (Baji Fist), 168–69, 170n10, 171n11; as sport, xv, 149, 156–57; Tai Chi, 148, 157; Wing Chun, 142, 145, 148, 163. *See also* Genres: kung fu and *wuxia*
Matsuda, Yusaku, 97
McCarey, Leo, *Elle et Lui*, 91
Media, 47, 54; Greater Chinese, x; Hong Kong, vii, x, 34, 66, 70
Mei Ah (distributor), 135
Memory, xv, 17, 100–101, 110, 116
Memphis, Tennessee, 118, 121, 123, 131–32

Mianzi and *lizi*, 141, 143–44, 149n1, 167–68

Mise en scène, 91

Mishima, Yukio, 49

Mok, Karen, 63

Mong Kok, 3, 7n1, 57, 60n1

Mong Kok Carmen. See *As Tears Go By*; Film titles

Mood, 24, 86, 92, 104, 111–12, 116

Morita, Yoshimitsu, *And Then*, 97

Morricone, Ennio, 59, 164, 165n5

Mother, Wong Kar-wai's, xiv–xv, 36–37, 40, 48, 98

Mu Shiying, xvi, 51–52; *Major Kuga*, 51; *A Platinum Statue of the Female Body*, 51

Murakami, Haruki, 27–28, 49–50; *Pinball, 1973*, 50

Music, xvi–xvii, 5, 41, 53, 59, 76, 80, 83, 87, 90–91, 94–98, 108–13; Latin American, 80, 84, 90; original film scores, 90, 95, 97, 111; popular music, 5, 59, 95–97, 111, 113; ready-made, 90, 95, 111; rondo, 97; rumba, 112; tango, 76, 79–80, 84, 111–12, 115; waltz, 90, 97, 111. *See also* Opera

Music composers, 90, 94–95, 97, 108, 111, 136. *See also specific musicians*

Muzha Line, Taipei, 104, 113n1

My Blueberry Nights, xi–xii, 115–28, 129–33, 136

Mysterious Box of Lunar Palace, The, 48. See also *Thief of Bagdad, The*

Neosensualism: Shanghai, 51–52; Japanese, 49, 52. *See also specific writers and titles*

Nevada, 118, 132

New York City, 116, 118–19, 121, 126, 128, 130–32

Nostalgia, 27, 137, 145

Numbers, 27, 45, 56, 100–101, 108–9

Opera, 112; Cantonese, 96; Italian, 7n1, 101, 108; Peking, 42, 96; Pingju, 96. *See also specific titles*

Ozu, Yasujirō, xv, 37, 89

Pan, Rebecca, 92, 96–97

Paradis Film, 93

Philippines, 11, 17, 53, 90, 98

Photography, 36–37, 79

Piazzolla, Astor, 79–80, 84, 136

Portman, Natalie, 119, 124

Postmodernism, 27, 53–54, 64

Preservation, 52, 135, 137, 143; of history, xv, 57–58, 102

Presley, Elvis, 98

Pressure, 9, 14, 34, 68, 86; from self-expectations, 19

Production process: deadlines, 5, 92; length, vii, xii, 9, 11, 18, 40, 70, 92, 101, 120, 124, 134, 142–43, 158; pre-production, xii, xvii, 9, 43, 77–78, 85, 120, 124, 126, 130, 142–43; produc-tion, xi–xii, 9, 78, 85, 93, 101, 133, 142; postproduction, xi–xii, xvii, 5, 9, 24, 26, 40, 108, 134, 159

Puig, Manuel, xvi; *Betrayed by Rita Hay-worth*, 52; *The Buenos Aires Affair*, 76; *Heartbreak Tango*, xvi, 50, 52; *Kiss of the Spider Woman*, xvi, 42, 50, 52

Qipao (Chinese dress), 104, 113n3, 115

Queen's Café, 58

Radio, 17, 25, 52, 80, 96; BBC, 40; drama, 52–53

Radio Television Hong Kong (RTHK), viii

Ray, Satyajit, 25

Rebel Without a Cause, 11, 15n3. See also *Days of Being Wild*; Film titles

Reis, Michele, 63–64

Rejection, characters' fear of, 23–24, 43, 48

Resistance against Japan (Second Sino-Japanese War), 144, 146, 165n2, 170n9

Revenge, 22, 50, 141–43, 145, 149, 156, 170n6

Rhythm, xii, 41, 77, 80, 83, 91, 96–97, 110–12, 119, 129

Rohmer, Éric, xv, 38

Romance of the Three Kingdoms, 41, 49, 55n4

Rooftops, 107–9

Rumors, xiii, 11–12, 34, 126, 146, 166. *See also* Media

Russian Revolution, 92

Sawada, Kenji, 97

Schedules: actors, 9, 18, 62, 101, 119, 121; screening, 5, 9, 19, 40

Scoring. *See* Music: original film scores

Scorsese, Martin, xvi; *The Age of Innocence*, 29; *Mean Streets*, 7, 39

Screenplays, viii, xi–xii, 8–9, 12, 18, 37, 40–42, 45, 59, 62, 78, 80, 89, 103, 106, 120, 128, 131–33, 142, 150n4, 152, 170n7

Scriptwriter, Wong Kar-wai as, ix, 4, 8–9, 37–39, 115

Second Wave of Hong Kong Cinema, viii, ix–x. *See also* Hong Kong New Wave

Seventh Voyage of Sinbad, 48

Sexiness, 115

Shanghai, x, xiv, xvi, xlxn3, 17, 35n3, 36, 40, 48, 59, 89, 92, 96, 101, 103, 105, 107, 113n3; style (Hai Pai), 51–52

Shanghainese: as ethnic group, xv; as language, x, 40; in Hong Kong, xiv–xv, 85–87, 92

Shaw Brothers studio, 102, 126, 128n2, 152, 154, 163–64

Shi Jianqiao, 141–42

Shi Zhecun: *The General's Head*, 51; *Spring Sun*, 51; *The Taxi Dancer in the Dusk*, xvi, xixn3, 51

Shooting film: in China, 22–23, 40, 43, 52, 143; on location, ix, 6, 9, 52, 69n4, 72, 90–91, 119, 159; at night, 6, 57, 127; in a small space, xv–xvi, 61–63, 92, 107

Singapore, 90, 101

Social class, 4, 22, 38, 51, 60n2, 72, 144

Space, 17, 23–24, 49, 56, 61, 87, 91–92, 98, 104–9, 130; as a character, xvi, 24, 107

Special effects, 35n2, 68, 70–71, 163

Spielberg, Steven, 54

Steenbeck, 80, 84n1

Steinbeck, John, xvi, 49

Story about Food, A (unproduced), 87–88

Storytelling, ix, 69, 130; characters, xi, xiv, xvi, 4, 16, 21–22, 26, 41, 103, 112, 117, 129–31, 143, 164; cue, 27–28, 37, 62, 164; dialogue, xvi, 13, 25, 37, 41, 44, 53, 56, 63, 66, 90, 106, 112, 116–17, 123, 127–28, 146, 150n5, 163, 167–68; ending, xiii–xiv, 5–6, 7n3, 22–24, 32, 43, 48, 64, 88–91, 97, 112, 117, 122, 145; flashback, 42; fragments, xii, 26, 42–43, 56; interior monologue and voice-over, xvi, 25, 42–43, 52–53, 66, 90, 128–30, 147; narrative, xvi, 26–27, 42, 56, 78–80, 116, 167; nonlinear, xvi, 59; plot, xi, 4, 9, 38, 40, 59–63, 108, 111–12; story outline, xi, 3, 18, 59, 77–78, 87–88; structure, xii–xiii, 16, 26–27, 37, 40, 42, 52, 93, 101, 116, 135, 164; tempo, 37, 41, 52, 90 91

Strathairn, David, 119

Summer in Beijing (unproduced), 71, 75n1

Suzuki, Seijun, *Yumeji*, 90, 97, 111

Taipei, 30, 104, 113n1, 123

Taiwan New Wave (Taiwan New

Cinema), 45, 46n8. *See also specific filmmakers*

Tam, Patrick Ka-ming, viii–x, xv, 7–8, 26, 33–34, 46n3; *Final Victory*, ix, 3–5, 33, 38–39

Tang, Alan Kwong-wing, 8, 38

Tarkovsky, Andrei, *Nostalgia*, xvi, 30

Television Broadcasts Limited (TVB), viii, ix, 12, 37, 66, 69n3, 149n2

Television commercials, 70–75

Temples, 52, 88, 141, 143

Texas, 132

Thief of Bagdad, The, 55n3

Torrijos, Omar, 52

Tosca (opera), 108

Tree hole, 112, 127

Trilogies, xiv, 39, 112, 166, 168

Truffaut, François, 91; *Le Peau Douce*, 111

Tsim Sha Tsui, 57, 60n2, 67, 69n4, 104, 113n1, 126

Tsui Hark, viii–x, 4, 42–43, 46n3, 53, 161n3, 164

2046, xiv–xvii, 85, 88, 90, 93, 94, 100–102, 104–13, 115–18, 122, 127, 129–30, 136, 138–39, 153, 157, 169

Umebayashi, Shigeru, 97, 111–12

University of Hong Kong, 27

Van Sant, Gus, xvi; *My Own Private Idaho*, 29

Wan Chai, xv, 57, 60n3

Wang Fuling, 94

Water Margin, 49, 55n4

Wayne, John, 37

Weisz, Rachel, 119

Wong, Barry Ping-yiu, xviii, 37–38

Wong, Faye, xi, xiii, 58, 70, 72–74, 93, 112

Wong Jing, 68–69, 69n5

Working relationships, with actors, xi–xii, 12–14, 18, 74, 81–82, 102, 118–19

Wuxia. See Genres: kung fu and *wuxia*

Xu Jinglei, 124

Yang, Edward, 39, 46n8; *A Brighter Summer Day*, 82; *Mahjong*, 82

Yim Ho, viii–ix

Yokomitsu, Riichi, xvi, 49–50, 52; *Head and Belly*, 49

Young, Charlie, 46, 60, 63

Yuen Woo-ping, 147–48, 163

Zhang, Max Jin, 145, 163

Zhang Yimou, xvi, 30–31, 35, 54n1; *Hero*, 142; *Ju Dou*, 30; *The Road Home*, 102; *To Live*, 30, 35n7

Zhang Yuan, xvi; *Beijing Bastards*, 31, 35n9

Zhang Ziyi, xii, 102, 112, 142

Zhao Wei, 124

Zhou Xuan, 96

Zhou Zuoren, xvi, 51

Zizhi Tongjian, 50, 55n5

CPSIA information can be obtained
at www.ICGtesting.com
Printed in the USA
LVHW031246090323
741071LV00001B/59